D0945249

Revision
Cognitive and Instructional Processes

STUDIES IN WRITING

VOLUME 13

Series Editor:

Gert Rijlaarsdam, *University of Amsterdam, The Netherlands*

Editorial Board:

Linda Allal, *University of Geneva, Switzerland*
Eric Espéret, *University of Poitiers, France*
David Galbraith, *Staffordshire University, UK*
Joachim Grabowski, *University of Heidelberg, Germany*
Ronald Kellogg, *St. Louis University, USA*
Lucia Mason, *University of Padova, Italy*
Marta Milian, *Universitat Autonoma Barcelona, Spain*
Sarah Ransdell, *Florida Atlantic University, USA*
Liliana Tolchinsky, *University of Barcelona, Spain*
Mark Torrance, *Staffordshire University, UK*
Annie Piolat, *University of Aix-en-Provence, France*
Païvi Tynjala, *University of Jyväskylä, Finland*
Carel van Wijk, *Tilburg University, The Netherlands*

Kluwer Academic Publishers continues to publish the international book series Studies in Writing, founded by Amsterdam University Press. The intended readers are all those interested in the foundations of writing and learning and teaching processes in written composition. The series aims at multiple perspectives of writing, education and texts. Therefore authors and readers come from various fields of research, from curriculum development and from teacher training. Fields of research covered are cognitive, socio-cognitive and developmental psychology, psycholinguistics, text linguistics, curriculum development, instructional science. The series aim to cover theoretical issues, supported by empirical research, quantitative as well as qualitative, representing a wide range of nationalities. The series provides a forum for research from established researchers and welcomes contributions from young researchers.

The titles published in this series are listed at the end of this volume.

Revision
Cognitive and Instructional Processes

edited by

Linda Allal
University of Geneva, Switzerland

Lucile Chanquoy
University of Nantes, France

Pierre Largy
University of Toulouse Le Mirail, France

KLUWER ACADEMIC PUBLISHERS
Boston / Dordrecht / New York / London

Distributors for North, Central and South America:
Kluwer Academic Publishers
101 Philip Drive
Assinippi Park
Norwell, Massachusetts 02061 USA
Telephone (781) 871-6600
Fax (781) 681-9045
E-Mail: kluwer@wkap.com

Distributors for all other countries:
Kluwer Academic Publishers Group
Post Office Box 322
3300 AH Dordrecht, THE NETHERLANDS
Telephone 31 786 576 000
Fax 31 786 576 254
E-Mail: services@wkap.nl

 Electronic Services <http://www.wkap.nl>

Library of Congress Cataloging-in-Publication Data

Title: Revision: Cognitive and Instructional Processes
Editors: Linda Allal, Lucile Chanquoy, Pierre Largy
ISBN: 1-4020-7729-7

A C.I.P. Catalogue record for this book is available
from the Library of Congress.

TABLE OF CONTENTS

INTRODUCTION

Revision Revisited

LINDA ALLAL* & LUCILE CHANQUOY**

*University of Geneva, Switzerland, **University of Nantes, France*

Revision is a fundamental component of the writing process. So fundamental that for some specialists writing is largely a matter of revising, or as Murray (1978) stated, "Writing is rewriting..." (p. 85). Experience with writing does not, however, automatically translate into increased skill in revision. Learning to revise is a lengthy, complex endeavor. Beginning writers do little revision spontaneously and even experienced writers encounter difficulties in attempting to improve the quality of their texts (Fitzgerald, 1987).

Although revision has been extensively dealt with in the writing and learning-to-write literature, this book proposes to "revisit" theory and research in this area through a series of new contributions. The introduction begins with an overview of what revision encompasses. It then examines two parallel interrogations that underlie the chapters assembled here, namely: (1) What are the implications of research on cognitive processes for instruction in revision? (2) What are the questions raised by instructional research for the investigation of cognitive processes of revision? A final section presents the chapters of this book.

1. AN OVERVIEW OF REVISION

Our starting point will be Fitzgerald's (1987) definition of the activity of revision:

> Revision means making any change at any point in the writing process. It involves identifying discrepancies between intended text and instantiated text, deciding what could or should be changed in the text, how to make desired changes and operating, that is, making the desired changes. Changes may or may not affect meaning of text and they may be major or minor. (p. 484)

A substantial number of researchers have proposed additional conceptual distinctions which enlarge or refine this definition (see Alamargot & Chanquoy, 2001, for a detailed presentation of major models and associated research).

Since the introduction of the well-known, hierarchical models of writing, starting with Hayes and Flower (1980), it is generally accepted that revision can intervene at any point in the writing process. The temporal relations between revision and the other sub-processes of writing – planning and translating or transcribing – can be characterized in three broad categories (Witte, 1985): (1) pretextual revision, which affects intentions, plans or mental formulations of text before transcription has occurred; (2) on-line revision, which is integrated in the process of transcription and entails changes made while reviewing a word or group of words that has just been written; (3) deferred revision, which takes place once a relatively complete draft – of a text or a sizeable part of a text (e.g., a chapter) – has been written.

Revision has been conceptualized primarily as a problem solving process activated by the identification of "discrepancies between intended text and instantiated text," as stated by Fitzgerald. This perspective is a central feature of the models developed by Hayes and his co-workers (Hayes & Flower, 1980; Hayes, Flower, Schriver, Stratman & Carey, 1987; Hayes, 1996), as well as of those proposed by other researchers, such as the CDO (compare – diagnose – operate) model of Bereiter and Scardamalia (1987), or the procedural model of Butterfield, Hacker and Albertson (1996). The pervasiveness of this perspective is evidenced by the fact that expressions like "problem detection," "problem diagnosis," "problem resolution," have often been treated as synonymous with revision. Some researchers have suggested, however, that revision may be initiated by discoveries made while writing, without any prior diagnosis of a problem present in the current instantiated text (Galbraith, 1992). The way an idea has been formulated may suggest a new orientation to be given to the text, and thus operate as a bottom-up form of proactive regulation of what is next written. The orientation taken by emerging text can also lead, retroactively, to modifications of already written text.

Revision includes a number of sub-processes that have been defined in various ways by different authors (see reviews by Alamargot & Chanquoy, 2001; Fitzgerald, 1987). Several main sub-processes are nevertheless present in all models, under varying designations. Revision entails, first of all, an activity of *reviewing*, that is, of reading or (re)processing existing text or existing mental formulations of text. Reviewing generally takes place with the aim of evaluating the adequacy of "text thus far" with respect to the writer's intentions or in relation to some other reference (e.g., conventions used in proof-reading for a journal). Hayes and Flower's (1980) initial conception of reviewing was later expanded to include several different types of reading (reading to comprehend, to evaluate, to define problems: see Hayes et al., 1987), and was subsequently reformulated in broader terms as a "text processing" (Hayes, 1996).

The reviewing process leads to decisions regarding actions to be taken. It may be decided that no action is warranted: A draft is reviewed, reflections are made about possible changes, but none are finally carried out. If, however, a modification is considered necessary or desirable, several strategies may be used, depending on the writer's goal. Revision strategies can be classified in two major categories: *editing*, which entails error correction and modifications designed to improve the adequacy of text without changing its general meaning; and *rewriting*, which entails transformations of text content (addition or deletion of segments), changes in text organization (sequencing of segments), and modifications of the meaning conveyed by a segment. These two strategies can be combined in a revision process that corrects errors while at the same time transforming content. The execution of these strategies involves the coordination of the writer's goals with a wide range of knowledge components (knowledge of content, of text grammar, of syntax, of spelling, etc). Depending on the writer's degree of expertise, some components intervening in revision are activated automatically whereas others require deliberate reflection. The progressive atomization of basic skills allows the writer to exercise intentional, reflective control over increasingly complex components. For example, the automatization of skill in spelling allows greater investment of the writer's cognitive resources in revisions linked to text organization and elaboration of content (Allal, Bétrix Köhler, Rieben, Rouiller Barbey, Saada-Robert, & Wegmuller, 2001; McCutchen, Covill, Hoyne, & Mildes, 1994).

Although the distinction between internal revision (what the author formulates mentally) and external revision (what is marked on a text) has existed for some time (Murray, 1978), many researchers have tended to restrict the term revision to the observed marks written on a text (e.g., Scardamalia & Bereiter, 1986). This usage has been reinforced by the development of various taxonomies of revision focused on different characteristics of observed changes in text. Most taxonomies (e.g., Allal, 2000; Chanquoy, 1997; Faigley & Witte, 1981; Hayes et al., 1987; Sommers, 1980) propose multidimensional classifications taking into account the meaning-preserving or meaning-transforming nature of a modification, the level of language affected by the change, the operations used to carry out a revision (addition, deletion, substitution, reordering), the effect of the revision (positive, neutral, negative). In order to differentiate more clearly the overall process of revision from the resulting products, Allal (2000) suggests using the term "transformation" for the changes actually carried out. This allows the term revision to keep an inclusive meaning referring to the processes which lead or, in some cases, do not lead to transformations of existing text.

Recent research has provided more in-depth specification of the cognitive processes involved in revision, including the role of working memory (McCutchen, 1996; Olive Kellogg & Piolat, 2001), the interaction between cognitive and metacognitive factors (Butterfield et al., 1996; Plumb, Butterfield, Hacker & Dunlosky, 1994), the progressive structuring of linguistic knowledge needed for writing and revision (Chanquoy & Negro, 1996; Totereau, Barouillet, & Fayol, 1998). Several chapters in this book pursue these lines of investigation.

2. COGNITIVE AND INSTRUCTIONAL PROCESSES IN REVISION

This book approaches the relations between the cognitive processes intervening in revision and the instructional processes brought into play in situations where students are learning to write and to revise. This intersection is still largely unexplored, but several examples can be given to illustrate the potential fruitfulness of these complementary and interacting directions of inquiry.

2.1 *Implications of Research on Cognitive Processes for Instruction in Writing and Revision*

The development of programs to teach writing and revision, as well as current research in this area, almost always refer to studies of the cognitive processes involved in revision. The models developed by Hayes and co-workers and by Bereiter and Scardamalia are well-known and the research on cognitive processes has had a substantial impact on instructional research and development. Two significant examples of this impact will be mentioned. First and foremost, research has fostered recognition that writing is a complex activity involving several sub-processes that require specific forms of instructional support. This has led to the development of instructional sequences that provide time for student investment in the different sub-processes (planning, translating, revision) and material (guidelines, examples, checklists, reminders) designed to facilitate each aspect of writing. In addition, direct instruction in cognitive strategies has been incorporated in many instructional approaches, such as the Self-regulated strategy development approach of Harris and Graham (1996) and the Cognitive strategy instruction in writing, proposed by Englert (1992).

A second example of the influence of cognitive process research on instructional research concerns the role of individual differences in writing. The importance of these differences (Berninger, Abbott, Whitaker, Sylvester & Nolen, 1995; Galbraith, 1996; McCutchen et al, 1994) means that any effective instructional approach needs to include ways of identifying the relevant types of student variation and, more importantly, the means of dealing with this variation. Student differences can be taken into account in an instructional program by two types of measures:

- compensatory measures, such as providing some students with forms of procedural facilitation (Bereiter & Scardamalia, 1987) that are not needed by other students;
- proactive, adaptive measures which allow students to make choices among several procedures for carrying out a writing task (e.g., letting students decide if they want to revise on-line or in a deferred manner; if they want to plan and then write, or use a multiple drafting strategy, Cf. Galbraith, 1996).

2.2 *Implications of Research on Instructional Processes for the Investigation of Cognitive Processes in Writing and Revision*

Most research on cognitive processes in revision has been conducted with little attention paid to the findings of instructional research. This is undoubtedly due to the out-dated, but still widespread tendency to consider instructional research as an "application" of research on cognitive processes. We believe that instructional research can in fact provide ideas and raise questions that may provide new directions for cognitive process research. To illustrate this assertion we will discuss two examples.

Several studies have shown that students' ability to make appropriate revisions, and particularly higher-level revisions of meaning and text structure, is affected by their knowledge of appropriate evaluation criteria (Englert, Raphael, Anderson, Gregg, & Anthony, 1989; Graham, Schwartz, & MacArthur, 1993). Direct instruction aimed at enhancing students' knowledge of evaluative criteria and their understanding of revision goals can have positive effects on the acquisition of revision skills (Fitzgerald & Markham, 1987; Hillocks, 1984). The results of these studies raise several questions for research on cognitive processes in writing. For instance, in an extension of the work by Butterfield and co-workers (Butterfield et al, 1986; Plumb et al, 1994), it would interesting to determine if there is a developmental shift in the relative importance of the factors (cognitive vs. metacognitive) accounting for students' revision competencies. Studies could also be conducted to identify the cognitive processes activated by different forms of presentation of evaluation criteria. It is possible that certain instructional guidelines and tools aimed at procedural facilitation of revision actually increase the cognitive load of the task due to inadequate formatting (e.g., formats causing "split attention" or other effects, see Sweller & Chandler, 1994).

A second example concerns the role of peer interaction in learning to write and to revise. A sizable number of studies of writing instruction have shown the positive impact of structured peer interaction on revision (Daiute & Dalton, 1988; Dipardo & Freedman, 1988; MacArthur, Schwartz & Graham, 1991; Saunders, 1989; Zammuner, 1995). The findings from these studies suggest that existing models of individual cognition need to be enlarged to take into account the "distribution of cognition" (Perkins, 1993) across participants and across supporting artifacts within a writing activity. Although this perspective is not new, it has not yet been widely integrated into the conception of experiments on cognitive processes of revision. Future research in this direction could be designed to study several aspects of peer interaction, from the point of view of distributed memory or of distributed metacognitive monitoring of revision processes.

3.   THE CHAPTERS IN THIS BOOK

In the first chapter, John Hayes addresses the two themes of this book. He reviews the evolution of the models of cognitive processes in writing developed with his co-workers and raises in particular the question: What triggers revision? He then examines the research on teaching judgmental skills to students for evaluating and improving text. Although the relevant findings from this research are quite meager, they generally substantiate the view that a better understanding of evaluation criteria can improve students' revision skills.

The following two chapters, by Annie Piolat, Jean-Yves Roussey, Thierry Olive, and Murielle Amada, and by Pierre Largy, Lucile Chanquoy, and Alexandra Dédéyan, focus on basic research designed to analyze cognitive processes involved in revision. They present experiments concerning the detection and the correction of errors that have been inserted into texts provided to students (undergraduates, in the Piolat et al. study; students of elementary and junior high grades, and undergraduates in the Largy et al. study). The first study shows the effects of different types of errors (linked to coherence, syntax, spelling) and of working memory capacity on the revisers' effectiveness. The experiments presented in the Largy et al. chapter concern the processes of knowledge proceduralization and implicit learning that form the basis of error detection in the area of subject-verb agreements.

The chapter by David Galbraith and Mark Torrance reviews research at the other end of the spectrum, that is, studies looking at how adult writers carry out revisions of relatively lengthy drafts which they have produced. It shows that revision takes different forms in the context of different drafting strategies and that multiple drafting offers an interesting alternative to the traditional outline-then draft strategy. The next chapter by David Holliway and Deborah McCutchen is also concerned with how authors, in this case fifth- and ninth-grade students, revise drafts they have composed in a communication context. It looks specifically at the question of the author's understanding of the reader's perspective and the resulting impact on revision.

The chapter by Amos Van Gelderen and Ron Oostdam discusses the implications of research on cognitive processes of revision for instruction, with a particular concern for second-language instruction. On this basis, the authors propose two dimensions for structuring instructional activities: explicitness of instruction (explicit vs. implicit treatment of writing and revising criteria), and focus of instruction (on linguistic meaning vs. on linguistic form).

The following two chapters deal with research on instructional activities carried out in elementary classroom or in experiments designed to approximate the main features of these settings. Charles MacArthur, Steve Graham, and Karen Harris present a well-documented review of the research on instruction in revision with "struggling writers" (i.e., students with learning disabilities). The findings of this research are relevant, we believe, for all young writers (in the elementary and early secondary grades) who encounter significant difficulties in learning to write and to revise. The studies reviewed show the positive impact of direct strategy instruction combined with peer interaction and word processing. The chapter by Linda Allal presents the rationale and the results of a year-long field experiment comparing two contrasting approaches to instruction: an integrated sociocognitive approach and a componential skills approach. The data show that the impact of the sociocognitive approach on students' revision skills is more pronounced in sixth than in second grade.

The next two chapters are concerned with a specific feature of instruction, namely, the role of peer interaction in the revision of narrative texts by elementary and junior high school students. The chapter by Pietro Boscolo and Katia Ascorti studies peer collaboration in the context of reciprocal revision: Students give each other feedback on their respective texts and discuss possible revisions. The problem of understanding audience perspective, present in the Holliway and McCutchen study, reemerges in this chapter. Yviane Rouiller presents research on peer collaboration during joint dyadic revision of a common text. A qualitative analysis compares highly productive and less productive dyads. The metacognitive reflections about revision expressed by students working individually and in dyads are also studied.

The final chapter of the book, by Gert Rijlaarsdam, Michel Couzijn, and Huub Van den Bergh, draws on all the preceding chapters to lay out a framework for future research on revision. This chapter examines different questions concerning the definition of revision, the justification of research on revision, the place of revision in writing instruction. The authors then present two prospective research agendas. The first concerns research on revision as a component of the writing process. It formulates key questions and enumerates the problems of generalization (across writing tasks and conditions; across writer profiles, cognitive functioning, levels of expertise) that confront researchers. The second agenda concerns research on revision in the context of learning to write. The questions proposed for this agenda concern the role of revision as a tool for learning about writing, the nature and effectiveness of feedback, the relative importance of pre-writing and post-writing activities, and the function of multiple drafting.

These agendas are ambitious and will thus require the development of multidisciplinary approaches and research groups in order to link systematically cognitive and instructional processes in the area of text revision.

WHAT TRIGGERS REVISION?

JOHN R. HAYES

Carnegie Mellon University, USA

Abstract. This chapter provides a brief review of empirical findings and theoretical positions concerning the conditions that lead writers to revise texts. The review identifies a need for further research in two directions. First, much of revision research is focused on revisions that are triggered by the discovery of text faults. More research is needed to explore revisions that are triggered by the discovery of opportunities for text improvement other than the correction of text faults. Second, more research is needed to identify effective means for teaching students to recognize and apply standards of text quality while they write.

Keywords: Writing, revision, writing instruction

1.   INTRODUCTION

Over the last quarter of a century the scientific community has made very substantial progress in understanding the process of revision. During this period there was considerable confusion among researchers about just what should be included as revision. Should revision refer only to changes in a completed draft? Should we consider changes made while text was being created as revision? Should we consider changes in the writer's plans before any text had been written as revisions? At present, there appears to be a fairly general acceptance in the research community for an inclusive definition such as the following articulated by Fitzgerald (1987): "Revision means making any change at any point in the writing process" (p. 484). In this chapter, I will use the term revision as Fitzgerald defined it.

My purpose in writing this chapter is to explore what we know and what we don't know about the cues and conditions that initiate the activity of revision. What is it that leads writers to change what they have written or what they had intended to write? I will trace some of the theoretical and empirical developments in the last quarter of a century that bear on this question and try to identify some of the gaps in our knowledge.

2. EARLY MODELS

In their 1980 model of the writing process, Hayes and Flower included revision, which they called "reviewing," as a major writing process parallel to planning and translating (see Figure 1). However, their discussion of the nature of the reviewing process is inconsistent. Their discussion presents two accounts that are not compatible with each other. In their first account, on pages 16 through 18, they describe reviewing as consisting of two sub-processes; reading and editing. Only the editing process was described in any detail. Editing was assumed to be a production system that responded automatically to faults such as misspellings, factual inaccuracies, lack of clarity, or inappropriate tone. When editing was triggered, it interrupted other processes and initiated procedures to fix the problem. As Alamargot and Chanquoy (2001) have pointed out, the view that problem detection automatically triggers problem correction has not survived critical evaluation. Of course, through extensive practice, certain aspects of editing may become automated. However, it seems unlikely that the activity of editing as a whole would ever become completely automatic even in highly practiced individuals.

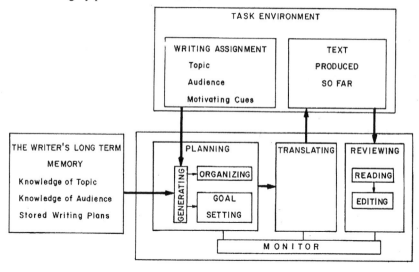

Figure 1. Hayes and Flower's (1980) general model of writing.

Hayes and Flower (1980) provide a second account of the nature of reviewing at the bottom of page 18. Here they describe reviewing and editing as processes that have distinctly different properties. They described reviewing as a reflective activity in which "the writer decides to devote a period of time to systematic examination and improvement of the text" (p. 18) rather than an automatic process like editing. Clearly, these two accounts are inconsistent. In later work, Hayes and his colleagues (Hayes et al. 1987; Wallace & Hayes, 1991; Chenoweth & Hayes, 2001) have emphasized the reflective nature of revision.

3.   DISSONANCE MODELS

At about the same time that Hayes and Flower proposed the model described above, a number of researchers were suggesting that the process of revision is triggered when writers notice a dissonance between what they intended to write and the text that they have actually written (Bridwell, 1980; Scardamalia & Bereiter, 1983; Sommers, 1980). This idea, most clearly elaborated in Scardamalia and Bereiter's well-known Compare, Diagnose, Operate, or CDO, model, is an attractive one. We can easily imagine that writers sometimes read their texts and say "No, that is n't really what I meant." However, revision often occurs in situations where there is no immediate experience of dissonance between what the writer intended to write and what appeared on the page. Indeed, dissonance models appear to be rather limited in the range of revision phenomena that they can account for, at least, for adult writers.

First, these models apply only to the revision of written text and not to the revision of text plans or goals for writing texts. This omission is an important one since revisions of writing plans and goals that occur during writing are often critical for improving the quality of the text.

Second, even when the text on the page is exactly what the writer intended at the time, he or she may decide later, looking at the text from another point of view, that it needs to be changed. Indeed, as Chanquoy (2001) has shown, delaying revision increases the frequency and depth of revision in 3rd-, 4th-, and 5th-grade students. This result would be very difficult to account for with a dissonance model.

Third, dissonance models appear to be designed primarily to apply to situations in which writers are revising their own rather than someone else's text. When we revise someone else's text, we may try to guess the intention of the original writer and change the text so that it matches what we believe was the writer's intention. More often, though, we revise text not because it did not match the writer's intention but rather because it was wordy, graceless, or because the writer wandered from the main point.

Finally, an additional problem with dissonance models is that they assume revision occurs only when there is something wrong with the text. In many cases, we revise not because we discover a fault but because we discover something better to say or find a better way to say what we have said.

4.   MORE RECENT MODELS OF REVISION

In 1987, Hayes, Flower, Schriver, Stratman, and Carey provided a model of revision that was substantially more detailed than Hayes and Flower's 1980 model. The 1987 model, shown in Figure 2, introduced a number of useful new features. These included a role for task definition, a model of evaluation as an extension of the reading process, and a sophisticated strategy selection process.

Task definition. A writer's task definition specifies:

- The writer's goals for revision, for example, whether revision is for grammatical correctness, clarity or elegance;
- the scope of the revision, for example, whether revision is to be local or global, and

- the procedures to be used, for example, should changes be deferred until the text has been read completely or not.

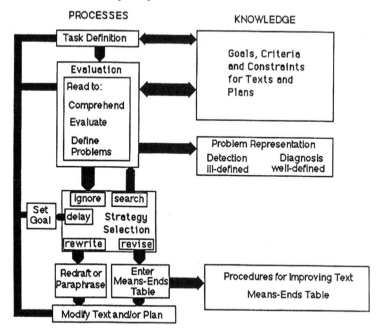

Figure 2. Hayes et al.'s (1987) model of revision.

Task definition provides a locus in the model for the metacognitive control of the revision process. The authors emphasized that the task definition varies from writer to writer. In particular, more experienced revisers have more elaborate and effective task definitions than do novices. Further, a writer's task definition may be modified dynamically as revision proceeds. If a writer finds that a text has many errors, he or she may decide to extract the gist of the text and rewrite it rather than to repair individual errors.

A model of evaluation. The authors made two important additions to the description of the reading process within revision. First, they chose a specific reading model, the multi-level model of Thibideau, Just, and Carpenter (1982), and adapted it for the purposes of revision. The reading model allowed for parallel processing of the text at many levels from decoding words and identifying grammatical structures to identifying gist and inferring the writer's intentions. Second, they distinguished among three modes of reading: *reading to comprehend, reading to evaluate,* and *reading to define problems.* Reading to comprehend is the most familiar reading process. In this type of reading, the reader's goal is simply to represent the text's message. Examples include studying and reading for pleasure. In reading to evaluate, the reader reads to comprehend but adds the goal of detecting text problems. In grading papers, teachers typically read to evaluate. In reading to define problems, the reader reads to evaluate but adopts the additional goal of fixing the problems that are detected. Thus, Hayes et al. (1987) saw problem detection and correction as dependent on the reader/reviser's goals.

The strategy selection process. Strategy selection is the process of deciding what to do after a problem has been detected. Options include:

- Ignoring the problem if it is too trivial or too difficult to correct,
- delaying action until a later time,
- searching for a better representation of the problem,
- repairing[1] the text, that is, fixing the detected problems,
- rewriting the text if it has more problems than the reviser chooses to repair.

The model represents the relation between the problems detected and the actions taken to repair those problems as a means-ends table (Newell & Simon, 1972). The authors note that the means-ends tables of experts are larger than those of novices because experts detect more problem types and have more procedures for fixing them than do novices.

The authors clearly recognize that revision may be initiated by the discovery of opportunities as well as by the detection of problems. Hayes et al. note how "searching for an example to illustrate a principle may lead to the discovery of a way to make contact with the special interests of the audience" (p. 204).

It seems reasonable to believe that the discovery of opportunities may be a very important part of the revision process of skilled revisers. However, the formal model is focused entirely on the detection and correction of problems and does not account for revisions triggered by discovered opportunities. Indeed, on page 207 Hayes et al. say "problem detection, then, is a necessary precondition for revision." Perhaps they would have better represented their position if they had said: "Detecting a problem is a necessary precondition for setting a goal to repair that problem." In any case, omitting a role in revision for the discovery of opportunities seems a serious limitation of the formal model.

Another shortcoming of this model is that it is really focused on revision that occurs when the reviser reads a transcribed text. The input to the revision process is reading rather than internally generated language that writers produce as they compose. Work by Kaufer, Hayes, and Flower (1986), Chenoweth and Hayes (2001), and Chenoweth and Hayes (2003) shows that writers do a great deal of revising as they compose. They revise sentences that have been completed; they revise sentences as they are being composed; and they revise ideas that have not yet been written down. Chenoweth and Hayes (2003) studied writers as they composed a single sentence on a word processor to describe a cartoon. Participants could either see the text as they typed or the text was invisible to them as they typed. The authors found that when the writers could see the text they were composing, they took 23% longer to compose a sentence than when they could not see their text. The difference could be attributed to the larger number of revisions that writers made when they could see the sentence they were composing than when they could not. Thus, even in the rela-

---

[1] *Hayes et al. (1987) actually called this option "revision." Since this is a subprocess of a larger process also called revision, I substituted the term "repairing" to avoid confusion.*

tively simple task of composing a single sentence, revision occupies a substantial portion of the writer's time during composition.

Dissonance models are better suited to describing revisions that occur while writers are composing texts and the Hayes et al. (1987) model is better suited to describe revisions that occur when revisers are modifying existing texts. Neither the dissonance models nor the Hayes et al. (1987) model gracefully integrates the processes involved in revising while creating new text with those processes involved in revising existing texts.

In 1996, Hayes introduced a new framework for describing writing processes and a new model of revision. The framework specifies three fundamental writing processes: language processing (e.g., reading, listening); reflection (e.g., problem solving, decision making); and language production (e.g., producing text or speech). The new revision model (shown in Figure 3) represents revision as a process in which the three fundamental processes are controlled by the writer's task schema.

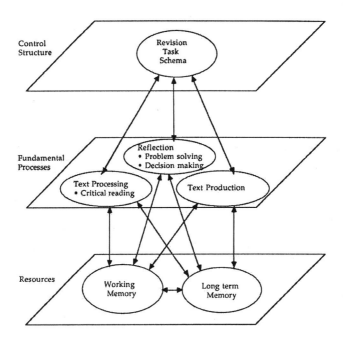

Figure 3. Hayes's (1996) new model of revision.

This model was designed to take into account claims such as those of Hayes et al. cited above that the writer has voluntary control of many aspect of the revision process. Some experimental support for such claims was provided by Wallace and Hayes (1991) who found that writers asked to revise a provided text could be induced to revise more globally simply by instructing them to do so. Wallace, Hayes, Hatch,

Miller, Moser, and Silk (1996) found the same result for writers asked to revise their own texts. In the Hayes (1996) model, the input to the revision process is text processing making this model more appropriate to revision of an existing text than the revision of a text being composed. However, I believe that this problem is easily fixed. Indeed, Chenoweth and Hayes (2001) have proposed a model of sentence generation that includes a revision process with the structure of the Hayes (1996) revision model that takes input both from internal processes for generating text and from reading. As modified by Chenoweth and Hayes (2001), then, the Hayes (1996) model can accommodate both the revising of texts as they are being created and the revising of texts that already exist

5.   WHAT KNOWLEDGE IS REQUIRED FOR DETECTION?

Can we detect a problem that we don't know how to fix? Hacker, Plumb, Butterfield, Quathamer, and Heineken (1994) have proposed an interesting hypothesis that appears contradictory to the widely held belief that one can detect a text problem but not know how to correct it. According to their hypothesis, knowledge of how to correct text problems is necessary for detecting those problems. I will call this the "correction-first" position because it holds that one must be able to correct a problem before being able to detect it. To support this position, the authors carried out a two-phase study. In the detection phase of the study, students were asked to circle problems in spelling, capitalization and punctuation, usage, and meaning in two text passages. In the correction phase, the students were asked to fix the same sorts of problems in short texts. In these short texts, the locations of the problems were identified for the student by highlighting the relevant words. This was done to insure that difficulties in detecting the problems were minimized.

Hacker et al. (1994) reasoned that if ability to detect a problem was contingent on having the knowledge of how to fix the problem, then two relations ought to be observed:

1)   If students identify a problem in the detection phase, they should be able to fix that problem in the correction phase.
2)   If students fail to fix a problem in the correction phase, then they should also fail to identify it in the detection phase.

Hacker et al. (1994) found support for both of these hypotheses. They observed that if students detected a problem, then the probabilities that they would be able to correct it were .91, .88, .93, and .76 for spelling, capitalization-punctuation, usage, and meaning. Further, they observed that if students failed to correct a problem, then the probabilities that they would fail to detect them were .57, .76, .74, and .80 for spelling, capitalization-punctuation, usage, and meaning errors. Thus, if students failed to correct a problem then they usually failed to detect them. The authors concluded that a necessary condition for detecting an error is knowing how to correct that error.

Although the correction-first position is an interesting one, I do not believe that the authors have made a strong case for it. First, their evidence, although consistent with the correction-first position, does not contradict some plausible alternative views. Let me outline an alternate view that I will call the "detection-first" position.

According to the detection-first position:
1) The ability to detect problems is necessary for correcting them, but
2) the ability to correct problems is not necessary for their detection.

That students are able to correct many of the surface level errors that they detect, as Hacker et al. (1994) observed, is not inconsistent with the detection-first position. In such cases, detection and correction may both require attending to the same set of cues. For example, in the case of spelling, detection may occur when the reviser notices a letter pattern on the page that does not match the memory image of any word. Further, the letter pattern may remind the reviser of a real word. If that word fits the grammatical and semantic context of the misspelled word, then the reviser may conclude that the retrieved word should be substituted for the misspelled word to correct the error. Thus, ability to detect and ability to correct may be correlated because they involve noticing some of the same cues. However, since more information is required to fix the problem than to detect it, we might predict that revisers will detect at least some problems that they fail to correct.

Embarrassingly often, I find myself facing my word processor, realizing that I have spelled a word incorrectly but not knowing for sure how to spell it correctly. It is at such times that I most appreciate my spell checker. In such instances, a partial knowledge of word patterns has allowed me to detect a problem but not to fix it. Even in the relatively simple domain of spelling, then, it is possible to detect a problem without having the knowledge needed to fix it.

Indeed, in the Hacker et al. (1994) study, participants were able to detect about 25% of the problems that they were unable to correct. Bartlett (1982) found that for some simple reference problems, students were unable to correct up to 42% of the errors that they detected.

In more complex cases, the cues used to detect a problem may be quite different from those used to correct it. As Hayes et al. (1987) have pointed out, if a text has many problems, revisers may decide to extract the gist of the text and to rewrite it in their own language rather than fix it. In this case, the information that the revisers used to detect problems in the text has little to do with the information they use to improve it. One can imagine that revisers may use the same rewriting strategy when they detect so-called "awkward" sentences. That is, they extract the sentence's gist and rewrite it without diagnosing what it was that made the original sentence awkward.

Hacker et al.'s (1994) second observation, that students are less likely to detect errors that they cannot correct, is also quite consistent with the detection-first position. Suppose that a student is so insensitive to the need for parallelism in lists that he or she fails to detect the problem even when the faulty list is pointed out (as in the correction phase of Hacker et al.'s study). We would expect that this student would not only fail to correct the problem in the correction phase but would also fail to detect the problem in the more difficult detection task posed by the detection phase of the study.

Thus, the data presented by Hacker et al. (1994) do not appear to differentiate between the detection-first and the correction-first positions. Further, the correction-first position seems to entail a serious pedagogical problem. If students must be able to correct problems before they can detect them, how do they ever learn to correct them? The correction-first position would seem to put the writing teacher in the unenviable position of trying to teach students to fix problems they cannot see.

6.   TEACHING THE JUDGMENTAL SKILLS REQUIRED FOR DETECTION

It has been observed that novice writers detect a smaller percentage of text problems they encounter than do experts (Butterfield, Hacker, & Plumb, 1994; Fitzgerald & Markham, 1987; Hayes et al., 1987). For example, Hayes et al. asked experts and novices to revise a text with 26 planted sentence-level problems. They found that the experts detected 58% of the problems but the novices detected only 36%. It was not that the novices were simply being careless. In some cases, they would read the same faulty passage as many as eight times and still fail to see the problem. In such cases, the novices appeared to be persistently insensitive to problems that the experts detected on the first pass.

The goal of helping revisers to become more sensitive to text problems is obviously an important one for writing education. Scholars such as Graves (1994) and Tierney, Carter, and Desai (1991) stress the importance of teaching students to evaluate their own writing. However, there is surprisingly little research on this issue reported in the literature and currently there does not seem to be a great deal of interest in it. Perhaps the reason is that many believe the problem is already solved, that is, that current methods for teaching text evaluation skills are successful. Unfortunately, they are not (Hillocks, 1986; Schriver, 1992), and because they are not, there is a major gap in our knowledge of how to teach revision.

I believe that we need to pay far more attention to methods for teaching writers the judgmental skills needed both to detect problems in text and to recognize opportunities for improving text. By judgmental skills, I mean the skills involved in attending to, recognizing, and evaluating complex patterns in text. For example, a student might fail to detect problems of parallelism because she is attending to the individual items in a list rather than to the relations among the items. Successful instruction would redirect the student's attention.

The primary model for teaching revision seems to be a tutorial one. According to this model, the student submits a draft to a knowledgeable tutor. The tutor comments on the draft relying on his or her expert sensitivity to stylistic and other features of writing. The student then reads the tutor's comments and revises the text. Through repetition of this process with numerous texts, the student is expected to acquire at least some of the tutor's sensitivities. This model appears to be widely used in classroom and professional settings. Here is an ad from a recent *Writer's Digest* (2001):

> Your instructor will be with you every step of the way, carefully reviewing your writing. He or she will give you feedback on both your ideas and your abilities – so you can build on your strengths, work on your weaknesses, and master the elements of all good writing. It is just the kind of personal attention you need to avoid the trial and error of being on your own. (p. 7)

Unfortunately the tutorial model does not appear to work very well. Hillocks (1986), who provides the most complete discussion of these issues, reviewed four procedures for teaching students to evaluate their own writing:

1)   Teachers commenting on students' final drafts,
2)   teachers commenting on students' intermediate drafts,
3)   students studying models of writing,
4)   students being taught sets of evaluative criteria.

Concerning the first two procedures, Hillocks reviewed the literature and concluded, "the available research suggests that teaching by written comments on compositions is generally ineffective" (p. 167).

He suggested that the reason for the failure of these procedures is that students may fail to understand the teachers' evaluative criteria. For example, when a teacher comments that a sentence is "awkward", the student may have no idea what the designation "awkward" means.

When students are taught by requiring them to study models of writing, they might be asked to read models of good writing, to read and identify features of good (and sometimes poor) writing, to attempt to imitate examples of good writing, or all three. Hillocks reported that the results of studies evaluating this method were mixed with some studies showing gains but others not.

The fourth procedure, teaching students sets of evaluative criteria, differs from the procedures just described in one critical way. It includes specific tests to insure that the students have acquired and can apply the criteria. The first three procedures attempt to teach students to recognize criteria relevant to writing quality by exposing the student to teacher comments or written models. Only the fourth procedure assesses whether or not the student has understood the criteria and can apply them.

Hillocks reports very positive results for this fourth procedure. Summarizing his review of a number of studies (Benson, 1979; Clifford, 1981; Farrell, 1977; Kemp, 1979; Rosen, 1973; Sager, 1973; Wright, 1975), he says:

> As a group, these studies indicate rather clearly that engaging young writers actively in the use of criteria, applied to their own and others' writing, results not only in more effective revisions but in superior first drafts. (p. 168)

That students' first drafts improve is important because it suggest that students are applying the criteria to their own text production process.

Sager's (1973) study provides a clear illustration of a procedure for teaching students criteria for evaluating the quality of texts. Sager studied sixth-graders in inner-city schools. Students in the experimental group were taught to use scales focusing on four aspects of writing quality: vocabulary, elaboration, organization, and structure. Each scale had four values ranging from 0 for the poorest quality to 3 for the best. High scores on vocabulary were given to essays that had a variety of new and interesting words rather than just common overworked ones. A high score on elaboration was given to essays that had an abundance of related ideas that flow smoothly from one idea to the next. High scores on organization were given if ideas were arranged in a way that was interesting and easy to follow and high scores on structure, if the story could be read aloud with ease. Students worked on one scale at a time, learning on one day what features earned a 0 and on other days what features earned 1, 2, or 3.

In introducing each scale, the teacher led a discussion of the features that a specific composition did or did not have. Students then received extensive practice in rating compositions both by themselves and in small groups. Differences of opinions about ratings were discussed and an attempt was made to achieve consensus among class members. If the compositions did not receive a 3, the students suggested improvements and made revisions. At first, the children rated for one component at a time, then two components, finally, all four. Toward the end of practice, students rated compositions individually to assess agreement without discussion. The estimated reliability of the scale when used by the children was .99 with component reliabilities ranging from .96 to .98.

Students in the control group studied the same four components of composition but followed the standard school curriculum. Both groups studied 45 minutes a day for five days a week for eight weeks. By comparing pre- and post-test essays, Sager found that the experimental group made significantly greater gains than the control group on all four aspects of writing quality. Hillocks (1986) calculated that the experimental/control effect size was .93 and the pre/post effect size for the experimental group was .82.

Many of the studies reviewed by Hillocks that explored the teaching of text-quality criteria were flawed in one way or another. In several of them, the effect of teaching criteria for quality was confounded with one or more other variables (Benson, 1979; Clifford, 1981; Farrell, 1977; Wright, 1975). Clifford listed 10 variables other than training on criteria for quality that differentiated his experimental and control groups. In an apparently unconfounded study, Rosen (1973) taught students organizational skills. She found significantly greater gains in the treatment group than in the control group in the organization of their essays. However, her results raise some questions because the experimental group showed greater gains than the control group on most of the variables measured in the study including punctuation, mechanics, and spelling. One of the studies, Kemp (1979) appears to have been focused on teaching stages of the writing process rather than criteria of writing quality. In the Sager study, the results may be questioned because the researcher taught all of the experimental students but others taught the control students. However, despite the presence of problems, the studies, as a group, do suggest strongly that teaching criteria for quality can improve students writing.

Two additional studies lend support to this conclusion. In a study by Rosow (1996), second-graders were taught to use scales focusing on three aspects of writing quality: focus, detail, and organization. Each scale had four values ranging from 0 for the poorest quality to 3 for the best. Rosow's instructional procedure was quite similar to that used by Sager. The objective of the research was to determine if the students could learn to rate their own compositions on focus, detail, and organization as adults would rate them. Although there are some weaknesses in the author's data analysis, the results do suggest that the students were able to evaluate at least the organization of their compositions as adults did.

A study by Schriver (1992) used a very different method to teach college students to detect readers' potential problems with texts. Schriver constructed a sequence of ten lessons on writing clarity. Each lesson was constructed as follows: First, participants read an unclear text and underlined those aspects of the text that they thought the intended readers of the text would find unclear. Second, the participants read a think-aloud protocol of an intended reader attempting to understand that text. Finally, the participants were asked to revise their initial judgements of clarity on the basis of the protocol.

The experimental group, consisting of five classes, studied the ten lessons as part of a writing curriculum. The control group consisted of five classes that used the standard writing curriculum that included peer critiquing, role-playing, etc.

Participants were pre-tested and post-tested by asking them to identify features in two popular science texts that students would find unclear. Schriver identified the text features that readers actually found unclear by collecting think-aloud protocols from 20 readers. Thus, she could determine whether the participants' predictions were accurate or not. The experimental group showed significant gains in predicting what readers would find unclear. The control group showed no change.

Together, these studies make it seem likely that teaching writers to recognize and apply criteria for text quality can substantially improve writing. Further, the participant populations in the studies reviewed here range from second grade to college suggesting that the benefits of teaching students to recognize and apply criteria of text quality may apply to a very broad range of writers.

7. CONCLUSION

Clearly, over the last quarter of a century, our understanding of what it is that triggers revision has increased substantially. Many empirical studies have been carried out and our models have become more sophisticated. However, two directions for further revision research emerge from this brief review.

First, there is evidence to suggest that teaching students to understand and apply criteria of text quality can yield substantial improvements in students' revision processes and in the quality of their first drafts. However, as noted earlier, the quality of this evidence could be improved. Therefore, further research designed to evaluate the effectiveness of this teaching method would be useful and could, potentially, lead to substantial improvement in writing instruction.

Second, we need to have a better understanding of the role that discovery plays in initiating revision. Research has focused on revisions that fix problems, for example, problems of faulty mechanics or poor organization. However, revisions that are stimulated by the discovery of new connections, new ideas, or new arguments seem intrinsically more interesting. Such revisions are likely to be associated with improvements in the substance rather than the form of the text. They may mark those occasions when the writer learns something through the act of writing. Indeed, when I was revising this text, there were several occasions when revisions were triggered by discoveries. In many cases, these discoveries were stimulated by editor's comments but, in others, they were stimulated simply by re-reading the text.

Unfortunately, we know very little about revisions triggered by discovery. A reasonable first step might be to document the occurrence of such revisions in protocol studies and to classify them by type and frequency. A second step would be to determine whether, as I have suggested, these revisions are associated with interesting changes in the substance of the text and in the thinking of the text's author.

PROCESSING TIME AND COGNITIVE EFFORT IN REVISION: EFFECTS OF ERROR TYPE AND OF WORKING MEMORY CAPACITY

ANNIE PIOLAT*, JEAN-YVES ROUSSEY*, THIERRY OLIVE**, & MURIELLE AMADA*

*University of Provence, France, ** University of Poitiers, France*

Abstract. Cognitive effort and temporal organization of the sub-processes of revision (reading to define problems, searching a solution and transforming the text) were investigated when writers revised either spelling, syntactical or coherence errors. Differences in working memory capacity of participants were also examined and cognitive effort of reading to understand and of reading to define problems was compared. Participants revised a text while being submitted to a secondary auditory probe task and to a directed retrospection task. Results showed that the type of errors did not affect the cognitive effort and temporal organization of the sub-processes of revisions. Efficiency of the revisers depended mainly on the type of errors and partially on their WM capacity. Finally reading to define problems appeared more effortful than reading to understand.

Keywords: Text revision, cognitive effort, time processing, spelling errors, syntactical errors, coherence errors

1. INTRODUCTION

According to Scardamalia and Bereiter (1991), becoming an expert writer means acquiring an ability to efficiently and frequently activate the writing processes of planning and of revision during a composition. Considered as an ill-defined problem, text composition indeed requires a deliberate control before and during the production (Boscolo, 1995; Butterfield, Hacker, & Albertson, 1996). Writing expertise cannot thus be reduced to the automatization of writing processes. On the contrary, learning to write principally consists in controlling the activation of the writing processes and especially revision processes (Lumbelli, Paoletti, & Frausin, 1999; Torrance, 1996). The aim of the research presented in this chapter was to investigate the level of efficiency in revising of undergraduate students by focusing on the activation and cognitive effort of the different sub-processes of revision.

Revision is regarded as a major process in the different models of writing (Berninger & Swanson, 1994; Hayes, 1996; Kellogg, 1994). At *minima*, it is described as a reviewing process that allows writers evaluating their text and as an editing process that allows writers modifying the problems they detect. Revision can intervene at any moment of the composition and thus interrupts the progress of planning or of translating. Flower, Hayes, Carey, Schriver, and Stratman (1986; see also Hayes, Flower, Schriver, Stratman, & Carey, 1987) largely contributed in identifying the different processes (e.g., evaluation, strategy selection, modifying) and knowledge (e.g., task definition, textual and rhetorical constraints, means-ends tables) involved in the activity of revision.

Since a fortnight years, the changes in the main models of revision concern the largest importance devoted to the deliberate control of text production (for a synthesis, see Piolat, 1998; Roussey, 1999). Hayes (1996) underlines that fundamental processes of reflection and of text processing underlie revision. He considers this activity as being particularly high demanding (see also Kellogg, 1994; Levy & Ransdell, 1995; Olive, Piolat, & Roussey, 1997) and not only as an automatic detection of errors, mainly of surface errors. Berninger, Whitaker, Feng, Swanson, and Abbott (1996), Kellogg (1996) or Hacker (1994) and Torrance and Jeffery (1999) have focused on the role of working memory in writing which function is to allocate executive resources to on-going operations via the central executive system (Baddeley, 1986, 1996, 2000).

Before going further, it is necessary to precisely distinguish the concept of resources, cognitive capacity and cognitive effort. According to Halford, Wilson, and Philips' (1998) conceptions, *resources* refer to the mental energy available at a given moment that cognitive processes require to operate (see Baddeley, 1996, 2000; "executive resources"). *Capacity* corresponds to the maximal amount of resources that is available to an individual. Excluding the changes related to development, ageing, level of expertise or emotional states, this capacity is stable but differs between individuals. Daneman and Carpenter (1980) and Gathercole and Baddeley (1993) assessed such individual differences with different tests of working memory span. These authors have shown how these individual differences affect language comprehension and production. Finally, *cognitive effort* corresponds to the amount of resources required by a given task (Kellogg, 1987, 1988; Olive et al., 1997). For instance, a revision task would be all the more complex, and therefore more demanding in resources, that writers have to activate and manage several processes.

2.   GOALS OF THE RESEARCH

To bring to the front the functional characteristics of revision, we examined how (i) complexity of the revision task, and (ii) individual differences in cognitive capacity affected revision performance and the temporal organization and cognitive effort of three sub-processes of revision, namely, reading to define problems, searching a solution, transforming the text.

First, the complexity of the revision task was manipulated by asking participants to edit errors at different linguistic levels. As already shown by Hayes et al. (1987), surface (spelling) revisions are quasi-automatically detected and writers can build well-defined representations of the problems. To edit such errors, means-ends tables stored in long-term memory and requiring little, if any, resources can be used. Consequently, revision of surface errors should imply a very low cognitive effort. By contrast, for global revisions, writers build ill-defined representations of the problems that require them activating high-demanding reflection processes. Consequently, revision of coherence errors requires a greater amount of resources than revision of surface errors. Accordingly, to manipulate demands of the revision task, participants revised errors of different levels of complexity (Hacker, Plumb, Butterfield, Quathamer, & Heineken, 1994; McCutchen, 1996). More precisely, they revised a text containing either spelling errors, or syntactical errors (i.e., errors in the microstructure), or coherence errors affecting the macrostructure of the text (Faigley & Witte, 1981). Revision of spelling errors that implies to check only one word should involve a lower cognitive effort than revision of syntactical errors that implies to check a sentence. And this last revision should be less demanding than revision of coherence errors that requires taking into account the whole text.

Furthermore, as cognitive capacity constraints the activation of the cognitive processes, individual differences in working memory capacity were examined. By contrast with participants with high-working memory capacity, participants with low working memory capacity should exhibit more difficulties in managing the distribution of resources between the sub-processes of reading to define problems, searching a solution and transforming the text. This, in return, should induce a different activation of these sub-processes of revision. Consequently, the low-working memory capacity participants should detect and revise the errors in the text less than the high-working memory capacity participants. Moreover, this difference between the low- and high-working memory capacity participants should interact with the type of error: a larger difference should be observed with high-demanding revisions than with low-demanding revisions.

Cognitive effort and temporal organization of the different sub-processes of revision were evaluated with the triple-task method (Kellogg, 1987, 1988; Olive, Kellogg, & Piolat, 2001; Piolat & Olive, 2000). Based on the dual-task paradigm, participants performed two tasks simultaneously (the primary and secondary tasks) that share working memory resources (Kahneman, 1973). The functional characteristics involved in such tasks do not only appear in artificial laboratory experiments. Indeed, coordinating several processes, focusing attention, inhibiting alternatives and scheduling responses are executive functions frequently engaged in cognitive activities such as reasoning, memory and language (Baddeley, 1996). In the present experiment, while participants edited errors inserted in a text (the primary task), they were simultaneously submitted to a secondary auditory probe task. As reaction times to the secondary probes reflect cognitive effort of the primary task, long reaction times indicate that the processes of revision require high cognitive effort, and conversely. Moreover, the triple task technique allows associating cognitive effort with the different sub-processes of revision. Indeed, after each probe, participants perform a directed retrospection task (i.e., identifying the process activated at the moment of the probe). With this task, it has been shown, for example, that planning and revising are more effortful than translating (Kellogg, 1994; Levy & Ransdell, 1995;

Olive et al., 1997). In the present experiment, it is thus possible to study cognitive effort of the multiple sub-processes of revision but also their activation, by analyzing the number of times participants retrospect about a particular sub-process. As Hayes et al.'s (1987) experimental findings showed, we predicted a different cognitive effort for each of the sub-processes of revision. According to Kellogg's (1996) propositions, it is expected that the process of reading to define problems be more effortful than the two other processes of revision.

Finally, another goal of the research was to compare the cognitive effort of reading to understand the text and of reading to define problems. Indeed, in his recent model, Hayes (1996) has pointed out the role of critical reading during composition. In order to compare these reading activities, the experiment was organized in two steps. In the first step, where cognitive effort of the activity of reading to understand was evaluated, all participants read a text in dual-task situation (being submitted to a secondary auditory probe task). In the second step, all participants revised the text in triple-task situation (being submitted to a secondary auditory probe task with directed retrospection). Thus, cognitive effort of reading to define problems, searching a solution and transforming the text was evaluated. According to Hayes et al.'s (1987) propositions, reading to define problems should require more cognitive effort than reading to understand.

3.   EXPERIMENT

3.1   Method

3.1.1   Participants

One hundred and six undergraduate students in Psychology of the University of Provence (France) participated in the experiment. Participants were randomly distributed in three groups according to the type of errors they had to revise (see Table 1) and were categorized in two groups of low- and high-working memory (WM) span following their scores at a test of working memory span.

Table 1. Number of participants in each experimental group, according to the type of errors (spelling, syntax, and coherence) and to the working memory capacity (Low- or High-WM)

| | Working memory capacity | |
	Low-WM	High-WM
Spelling	20	19
Syntax	17	15
Coherence	19	16

3.1.2   Test of Working Memory

A French adaptation (Desmette, Hupet, Schelstraete, & Van der Linden, 1995) of the Reading Span Test of Daneman and Carpenter (1980) was used. Participants performed the short version (3 series). All blocks of each series were performed even if participants failed in remembering the words before ending a series. The working memory span of participants corresponded to the size of the larger block they achieved in at least two series out of three. Participants were categorized as low- or high-WM span according to the median of the reading span score (Median = 2,5; ranging from 1 to 4,5). However, participants whose reading span score was equivalent to the median split into the two groups of WM capacity according to their total number of words correctly recalled. This concerned only eight participants.

3.1.3   Texts

The text used in the experiments was extracted from the *Journal des Psychologues* (a French magazine on psychology). Its topic concerned the psychoanalysis of children according to the conceptions of Anna Freud and Melanie Klein. This original text was considered as the "correct" text (362 words). An English abstract of this text is presented below:

> Anna Freud and Melanie Klein are child psychoanalysts who adopted different theoretical approaches and practices to psychoanalyze children. For Anna Freud, the psychoanalytic cure gives to the analyst a status of educator. Melanie Klein opts, for her part, for an analysis of the child that is conformed to that of adults. Child psychoanalysts must think about these two attitudes.

Three versions of the text (the experimental texts) were constructed, each version containing either spelling, syntactic or coherence errors but in different numbers. Indeed, in a preliminary study, we observed faster revision with surface errors (spelling and syntactic errors) than with global errors (coherence errors). Furthermore, by contrast with global errors, surface errors were more often solved, and easier to detect and to correct. Consequently, the three experimental versions of the text contained a different numbers of errors: 24 spelling errors, 12 syntactic errors, and 6 coherence errors (see Appendix).

In order to compare the performance of participants for the three types of errors, it was important that they have not to re-write the text. Indeed, the quantity of linguistic elements that might be re-written can vary at a local level (e.g., a letter) or at a global level (e.g., several sentences) of the text. Consequently, the nature of the errors that were inserted in the text depended on how they had to be edited. Half of the errors were produced by displacing an element and the other half was produced by adding an element. Thus, to edit the errors in the three versions of the text, participants had either to move the problematical zone by surrounding it and by indicating with an arrow the "good" place of insertion or to suppress it by crossing it. Participants did not have to write but only to indicate a transformation operation with the same graphical signs.

More precisely, the text with spelling errors was constructed by adding a letter in 12 words or by moving a letter in 12 words. The errors introduced had no grammatical consequences. Several grammatical categories were concerned (adjective, noun, adverb and verb; examples of errors needing the suppression of a letter: *réielle*, *persepective*, *provocquer* instead of *réelle*, *perspective*, *provoquer*; examples of errors needing the displacement of a letter: *téorhique*, *implusion*, *enrte*, *suppleér* instead of *théorique*, *impulsion*, *entre*, *suppléer*).

The text with syntactical errors was constructed by adding a word in 6 sentences or by displacing a word in 6 sentences. Several grammatical categories were concerned (verb, noun, verbal expression; example of error needing the suppression of one or more words in a sentence: *très* added before *considérablement* in the second sentence of the first paragraph; examples of errors needing the displacement of one or more words in a sentence: *toute intervention pédagogique* before, instead of after *le psychanalyste refuse...* in the fifth sentence of the third paragraph).

The text with coherence errors was constructed by adding a sentence in a paragraph (3 sentences; for example: *L'intelligence concrète désigne des activités qui s'exercent sur des objets manipulables* sentence added in fourth position in the second paragraph that had to be crossed), by displacing a sentence in a paragraph (2 sentences; for example: *En outre, l'analyste doit obtenir des renseignements sur la structure familiale et suppléer au manque des parents à être de bons pédagogues* sentence in second position in the second paragraph that had to be moved in fifth position in this same paragraph) or by displacing a sentence between two paragraphs (1 sentence: *De plus, le psychanalyste refuse toute intervention pédagogique et il n'a pas besoin de renseignements sur la situation du jeune patient* sentence in last position in the second paragraph that had to be moved in fifth position in the third paragraph). The six errors were randomly distributed in the text.

3.1.4   Apparatus

The experiment was computer-assisted (Macintosh PowerPC) and was conducted with the experimental software SCRIPTKELL (Piolat, Olive, Roussey, Thunin, & Ziegler, 1999) that allows researchers to set either a dual-task (with only probes) or a triple task (with probes and directed retrospection). During the reading task, probes were randomly distributed in an interval between 5 and 15 seconds with a mean of 10 seconds. During the revision task, probes were randomly distributed in an interval between 15 and 45 seconds with a mean of 30 seconds. The random distribution of the probes prevented participants from anticipating their reactions to the probes. The software provided detailed individual protocols for each step of the experiment by recording all reaction times to probes with, in the second step, the process designated by the participants after each reaction.

3.1.5   Procedure

The two steps of the experiment (that lasted each about 30 minutes) were separated by at least a week.

The first step of the experiment (which goal was to evaluate cognitive effort of the process of reading to understand) begun by training participants to the probe task. Each participant was informed that he/she would occasionally hear auditory signals in variable intervals distributed by the computer. The instruction required that the participant systematically reacted to each probe by pressing the mouse of the computer with his/her non-dominant hand. This task allowed computing the mean baseline RT of each participant.

After this training, participants read the correct version of the text as many times they needed to understand it because they were informed that after this reading, they would have to answer questions about its content. While reading the text, participants reacted to secondary auditory probes by pressing the mouse of the computer with their non-dominant hand. In order that they do not forget to react as quickly as possible to the probes, a panel on which was written "React as quickly as possible to the probes" was displayed in front of them. When participants achieved their reading, they had to press a special key of the keyboard to stop the program.

Then, participants judged whether three brief affirmative sentences about the content of the text were correct or not, this, in order to control if they paid attention to the text during their reading. The mean score of comprehension of all participants was about 2.5 (on 3) and no significant differences were observed between the experimental conditions.

Finally participants' working memory capacity was assessed with the Reading Span Test. In concrete terms, a series of sentences, each printed on white sheets of a notebook, were presented to participants that had to read aloud each sentence at their own rhythm and without pausing between sentences (the experimenter turned the pages of the notebook as soon as a sentence was read). The task of the participants was to memorize the last word of each sentence. When a blank sheet appeared (at the end of each block), participants recalled all memorized words. The recall was unlimited in time and unordered. To avoid recency effects, participants could not begin with the last word they read. When this instruction was not respected, recall was judged as being incorrect.

During the second step of the experiment, processing time and cognitive effort of reading to define problems, searching a solution and transforming the text were evaluated. Participants were first trained to the directed retrospection task. The experimenter showed to the participants the different labeled keys they had to use to categorize their own thinking during the task and defined the three sub-processes of revision. A fourth label, "Other", allowed participants indicating a thought that did not concern the revising task (this label has not been used by participants in the experiment). Furthermore, participants categorized twelve written "thoughts" of a fictitious writer revising different levels of text. When participants made an error, the experimenter spoke with them and reminded them the correct meaning of each of the three labels.

Then, participants performed the same probe task to compute their mean baseline RT. A statistical analysis of the baseline RTs showed that across conditions participants did not react differently in the two steps of the experiment, although participants were reliably slower in the spelling condition (545 ms) than in the two other conditions (Syntax = 527 ms; Coherence = 504 ms; $F(2,100) = 3.58$, $p < .04$). Nevertheless, this difference does not impair the comparison between the three conditions because (a) participants were randomly distributed in the three conditions, and

(b) cognitive effort was evaluated with RT interferences in which the baseline RT was subtracted.

When their mean baseline RT was computed, participants begun to revise one of the three experimental texts (that contained either spelling, syntactical or coherence errors) in the triple-task situation. They received instructions concerning the way to edit the errors (by crossing or surrounding-displacing a wrong element). Before beginning the revising task, the experimenter announced that the text was the same than in the first step of the experiment and then read aloud the abstract of the text to remind its topic to the participants. This prevented participants from reading the text to understand it (as they did in the first step) and engaged them in reading the text to evaluate it. Participants were also instructed that they would occasionally hear auditory signals during the revising task. For reacting to the probes, they received the same instruction than in the first step of the experiment. However, they were also asked to indicate their thoughts with a labeled key after each reaction to a probe. RT interferences were again computed and were then associated with the label (i.e., the sub-processes of revision) designated by the participants. During the revision task, the experimenter noted the order in which participants made the corrections. Once participants decided that the text was satisfying, they had to press a special key of the keyboard to stop the program.

3.2 *Variables*

The variables that were analyzed accounted for the way the task was realized, the efficiency of the revisions performed by participants and the temporal organization and cognitive effort of reading to define problems, searching a solution and transforming the text.

Task-related Variables
- The length of the task, in minutes, informed on the time each participant needed to revise the text.
- The number of corrective passages was computed by analyzing the order of transformation of errors according to their place in the text. This variable informs on the number of times participants scanned the text to find errors. When doing more than one scanning, participants can re-read the text to search new problems or to find a solution of an error they did not edit at the first reading.

Efficiency of Writers' Revisions
- The percentage of correct revisions was computed for each participant by dividing the number of correct revisions by the number of expected revisions. A revision was scored as correct when (a) the suppression of the target was complete, and (b) the target was moved at the correct position or when the non-problematic zone was moved beside the target.
- The percentage of incorrect revisions was computed for each participant by dividing the number of incorrect revisions by the number of expected revisions. An incorrect error corresponded to the move of a target that had to be sup-

pressed or to the suppression of a target that had to be moved. Moving a target to an unexpected place also constituted an incorrect revision. This variable, that is not the complementary of the previous one (because some targets may have not been processed), informs on errors correctly diagnosed but for which participants did not find a solution.

- The number of unexpected revisions. This variable concerns revisions that did not correspond to revisions of errors inserted in the text or to partial revisions of targets. This variable informs on diagnosis' failures of participants.

Processes-related Variables

- The cognitive effort of the sub-processes of reading to understand, reading to define problems, searching a solution and transforming the text was assessed by RT interferences that were calculated by subtracting for each participant their mean baseline RT from the RTs collected either in dual- or triple-task.
- The activation of the processes was estimated by computing the percentage of time a sub-process of revision was designated by each participant (number of time a process is designated divided by the total number of processes designated during the triple task situation).

4. RESULTS

4.1 *Task-related Variables*

Results showed a main significant effect of the type of errors on the length of the task. Thus, participants took longer to revise problems of coherence (9.53 min.) than syntactical (8.01 min.) and spelling errors (6.08 min.), $F(2,100) = 12.11$, $p < .001$. The WM span did not affected the length of the task (low-WM = 8.26 min. vs. high-WM = 7.50 min.), $F(1,100) = 1.68$, $p = .19$ (see Figure 1). No significant interaction was observed.

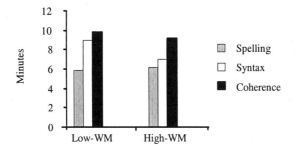

Figure 1. Length of the task (in minutes) according to the type of errors (spelling, syntax, and coherence) and to the working memory capacity (low-WM or high-WM).

Results on the number of corrective passages (see Figure 2) revealed a main effect of the type of errors. Participants made more corrective passages with coherence errors (2) than with syntactical (1.4) and spelling errors (1.2), $F(2,100) = 18.41, p < .001$. No other main effect of the WM-span was observed (low WM = 1.56 vs. high-WM = 1.51), $F(1,100) < 1$. No significant interaction was observed.

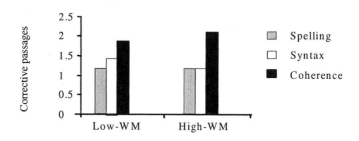

Figure 2. Number of corrective passages according to the type of errors (spelling, syntax, and coherence) and to the working memory capacity (low-WM or high-WM).

4.2 *Efficiency of Writer's Revisions*

Findings on the efficiency of writers' revisions are presented in Table 2. Participants made reliably more correct revisions with spelling errors than with syntactical and coherence errors, $F(2,100) = 69.34, p < .001$. No main effect of WM capacity was observed (low-WM = 53% vs. high-WM = 59.3%), $F(1,100) = 3.77, p > .05$. The type of errors and WM capacity factors reliably interacted. There was a significant effect of WM capacity only on the proportion of spelling errors correctly revised (high-WM = 86.7% vs. low-WM = 74.8%), $F(1,100) = 5.38, p < .03$.

The type of errors also reliably affected the proportion of incorrect errors, $F(2,100) = 17.67, p < .001$. The proportion of incorrect revisions was lower with spelling errors than with syntactical or coherence errors. No main effect of WM capacity was observed (low-WM = 11.14% vs. high-WM = 8.71%), $F(1,100) = 1.63, p > .20$ (see Table 2). No significant interaction was observed.

The number of unexpected revisions was also affected by the type of errors, $F(2,100) = 6.39, p < .003$. Participants made less unexpected revisions with spelling errors than they made with syntactical or coherence errors. WM capacity reliably affected the number of unexpected revisions (low-WM = 1.3 vs. high-WM = 0.80, $F(1,100) = 3.94, p < .05$). No significant interaction was observed.

Table 2. Percentage of correct and incorrect revisions and number of unexpected revisions according to the type of errors (spelling, syntax, and coherence) and to the working memory capacity (low-WM or high-WM)

	Spelling			Syntax			Coherence		
	High-WM	Low-WM	*m*	High-WM	Low-WM	*m*	High-WM	Low-WM	*m*
Type of revisions									
Correct	86.7	74.8	*80.74*	50.5	48.0	*49.29*	40.6	36.8	*38.71*
Incorrect	1.3	3.0	*2.15*	12.1	17.2	*14.65*	12.7	13.2	*12.95*
Unexpected	0.2	0.8	*0.50*	0.8	1.3	*1.07*	1.4	1.6	*1.50*

4.2 Processes-related Variables

Processing time and cognitive effort of the sub-processes of revision. As indicated in Table 3, the type of errors did not affect RT interference, $F(2,81) < 1$, nor did WM capacity (low-WM = 531 ms vs. high-WM = 547 ms), $F(1,81) < 1$.

Table 3. Cognitive effort (RTs interference in ms) of the sub-processes of revisions according to the type of errors (spelling, syntax, and coherence) and to the working memory capacity (low-WM or high-WM).

	Reading			Searching			Transforming			
	High-WM	Low-WM	*m*	High-WM	Low-WM	*m*	High-WM	Low-WM	*m*	*M*
Type of errors										
Spelling	411	420	*415*	629	477	*553*	591	561	*576*	*515*
Syntax	481	504	*493*	555	630	*593*	512	681	*596*	*560*
Coherence	506	406	*456*	596	480	*538*	644	621	*632*	*542*
			455			*561*			*601*	

However, across conditions, RTs interference of the sub-processes of revision significantly varied, $F(2,162) = 27.78$, $p < .001$. Analysis of contrasts revealed that RTs interference was lower for the sub-process of reading to define problems than for searching a solution and than for transforming the text, $F(1,81) = 73.01$, $p < .001$. This effect is observed for each type of errors (spelling: $F(1,81) = 34.96$, $p < .001$; syntax: $F(1,81) = 15.28$, $p < .001$; coherence: $F(1,81) = 25.11$, $p < .001$). Furthermore, results showed a reliable interaction between the sub-processes and WM capacity factors, $F(2,162) = 3.24$, $p < .05$. Participants with low-WM showed higher RTs interference with probes associated with transforming (621 ms) than with searching a solution (529 ms), $F(1,81) = 8.29$, $p < .006$. By contrast, such a difference was not observed with high-WM participants (searching a solution = 593 ms; transforming = 582 ms), $F(1,81) < 1$.

With regard to the activation of the sub-processes of revision (see Table 4), no effect of the type of errors ($F(2,80) < 1$) and of WM capacity was observed, $F(1,80) < 1$. Across conditions, the sub-processes of revision were however differently activated, $F(2,160) = 67.95$, $p < .001$. More precisely, reading to define problems was more activated (49.6%) than searching a solution (27.8%) and than transforming the text (22.6%), $F(1,80) = 101.31$, $p < .001$. This effect was observed with the three types of errors (spelling: $F(1,80) = 25.89$, $p < .001$; syntax: $F(1,80) = 22.91$, $p < .001$; coherence: $F(1,80) = 57.32$, $p < .001$).

Table 4. Activation (in %) of the sub-processes of revisions according to the type of errors (spelling, syntax, coherence) and to the working memory capacity (low-WM or high-WM)

| | Reading | | | Searching | | | Transforming | | |
	High-WM	Low-WM	*m*	High-WM	Low-WM	*m*	High-WM	Low-WM	*m*
Type of errors									
Spelling	44.9	50.1	*47.5*	23.7	25.3	*24.5*	31.3	24.5	*27.9*
Syntax	49.3	44.4	*46.8*	30.5	37.2	*33.8*	20.2	18.4	*19.3*
Coherence	55.9	53.0	*54.4*	23.8	26.4	*25.1*	20.3	20.6	*20.5*
			49.6			*27.8*			*22.6*

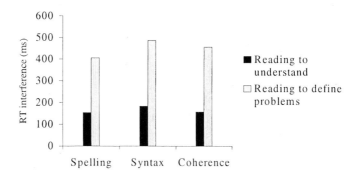

Figure 3. Cognitive effort (RT interference in ms) of reading to understand and reading to define problems according to the type of errors (spelling, syntax, and coherence).

Cognitive effort of reading to understand vs. reading to define problems. Results showed that across conditions, RT interference was higher for reading to define problems (449 ms) than for reading to understand (165 ms), $F(1,100) = 292.42$, $p < .001$ (see Figure 3). This difference was again observed with the three types of errors (spelling: 415 ms vs. 155 ms, $F(1,100) = 84.80$, $p < .001$; syntax: 492 vs. 183 ms, $F(1,100) = 101.89$, $p < .001$; coherence: 456 ms vs. 157 ms, $F(1,100) = 105.96$, $p < .001$). Furthermore, neither main effect of WM capacity nor significant interaction were observed.

5.   DISCUSSION

Three reports can be drawn from the findings of this experiment. Two are related to the linguistic level of the errors and to working memory capacity of participants. The third concerns the cognitive effort associated to the different sub-processes of revision and to reading to understand.

First, as expected, revising different types of errors does not impose the same level of difficulty to the revisers. Indeed, spelling errors were the more often successfully revised errors, followed by syntactical errors and then by coherence errors. This finding is confirmed by results on incorrect and unexpected revisions. These two kinds of revisions were less frequent in the text with spelling errors than in the text with syntactical errors, and they were the more numerous in the text with coherence problems. Thus, as expected, the text with syntactic errors constituted an intermediate difficulty in comparison with revision of spelling and of coherence. This scale in the difficulty to revise errors at different linguistic level is also illustrated by a different number of corrective passages and consequently to the duration of the task that is also scaled according to the kind of error. A single reading of the text is sufficient for revising the majority of spelling errors whereas one or two readings are necessary to revise less efficiently syntactical errors and at least two readings are necessary to revise only one third of the coherence errors. This result is in conformity with the findings of Hayes et al. (1987). Thus, the findings first indicate that revising coherence errors is difficult, even when such errors are less numerous than surface ones as it was the case in the present experiment. This clearly shows that complexity of revision does not depend on the number of errors that have to be corrected but on their nature. However, this change in the difficulty related to the linguistic level of the errors is not associated to a different cognitive effort, as if revision of spelling, which is the most successful, engaged all cognitive resources of participants. This interpretation is supported by results on working memory capacity.

Indeed, with regard to the writer's working memory capacity, the hypothesis that participants with high working memory capacity should be more successful in revising high demanding errors (syntactical and coherence errors) than low working memory participants was not confirmed. A significant effect of the working memory span was observed only on the number of correct revisions of spelling errors. Thus, revisers with high and low working memory capacity exhibited slightly different skills for the control of spelling. This difference may be explained by their ability to detect errors but also by the extent of possible solutions (e.g., means-ends table of Hayes et al., 1987). Indeed, revisers with low working memory span are less good at detecting errors (they made more unexpected revisions) and they applied less correct solutions (correct revisions) than revisers with high working memory span. Thus, the Reading Span Test that accounts for the working memory capacity available during reading might allow predicting only the success in spelling revision. However, being more skilled (or being more knowledgeable) does not imply a low cognitive effort for revisers with high working memory capacity. The cognitive effort allocated to the sub-processes of revision did not vary according to neither working memory span nor the type of errors that had to be edited. It seems that for controlling each of these linguistic levels, revisers engaged all their available resources but took more time trying to solve more difficult problems. Such a relation between cognitive effort and time spent on revision must be confirmed by other experiments. Evidence for such a relation will surely question skilled writing in different terms: when writers control their text, they engaged in effortful processes. And within a difficult task and in order to face a lack of resources, writers do not give up what they manage with difficulty; they increase the duration of the activity.

Regarding the cognitive effort and activation of the sub-processes of revision, two new results emerged from this experiment. First of all, and by contrast with hypothesis, reading to define problems is the less expensive of the sub-processes of revision whereas it is the more frequently activated, and this with all kinds of errors. The fact that in this research, by contrast to Kellogg's (1996) propositions, the process of transforming is relatively expensive is presumably related to the procedure of unusual graphic corrections imposed to the revisers. This experiment must be replicated by leaving participants to revise the text as they usually do. It will be thus possible to better evaluate the cognitive effort of transcription when revising a text. Indeed, it has been shown that during the written production of sentences (Bourdin & Fayol, 1996) and text composition (Olive & Kellogg, 2002), these processes are high-demanding in children but little, if any, in adults.

The second interesting result concerns the experimental validation of Hayes et al.'s (1987) propositions. Reading to understand is much less expensive than reading to define problems (see Flower et al. (1986) for a detailed description of the functional differences between these two kinds of reading). As indicated by the findings of this experiment, reading to define problems is almost three times more expensive than reading to understand. This suggests that even if writers only read a text to evaluate it, without carrying out any modification in the text, this reading is particularly expensive.

To conclude, it should be noted that the present results were little affected by participants' working memory capacity. Only, performance in spelling revision was affected. Further research must be carried out to better understand how capacity in working memory is related to functional differences of writing and, particularly, of revision. One way to explore such an issue may consist in systematically analyzing the relation between the difficulty of the errors that have to be corrected and individual differences in working memory capacity. In sum, this study indicates that even for undergraduate students who frequently use to produce a great amount of written documents in their studies and who have reached a high degree of expertise, text revision remains an expensive exercise, much more expensive than reading. It is important to notice that this activity is always high demanding, even when it concerns spelling. The present findings are convergent with previous research that evaluated cognitive effort of planning, translating and revising and that showed that revision is sometimes even the more demanding writing process (Kellogg, 1994; Olive et al. 1997; Piolat, Roussey, Olive, & Farioli, 1996; Piolat, Kellogg, & Farioli, 2001). The findings are also convergent with previous research that have shown a poor performance of revisers in controlling coherence of the texts and they raise the question about how to succeed in getting more efficient controls. Even if such a question is not new and has already been raised particularly with young writers (Beal, 1990), it has to be developed more deeply. Indeed, several works have studied the means that enhance efficiency of deep revisions, such as teaching the goal of revision (Wallace & Hayes, 1991), strategies (MacArthur, Graham, Schwartz, & Schafer, 1995), collaborative writing (Daiute, 1990), or guiding reviser activity (Berninger et al., 1996; Scardamalia & Bereiter, 1983). These works have however a limited scope. Indeed, either they concerned students with particular characteristics (MacArthur et al., 1995, disabilities), either they constitute punctual research on only one particular task (Wallace & Hayes, 1991), either their results are contradictory (Chanquoy, Piolat, & Roussey, 1996). Therefore, it seems, as Bisaillon (1992) reported, that revision is not explicitly and systematically taught in normal teaching. Perhaps this constitutes an explanation of the mixed success of the undergraduate students of this research despite the important cognitive effort they developed.

APPENDIX

A. ORIGINAL TEXT

LES PSYCHANALYSTES FACE AUX ENFANTS

Anna Freud et Mélanie Klein, des psychanalystes célèbres, ont été les précurseurs de la cure psychanalytique des enfants. Les deux approches divergent considérablement au niveau conceptuel. Elles posent le problème des contraintes méthodologiques associées à l'analyse des enfants.

En effet, les psychanalystes qui se réclament de la conception proposée par Anna Freud tentent d'appliquer la méthode analytique destinée aux névrosés adultes, tout en utilisant un cadre théorique qui dépasse largement la psychanalyse. Parce que l'enfant n'a pas conscience de son symptôme et n'a pas la volonté de guérir, il est nécessaire de le rendre analysable. Aussi, ces praticiens préconisent d'instaurer une phase préparatoire à l'analyse où tous les moyens sont bons pour «attirer» l'enfant, afin de provoquer de sa part un transfert positif. L'ascendant pris par le psychanalyste sur le jeune patient, grâce à ce transfert positif, doit servir d'amorçage au processus analytique. En outre, l'analyste doit obtenir en permanence des renseignements sur la structure familiale et suppléer au manque des parents à être de bons pédagogues. Aussi, dans cette démarche, le psychanalyste est un «éducateur bienveillant».

Au contraire, sous l'impulsion de Mélanie Klein, d'autres psychanalystes préconisent de pratiquer avec les enfants la psychanalyse, rien que la psychanalyse. Selon eux, l'analyse peut être utilisée avec tous les enfants, les enfants normaux compris. Ces praticiens recourent à l'angoisse et au sentiment de culpabilité de l'enfant comme signes interprétables. Ainsi, la construction d'un transfert forcément positif dès le premier contact avec l'enfant n'est pas nécessaire. De plus, le psychanalyste refuse toute intervention pédagogique et il n'a pas besoin de renseignements sur la situation réelle du jeune patient. Par sa parole, l'enfant est l'unique promoteur de son changement et de son évolution. Seule sa parole compte. Ainsi, dans cette perspective, l'analyste est une tierce personne absolument impartiale en position d'écoute pure.

En tout état de cause, ces divergences méthodologiques ne doivent pas faire oublier un problème essentiel, celui de la possibilité d'entreprendre une analyse avec un enfant. Chaque analyste, au-delà des oppositions entre les écoles et les courants psychanalytiques, doit résoudre ce problème qui se pose de façon renouvelée chaque fois qu'il reçoit un nouvel enfant.

B. TEXT WITH COHERENCE ERRORS

Anna Freud et Mélanie Klein, des psychanalystes célèbres, ont été les précurseurs de la cure psychanalytique des enfants. Les deux approches divergent considérablement au niveau conceptuel. Elles posent le problème des contraintes méthodologiques associées à l'analyse des enfants.

En effet, les psychanalystes qui se réclament de la conception proposée par Anna Freud tentent d'appliquer la méthode analytique destinée aux névrosés adultes, tout en utilisant un cadre théorique qui dépasse largement la psychanalyse. **En outre, l'analyste doit obtenir en permanence des renseignements sur la structure familiale et suppléer au manque des parents à être de bons pédagogues****. Parce que l'enfant n'a pas conscience de son symptôme et n'a pas la volonté de guérir, il est nécessaire de le rendre analysable. Aussi, ces praticiens préconisent d'instaurer une phase préparatoire à l'analyse où tous les moyens sont bons pour «attirer» l'enfant, afin de provoquer de sa part un transfert positif. **L'intelligence concrète désigne des activités qui s'exercent sur des objets manipulables***. L'ascendant pris par le psychanalyste sur le jeune patient, grâce à ce transfert positif, doit servir d'amorçage au processus analytique. Aussi, dans cette démarche, le psychanalyste est un «éducateur bienveillant». **De plus, le psychanalyste refuse toute intervention pédagogique et il n'a pas besoin de renseignements sur la situation réelle du jeune patient*****.

Au contraire, sous l'impulsion de Mélanie Klein, d'autres psychanalystes préconisent de pratiquer avec les enfants la psychanalyse, rien que la psychanalyse. **Les questionnaires d'attitude sont des instruments dont l'importance dans les études sociologiques est considérable***. Ces praticiens recourent à l'angoisse et au sentiment de culpabilité de l'enfant comme signes interprétables. Ainsi, la construction d'un transfert forcément positif dès le premier contact avec l'enfant n'est pas nécessaire. Par sa parole, l'enfant est l'unique promoteur de son changement et de son évolution. **Selon eux, l'analyse peut être utilisée avec tous les enfants, les enfants normaux compris****. Seule sa parole compte. Ainsi, dans cette perspective, l'analyste est une tierce personne absolument impartiale en position d'écoute pure.

En tout état de cause, ces divergences méthodologiques ne doivent pas faire oublier un problème essentiel, celui de la possibilité d'entreprendre une analyse avec un enfant. **Le praticien doit continuellement veiller à sa propre santé***. Chaque analyste, au-delà des oppositions entre les écoles et les courants psychanalytiques, doit résoudre ce problème qui se pose de façon renouvelée chaque fois qu'il reçoit un nouvel enfant .

*   semantically unrelated sentence to suppress
**   sentence to displace inside the same paragraph
***   sentence to displace in a other paragraph

C. TEXT WITH SPELLING ERRORS

Anna Freud et Mélanie Klein, des psychanalystes célèbres, ont été les précurseurs de la **curre** (cure) psychanalytique des enfants. Les deux approches **divregent** (divergent) considérablement au niveau conceptuel. Elles posent le problème des contraintes méthodologiques associées à l'analyse des enfants.

En effet, les **spychanalystes** (psychanalystes) qui se réclament de la conception proposée **part** (par) Anna Freud tentent d'appliquer la méthode analytique destinée aux névrosés adultes, tout en utilisant un cadre **téorhique** (théorique) qui dépasse largement la psychanalyse. **Prace que** (Parce que) l'enfant n'a pas conscience de son symptôme et n'a pas la volonté de guérir, il est nécessaire de le rendre analysable. **Eaussi** (Aussi), ces praticiens préconisent d'instaurer une phase préparatoire à l'analyse où tous les moyens sont bons pour «attirer» l'enfant, afin de **provocquer** (provoquer) de sa part un transfert positif. L'ascendant pris par le psychanalyste sur le jeune patient, grâce à ce transfert **possitif** (positif), doit servir d'amorçage au processus analytique. En **houtre** (outre), l'analyste doit obtenir en permanence des renseignements sur la structure familiale et **suppleér** (suppléer) au manque des parents à être de bons pédagogues. Aussi, dans cette démarche, le psychanalyste est un «éducateur bienveillant».

Au contraire, sous **l'implusion** (l'impulsion) de Mélanie Klein, d'autres psychanalystes préconisent de pratiquer avec les enfants la psychanalyse, rien que la psychanalyse. Selon eux, l'analyse peut être utilisée avec tous les enfants, les enfants normaux **compirs** (compris). Ces praticiens **reucourent** (recourent) à l'angoisse et au sentiment de culpabilité de l'enfant comme signes **interpértables** (interprétables). Ainsi, la construction d'un transfert forcément positif dès le premier contact avec l'**anfent** (enfant) n'est pas nécessaire. De plus, le psychanalyste refuse toute intervention pédagogique et il n'a pas besoin de renseignements sur la situation **réielle** (réelle) du jeune patient. Par sa parole, l'enfant est l'unique promoteur de son changement et de son **évollution** (évolution). Seule sa parole compte. Ainsi, dans cette **persepective** (perspective), l'analyste est une tierce personne absolument **impartialle** (impartiale) en position d'écoute pure.

En tout état de cause, ces divergences méthodologiques ne doivent pas faire **oubiler** (oublier) un problème essentiel, **celiu** (celui) de la possibilité d'entreprendre une analyse avec un enfant. Chaque analyste, au-delà des oppositions **enrte** (entre) les écoles et les courants psychanalytiques, doit **réssoudre** (résoudre) ce problème qui se pose de façon renouvelée chaque fois qu'il reçoit un nouvel enfant.

D. TEXT WITH SYNTACTICAL ERRORS

Anna Freud et Mélanie Klein, des psychanalystes célèbres, ont été **lancés*** les précurseurs de la cure psychanalytique des enfants. Les deux approches divergent **très*** considérablement au niveau conceptuel. Elles posent le problème des contraintes méthodologiques associées à l'analyse des enfants.

En effet, les psychanalystes qui se réclament de la conception proposée par Anna Freud tentent d'appliquer la méthode analytique destinée aux névrosés adultes, tout en utilisant un cadre théorique qui dépasse largement la psychanalyse. Parce que l'enfant n'a pas conscience de son symptôme et n'a **de guérir**** pas la volonté, il est nécessaire de le rendre analysable.

Aussi, ces praticiens préconisent d'instaurer **dans l'installation*** une phase préparatoire à l'analyse où tous les moyens sont bons pour «attirer» l'enfant, afin de provoquer de sa part un transfert positif. L'ascendant pris par le psychanalyste sur le jeune patient, grâce à ce transfert positif, doit servir d'amorçage au processus analytique. L'analyste doit obtenir en permanence des **en outre**** renseignements sur la structure familiale et suppléer au manque des parents à être de bons pédagogues. Aussi, dans cette démarche, le psychanalyste est un «éducateur bienveillant».

Au contraire, sous l'impulsion de Mélanie Klein, d'autres psychanalystes préconisent **en proposant*** de pratiquer avec les enfants la psychanalyse, rien que la psychanalyse. Selon eux, l'analyse peut être utilisée avec tous les enfants, **à la clé*** les enfants normaux compris. Ces praticiens recourent à l'angoisse et au sentiment de culpabilité de l'enfant comme signes interprétables. Ainsi, la construction d'un transfert positif **forcément**** dès le premier contact avec l'enfant n'est pas nécessaire. De plus, **toute intervention pédagogique**** le psychanalyste refuse et il n'a pas besoin de renseignements sur la situation réelle du jeune patient. Par sa parole, l'enfant est l'unique promoteur de son changement et de son évolution. Seule **seulement*** sa parole compte. Ainsi, dans cette perspective, l'analyste est une tierce personne absolument impartiale en position d'écoute pure.

Ces divergences méthodologiques ne doivent pas faire oublier un problème essentiel, celui de la possibilité d'entreprendre une analyse avec un enfant **en tout état de cause****. Chaque analyste, au-delà des oppositions entre les écoles et les courants psychanalytiques, doit ce problème qui **résoudre**** se pose de façon renouvelée chaque fois qu'il reçoit un nouvel enfant.

| * | word(s) to suppress |
| ** | word(s) to displace in the same sentence |

ORTHOGRAPHIC REVISION: THE CASE OF SUBJECT-VERB AGREEMENT IN FRENCH

PIERRE LARGY*, LUCILE CHANQUOY**, & ALEXANDRA DÉDÉYAN***

* University of Toulouse Le Mirail, France, ** University of Nantes, France, *** University of Rouen, France

Abstract. The chapter presents two experiments carried out on orthographic revision with children and adults. The first experiment aims to investigate the stage during which 'rule proceduralization', with regard to subject-verb agreement, occurs. On analysing the performance obtained from primary school children in two types of tasks: (1) to agree a dictated verb in context; (2) to detect and correct an error involving this kind of agreement, we found that there is a period (second and third years of primary school) during which children prove to be more able to detect and correct an agreement error, than to produce this agreement during writing. These results are explained in terms of the cognitive cost difference between these activities. The second research aims to study development of expertise in the detection of such agreement errors. Analysis of the performance of primary and secondary school children and adults, in a task consisting in detecting agreement errors in sentences presented one by one on a computer screen, reveals an expert profile of error detection, certainly due to an implicit learning of spatial co-occurrences between morphemes. From the point of view of the cognitive processes involved in production and revising, these results allow discussion, on the one hand, of the phenomenon of knowledge proceduralization (automatization of agreement processing for writing; automatization of agreement error detection processing), and on the other hand, of the role of implicit learning in the management of agreements.

Keywords: Orthographic revision, subject-verb number agreement, agreement errors, error detection, spelling expertise

1. INTRODUCTION

The main purpose of this chapter is to analyze how writers revise a specific grammatical agreement in French: the subject-verb number agreement. The results of the two experiments described here – each being carried out in a cognitive and developmental perspective – allow a better understanding of the processes used by both novice and expert writers to detect errors. In addition, these results, along with the questions they raise, enable us to discuss the way grammatical agreement can be taught at school.

Until recently, little research had been done on the revision in the area of grammatical agreements. This situation is probably due to the fact that the study of grammatical spelling entails many problems. First, investigations dealing with written production have long been outnumbered by studies concerned with oral language. The noticeably less advanced models, among other clues, clearly betray the fact that writing is lagging behind (see Bock, 1995). Moreover, studies in the field of writing have been mainly focused on conceptual aspects, considering spelling as a "low-level" activity (see Alamargot & Chanquoy, 2001 for a review). Finally, most models of spelling acquisition exclusively concern lexical spelling (for example, Ehri, 1986; Gentry, 1982; Morris, 1983), to the detriment of grammatical spelling. This observation is due to the fact that spelling has chiefly been studied through its relationships with reading (Rieben, Fayol, & Perfetti, 1997). More generally, grammatical spelling suffers from the weak position that it occupies within the English language, a language for which the great majority of research about writing is carried out.

The scarcity of research on the revision of grammatical spelling can also be accounted for by the difficulty to study this process without previously having a clear view of the declarative and procedural knowledge necessary for the production of spelling rules. Numerous studies connected with the activity of revision in primary school's children are thus limited to a comparison between the detection of surface (or formal) errors (including grammatical errors) and meaning errors (see for example: Cameron, Edmunds, Wigmore, Hunt, & Linton, 1997), essentially because of a lack of information about children's competencies, for a given age level and a given area.

The purpose of this chapter is therefore to study the specific case of the revision of the subject-verb agreement in written French. The relevance of this topic is developed after a general presentation of the activity of revision within models of text production.

2.   THEORETICAL PART

2.1 Research on Text Production

Studying the revision of an agreement leads to the necessity to take into account two research categories. On the one hand, studies relative to text production, because the revising process is one of the fundamental writing processes and is systematically present within writing models and, on the other hand, research on the agreement production, because it describes the development stages of the agreement procedure.

Revision is one of the three main processes in Hayes and Flower's (1980) original model. This model is made of three major components: (1) the task environment, including all the factors external to the writer that influence the task realization; (2) the set of cognitive processes implied in writing: planning (deciding what and how to write), translating (transforming plans into written texts) and revising (correcting the text in order to improve it); (3) the writer's long-term memory containing all the necessary pieces of knowledge in order to produce a text (for a detailed description and a discussion of this model, see Alamargot & Chanquoy, 2001). In this perspective, revision is conceived as an autonomous process including the re-reading activity of the already produced text as well as procedures used for correcting it (Piolat & Roussey, 1991-1992). More generally, revision is considered as a recursive activity that can appear at any moment during the writing process, before, during or after each writing period (Faigley & Witte, 1984).

Research carried out on revision generally distinguishes between formal (e.g., surface aspects: spelling, punctuation, etc.) and meaning revisions. The analysis of the nature and quantity of revisions has made obvious the effect of age and/or expertise level (for example, Chanquoy, 2001). Among other aspects, formal revisions have been shown to be persistently more frequent than those concerning the meaning of the text (Chanquoy, 1997, 2001; Yagelski, 1995), and that they mainly consist in low-level changes in novice writers (Roussey, 1991). The failure of revision is often explained in terms of cognitive overload in working memory (McCutchen, Kerr, & Francis, 1994). This overload would possibly take place during the revising process or before, that is during writing. Hacker (1994) considers that writers revise more the text surface than its meaning because formal revisions are cognitively less demanding. In children, Fayol, Gombert, and Baur (1987) have shown that the control of the text quality is largely limited. These authors have analyzed children's (7-8 years of age) behaviors while the latter were revising narrative texts. They have clearly established that the few alterations children made mainly concern spelling and very rarely the elaboration of the story. The authors explain this restriction of the revising activity by the important processing cost of the revision of a text structure.

The activity of revision is described as a composite activity, with three main operations: detection, diagnosis and modification (e.g., correction of an agreement error; rewriting). Revision failure is generally imputed to the detection operation. For example, to understand why children fail to revise semantic aspects of the text, Beal (1990) has studied the performances of children of 10 and 12 years of age for the detection and correction of meaning errors. This author observes that older children detect more meaning errors than 10 year-olds. However, when younger children detect an error, they correct it as efficiently as older children. Furthermore, when the author points out errors, the developmental differences observed during correction are less salient. It seems therefore that the initial problem that the novice writer is faced with during revision is how to locate the error and not how to correct it. Hacker, Plumb, Butterfield, Quathamer, and Heineken (1994) confirm this interpretation with teenagers and adults. They show that if to know how to correct an error is a necessary condition for its detection, this knowledge is, however, not sufficient.

Hayes, Flower, Schriver, Stratman, and Carey (1987) situate the detection operation within a revising model, which is organized in four steps. The first stage consists in defining the dimension to be revised. The second step is devoted to the reading of the text following the chosen dimension in order to find possible problems. The third stage corresponds to the decision to modify or not the text. After detection, diagnosis and decision to intervene, the fourth step consists in implementing technical means to modify the text. The revision process therefore results from this sequencing and the success of these different operations, from text rereading to modification, detection being here an essential stage.

To sum up, revision is a cognitively costly activity. The revision of dimensions such as spelling, considered as a formal correction, is less costly than those linked to semantic aspects (Chanquoy, 2001). Nevertheless, even lower-level dimensions require some attentional resources in order to be revised. A good way to analyze the detection operation is to study the particular case of the subject-verb agreement in written French.

2.2 *Relevance of Subject-Verb Agreement in Written French*

The case of the subject-verb agreement is particularly well-indicated to study the activity of revision in the area of grammatical spelling. First of all, the subject-verb agreement follows in French a simple grammatical rule: a singular noun requires a singular agreement for the verb and a plural noun leads to a plural agreement of the verb. Moreover, the verb agreement has been extensively studied for about ten years in the French written language (since Fayol & Got, 1991), as well as in the English oral language (since Bock & Miller, 1991). Recent experiments carried out in written French have allowed to describe how beginner and expert writers understand and produce number inflections of the verb (Chanquoy & Negro, 1996; Fayol, Hupet, & Largy, 1999; Negro & Chanquoy, 2000a & 2000b; Totereau, Thevenin, & Fayol, 1997). Finally, the verb agreement in French has permitted to study the management of inaudible inflections. Indeed, for the majority of verbs, the singular inflections (-*e*) and the plural inflections (-*ent*) do not lead to a phonological distinction between singular and plural forms (e.g., *il parle* [paRl] he speaks / *ils parlent* [paRl] they speak). Conversely, in English, the verb is differently pronounced according to whether it agrees with the singular or with the plural (e.g., speaks [spi:ks] / speak [spi:k]). The study of the subject-verb agreement in French therefore makes it possible to study processes implied in the management of the inflectional morphology, independently of the effect of the phonological marking of the verb number.

This particularity has been useful for research concerning the production of inflections of verb and noun number in French. Indeed, there is in this language a similar configuration in the case of the plural of nouns: there is no phonological difference between the singular and the plural for most nouns (e.g., *lit* [li] / *lits* [li]) while this difference exists in English (e.g., bed [bed] / beds [bedz]). The inflectional marking of plural has been demonstrated to be more than a simple transcription of phonemes into graphemes. In the same way, it is probable that the revision of an agreement is not limited to the search for an appropriateness between phonemes and graphemes.

Studying the production of subject-verb agreement, Largy, Fayol, and Lemaire (1996) took advantage of this silent morphology to show that the agreement processes are permeable to the semantic characteristics of the words to generate. By dictating sentences to adults, using a double task procedure (i.e., keeping a series of words in memory while transcribing sentences), the authors observe more agreement errors in sentences such as "*Le jardinier sort les légumes et il les asperge*" (The gardener takes the vegetables out and he sprinkles them) that in sentences such as "*L'éléphant voit les clowns et il les asperge*" (The elephant sees the clowns and it sprinkles them). They thus show that, when the noun and the verb are homophones (i.e., in French, *asperge* is both a verb conjugated in the present with the third person singular and a singular masculine noun), the semantic context of the sentence has an impact on the selection of the plural inflection. The error consists here in agreeing the verb *asperger* (to sprinkle) as if it were a noun (*asperge* [asparagus]) when the context of the sentence evokes the semantic field of the garden and vegetables ("*Le jardinier sort les légumes et il les asperges*").

More recently, Largy and Fayol (2001) have underlined the effect of phonological factors on agreement accuracy. Adults in a double task situation make significantly more agreement errors with verbs which do not allow them to clearly distinguish the singular form from the plural form (e.g., *accuser* [to accuse]: the singular (*accuse*) and the plural (*accusent*) are pronounced in the same way: [akyze]) than with verbs for which this distinction is possible (e.g., *trahir* [to betray]: *trahit* [tRai] for the singular *vs. trahissent* [tRais] for the plural). Thus, sentences as "*La bande des résistants accuse*" (The band of rebels accuse) are more frequently erroneous than sentences as "*La bande des résistants trahit*" (The band of rebels betrays). The observed error is an error of proximity agreement: "*La bande des résistants accusent*" (The band of rebels accuse).

The study of the French verb agreement seems therefore particularly relevant in order to study revising processes independently of the phonological marking of the verb number.

2.3 *Research on Subject-Verb Agreement*

In French, the orthographic competence in the management of the subject-verb number agreement is linked to the learning of a rule, to the written production of often inaudible inflections, but also to the writer's capacity of re-reading a text in order to find errors. Agreement errors are frequent in beginner writers but they are equally observed in experts, which have a regular practice of writing (Chanquoy & Negro, 1996; Fayol & Got, 1991; Fayol & Largy, 1992; Fayol, Largy, & Lemaire, 1994; Largy, Chanquoy, & Fayol, 1994; Largy et al., 1996; Negro & Chanquoy, 1999, 2000a & b). Although beginner's errors must be clearly distinguished from expert's, chiefly because their origin is different, the spontaneous agreement production is nevertheless, on the whole, frequently erroneous in written French. Consequently, it is important for both types of writers to develop competencies in spelling revision.

Before analyzing how agreement is revised, it is of course necessary to observe how it is produced. Many studies have been devoted to the development of the agreement procedure in French (see for example: Fayol et al., 1999; Largy, 1995; Totereau, Barrouillet, & Fayol, 1998; Totereau et al., 1997). Most of these studies have used the same experimental paradigm. It consists in dictating items (sentences, phrases or words) to participants of different ages and/or school levels while varying the degree of cognitive resources necessary to manage the agreement. The limitation of these resources is obtained by adding to the main task a secondary task, cognitively demanding. The authors then compare the different types of errors produced, with or without a secondary task.

In this view, the analysis of errors carried out by Fayol et al. (1999) has brought to the fore three main stages in the development of the agreement procedure. By dictating to second, fourth, and fifth year primary school children sentences built as follows: "Noun1 of Noun2 + Verb" (e.g., *"Le chien des voisins arrive"* [The dog of the neighbors arrives]), in which Noun1 and Noun2 differ in number, the authors observe, with two different conditions (recall of sentences without added task *vs.* with added task), three main types of errors characterizing, according to them, three acquisition steps. They first observe a systematic failure of agreement when one or both nouns are plural, then a "fragile" agreement, frequently erroneous with a secondary task, and finally the characteristic expert error, which is, with the added task condition, an agreement error of proximity (i.e., *"Le chien des voisins arriv<u>ent</u>"* [The dog of the neighbors arriv<u>e</u>]). Fayol et al. (1999) explain these three types of errors as follows.

As early as their second year of primary school, children have to learn that, in writing, some inflections indicate the plural at the end of words (e.g., *-s* for nouns and e.g., *-ent* for verbs conjugated with the third person plural) and that these marks are generally not pronounced and, as a consequence, not audible. Before this learning, most of the oppositions between singular and plural met by children are due to the opposition between singular articles – definite (*le* / *la* [the]) or indefinite (*un* / *une* [a]) – and plural articles (definite: *les* [the] or indefinite: *des* [some]). In oral language, these articles are often the unique markers that indicate the number of the noun they relate to (Dubois, 1965; Jarema & Kehayia, 1992). Conversely, in written production, the number of nouns and verbs is systematically marked (with very rare exceptions for nouns, such as: *nez* (singular) / *nez* (plural) [nose / noses]). However, plural and singular nouns, as well as regular verbs conjugated with the third person singular or plural, are most often homophonous. Thereby, children have to discover the existence of a specific written morphology that has no correspondence with oral language. Consequently, the first stage of the acquisition of the written morphology is to learn that the notion of plurality in a sentence has to be expressed by adding *-s* to nouns and *-ent* to verbs. This first step consists in encoding the morphology of noun and verb number under a declarative form.

The discovery of written marks indicating plural does not imply that these marks can be immediately written. Indeed, to agree nouns and verbs, children have to differentiate nouns from verbs and to apply condition-action rules (or *algorithms*; see Anderson, 1983, 1993) such as: "If a word is a noun and if this noun is plural, then it is necessary to add a morpheme *–s* at the end of the noun; if a word is a verb and if the subject of this verb is plural, then the morpheme *–nt* has to be added to the verb." The laborious and slow application of such production rules characterizes a second stage: The writer has to access a declarative knowledge in long-term memory, in order to test the appropriateness of the conditions and actions with the situation s/he is processing, so as to edit the correct word. As it is not still automated, the application of such a procedure mobilizes a lot of cognitive resources. This procedure is then not efficient when the writer must manage in parallel a cognitively costly secondary task.

The third stage is conceived as the passage from the laborious application of the agreement algorithm to a direct retrieval in long-term memory of root/inflection associations (Logan, 1988a, 1988b, 1992). As children increasingly read and write sentences and texts, they more and more frequently meet the following sequence: "Article + Noun + Verb (+ Complement)", which is in French the most canonical sequence of words (Dubois, 1965). The frequency and the regularity of these multiple exposures would lead children to shift from a strongly controlled algorithmic activity to a direct, rapid and costless access in memory to the correct morpheme. Indeed, during reading, children frequently meet linguistic associations such as "Article + Noun" and "Noun or Pronoun + Verb", and their associated plural inflections. There would thus be a form of implicit learning for the agreement (Perruchet, 1998). This phenomenon has to be added to the practice of text production, these two phenomena leading to the agreement procedure as a direct retrieval from long-term memory of the correct morpheme. Thus, as the practice of subject-verb increases, it becomes increasingly automated and autonomous. Proximity agreement errors, which characterize expert performances, are contemporary to this passage from a costly processing of agreement to a direct retrieval of morphemes from memory (see, concerning this topic, Anderson & Fincham, 1994).

2.4 Revision of Subject-Verb Agreement: Some Hypotheses

As a conclusion, a weak link can be observed between studies dealing with text production, including those on revision, and research on the production of grammatical agreements under sentence dictation, as each resorts to specific models.

Investigations on the production of agreements are essentially based on an adaptation to written production of Levelt's (1989) model of oral language production and cannot thereby be analyzed according to the general models of text production. What may bridge the gap between these two types of studies is the way they apprehend expertise, as both refer to the theory concerning the capacity of attentional resources (Just & Carpenter, 1992) and to the working memory model (Baddeley, 1986; 1990). Hence, expertise, both in the field of agreement production and text revision is usually described as an ultimate stage enabling the writer to manage his written production more efficiently and with a lower cost. Based on this concept of attentional resources, this chapter tries to highlight two levels of achievement in the case of the subject-verb agreement, the first one characterizing the novice's behavior, the second describing the expert's.

Indeed, as shown previously, the beginner (or novice) writer would rely on the cognitively costly application of an algorithm of agreement verification. This algorithm would consist in condition-action rules (Anderson, 1983, 1995), close to rules used during agreement production, since using the same propositions, such as: "If a word is a verb, if the subject of this verb is plural and if this verb does not present the morpheme –ent, then it is necessary to add this morpheme to the verb." Although experts are also able to access and use this algorithm, they do so less systematically than novices. Indeed, we postulate that the repeated practice of written language can facilitate the spelling revision activity by substituting to the nearly systematic application of this algorithm the use of prototypic configurations stored in long-term memory. Thus, in the case of the subject-verb agreement, the co-occurrence of the inflectional morphemes *–s* and *–ent* on two successive words would allow the expert to consider that the agreement is correct, without any necessary verification. The revision expertise could then be defined as the immediate recognition of prototypical agreement configurations, just like writing expertise (for agreement), which is considered by Fayol et al. (1999) as a direct retrieval from memory of roots/inflections associations (Logan, 1988a, 1988b, 1992). The important frequency of co-occurrences such as "noun *–e* + verb *–e*" and "noun *–s* + verb *–ent*" during reading as well as writing could then explain this implicit learning.

3.   EXPERIMENTS

3.1 *Experiment 1*

In this first study, second, third and fourth primary school graders were asked to perform two tasks. The first task consisted in writing under dictation verbs that were singular or plural. The second one was a detection and correction task of agreement errors among sentences. As the revision algorithm relies on the same knowledge that the production algorithm, it is predicted that, during first primary school years, children should make subject-verb agreement errors as well as detect and correct such errors. Moreover, because the performance related to agreement production is largely constrained by the writing activity itself (e.g., graphic and orthographic constraints; see Bourdin & Fayol, 1994), differences between production and revision should decrease as school grades increase, due to better performances in the production task. We also predict that the stage during which the child proves to be competent in terms of agreement production is systematically preceded by another stage in which the same child is more successful in revision than in production.

3.1.1   *Method*

Seventy-two children, regular at school, coming from a same primary school, participated in the experiment; there were 24 children in each of the following grades: second (mean age: 7;6), third (8;5) and fourth (9;6). These children had not followed any specific training to orthographic detection or correction.

Thirty-two noun-verb pairs had been selected (e.g., *bague/briller* [ring/to shine]; see Appendix A). Experimental items were constructed according to the classic French grammatical structure "Article + Noun + Verb" (e.g., "*La bague brille*" [The ring shines]). Nouns and verbs were simple words taken from the reading book (Gafi, 1998) used in the school where the experiment was carried out. None of these nouns or verbs began by a vowel, so as to avoid phonological information connected with plurality as might be the case with the French "liaison" phenomenon (Largy & Fayol, 2001). There were as many masculine nouns as feminine nouns. All the verbs were French first group verbs and were systematically conjugated in the third person singular or plural of the indicative present. The noun and verb length never exceeded three syllables.

For the production task, half of the experimental items was singular, and the other half was plural. For the revision task, half of the items appeared without agreement error, and were singular or plural in one sentence out of two. Half of the other experimental items was incorrect (agreement error). There were two types of errors: (1) illicit plural inflection (e.g., "*La bague brillent*" [The ring shine]); (2) no plural inflection (e.g., "*Les bagues brille*" [The rings shines]).

All the items were printed in a booklet, with one item per page: 32 experimental items were mixed with different categories of filler items so as to avoid any special focus on the subject-verb agreement during production or revision activities.

For the production task, the article and the noun were printed on each page of the booklet. Children had to write down the verb once the experimenter had read the complete item (e.g., Article + Noun + Verb). For the revision task, the complete item appeared on the booklet. Children had to correct possible errors once the experimenter had read the complete item. The item was presented as being likely to contain an orthographic error.

3.1.2   Results

Three categories of errors were found in production and in revision. They concerned: (1) exclusively the word inflection (noted $R^{+}I^{-}$), (2) exclusively its root (noted $R^{-}I^{+}$), or (3) both the root and the inflection (noted $R^{-}I^{-}$).

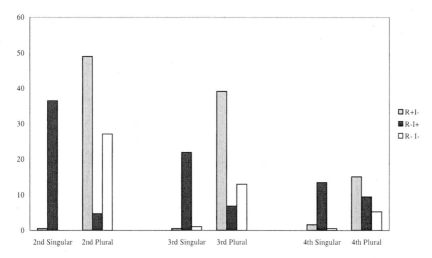

Figure 1. Production: Percentages of the 3 types of errors ($R^{+}I^{-}$: right root and erroneous inflection; $R^{-}I^{+}$: erroneous root and right inflection; $R^{-}I^{-}$: erroneous root and erroneous inflection) in relation with the number of the verb (singular vs. plural) and the school level (second, third and fourth years of primary school).

In production (see Figure 1), sizeable but decreasing number of root errors is observed from second to fourth primary school year: 61% were confusions about the phoneme-grapheme correspondence ("translation" problem: "*sircule*" instead of "*circule*" [circulates]), 23 % concerned letters that had to be doubled ("*chaufe* instead of "*chauffe*" [warms]), 15 % dealt with an absence of accent ("*brule*" instead of "*brûle*" [burns]), and finally only 1% were unreadable root (problem of handwriting). Considering that the production of the root has a non negligible cost for these young children, performances for agreement production have been analyzed only when the root was correctly written. Thus only the first category of errors (R^+T^-) has been considered for the analysis. In this case, few errors were observed in the singular: 1 error in second and in third grade, and 3 errors produced by one fourth grader. All of them consisted in agreeing a singular verb in the plural with a *–ent* inflection.

Consequently, the performance for the production task about the verb agreement has been analyzed only when children had to produce the plural inflection *–ent*. On this condition, two types of errors were found: (1) absence of the *–ent* inflection (40 %) and (2) presence of an incorrect plural inflection corresponding to a noun inflection (e.g., *–s*; 60 %). In addition, this last type of error increased with grade (51/94 in second grade, 44/75 in third and 24/29 in fourth). With grade progression, children increasingly often agree the verb, even if there still is a confusion between verb and noun inflections in the plural. However, in both cases the agreement was erroneous and the two categories of errors were put together in the analysis of variance described below.

Concerning the revision task, Figure 2 presents only two error categories because only one (R^-T^-) error was produced in third grade. Moreover, this Figure only concerns errors made during the revision of an erroneous agreement. Indeed, very few revision errors were observed in the case of a correct agreement (0 for the singular, 3 for the plural). These errors were produced by two second graders and consisted in suppressing the *–ent* inflection and to replace it by the *–s* inflection. 11 items (6 in second grade, 2 in third and 3 in fourth) with a correction of the noun root (the subject of the verb) were eliminated, as well as those that presented a modification of the verb root.

The number of revision errors was more important with the absence of verbal inflection in the plural than with incorrect inflection. Thus, children made more revision errors with items as "*Les chiens mange*" [The dogs eat*s*] than with sentences as "*Le chien mangent*" [The dog eat], when these items were presented both orally and visually. To understand this difference, it is necessary to specify the nature of errors committed in both cases. Indeed, with an erroneous verb inflection, the errors were exclusively a non-suppression of the erroneous *–nt* inflection. Conversely, without plural inflection, there were two types of errors: (1) no addition of the missing *–nt* inflection or (2) addition of a plural *–s* inflection (e.g., addition of noun inflection instead of verb inflection: violation of grammatical category). This second category increased with grades (31/63 in second grade, 27/41 in third and 17/20 in fourth). It looks as if, in the course of these three school years, children were gradually able to better detect the inappropriateness between verb inflection and the subject number, but, in order to correct this error, were able to make a confusion between noun and verb inflections.

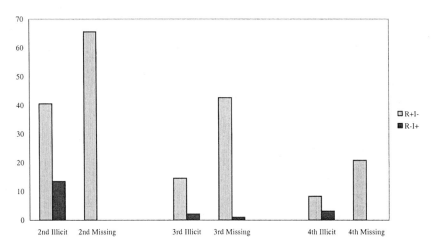

Figure 2. Revision: Percentages of the 2 types of errors (R^+I^-: right root and erroneous inflection; R^-I^+: erroneous root and right inflection) in relation with the type of introduced errors (illicit inflection vs. missing inflection) and the school level (second, third and fourth years of primary school).

The following analysis aims at comparing children's performances during the production of plural verb inflections (*–ent*) with their performances during the revision of a subject-verb agreement error. A correct revision needs to detect and to correct an incorrect verb inflection (i.e., to suppress the incorrect *–nt* inflection or to add the correct *–nt*). The dependent variable is the percentage of items for which the plural inflection was correctly produced or revised, this percentage being calculated in relation to the number of correctly produced or correctly revised items, indifferently from the accuracy of the inflection. These data have been computed with a 3 (School level: second, third or fourth grade) x 2 (Type of task: production or revision) analysis of variance with repeated measures on the last factor. This analysis was performed both with participants (*F1*) and with items (*F2*) as random factor. Percentages of items correctly produced and revised appear in Figure 3.

The grade level was significant: 35.4% of success in second, 60.1% in third to 82.9% in fourth grade, $F1(2,69) = 13.53$, $p < .0001$; $F2(2,124) = 48.86$, $p < .0001$. The percentage of successful revisions (66.9%) was significantly higher than those observed in production (52%), $F1(1,69) = 31.09$, $p < .0001$; $F2(1,62) = 5.32$, $p < .03$.

As it was predicted, the interaction between the school level and the type of task was significant with participants, $F1(2,69) = 4.7$, $p < .01$, and only marginally significant with material, $F2(2,124) = 2.8$, $p < .06$. This interaction shows that the effect of the type of task was significant in second, $t(23) = 3.52$, $p < .002$, and third grade, $t(23) = 5.77$, $p < .0001$, and not in fourth grade, $t(23) < 1$.

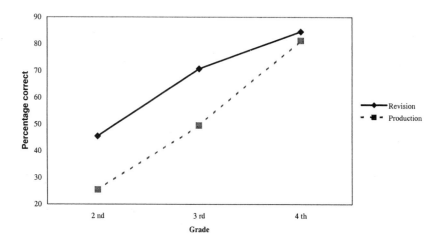

Figure 3. Percentages of correctly realized items in relation with the type of situation (production vs. revision) and the school level (second, third, and fourth grade).

A study of children's individual profiles showed that the success in both tasks (production and revision) occurred quite late in primary school. It was only from the fourth grade that it was largely observed (with a criterion of 75% of success at least by task: 4 second graders; 7 third graders; 17 fourth graders). Thirteen children massively failed in both tasks (with a criterion of 25% of success, or less: 10 second graders; 2 third graders; one fourth graders). Most of the other children (10 second graders; 15 third graders; 5 fourth graders) obtained better results in revision than in production. Only one fourth grader made fewer errors in production than in revision.

These results were compatible with our hypothesis. In beginner writers, producing and revising an agreement seem to rely on the application of an algorithm mobilizing the same set of knowledge. Indeed, the study of individual profiles has shown that, when performances differed between the two tasks, the revision of the agreement was quite systematically better achieved than its production. Moreover, this difference was mainly observed in younger children for whom graphic transcription was not yet automated (Bourdin & Fayol, 1994). Differences observed between verb agreement revision and production seem to be only due to the highest cognitive cost of the production task.

The simplicity of the task and of items used in the first experiment do not enable us to characterize the expertise in verb agreement revision. To make this possible, a second experiment was carried out, with more complex experimental items, built as follows: "Noun1 of Noun2 Verb", and imposing a constraint on the time that can be devoted to the detection of potential errors.

3.2 *Experiment 2*

In this second experiment, primary school graders, junior high school and adult students had to detect agreement errors in sentences appearing one after the other on a computer screen, by answering with two keys on a joystick. Experimental sentences to be revised were constructed as follows: "Noun1 + of + Noun2 + Verb." The verb agreement was correct or erroneous. Finally, a constraint was imposed (or not) on the time participants had to realize the revision task. Performances were assessed on the basis of the percentage of erroneous sentences that participants have judged correct (labeled "missed" errors).

Analyzing the number of "missed errors", rather than the number of "false alarms", was relevant to outline a profile of errors characterizing the use of an expert procedure during revision. Since in production, the expert writer often handles the subject-verb agreement through proximity (i.e., proximity concord, see Francis, 1986), it is thus possible to postulate that this could be equally the case during agreement revision. Some of the experimental complex sentences were built in order to delude participants, who focused on the presence or absence of proximal co-occurrence between inflections (–s of a noun and –ent of a verb) to determine if the agreement was correct or not. Indeed, as the number (singular *vs.* plural) of Noun1 and Noun2 varied, participants had to judge sentences in which the subject-verb agreement was erroneous but which also contained a proximity agreement (e.g., "*La tige des tulipes cassent*" [The stem of tulips break] or "*Les pavés de la route glisse*" [The cobbles of the road slips]). If the expert writer uses such a procedure to revise more rapidly and to lesser cost, more "missed" items should be found in the detection of sentences where Noun1 and Noun2 differ in number than in those where Noun1 and Noun2 have the same number. Moreover, this effect should be observed more specifically when participants, constrained by an instruction of rapidity (time constraint), will thus use an expert procedure (proximity agreement), generally efficient, but leading to detection errors with such sentence construction. Finally, this effect should appear late in the process of schooling. Indeed, the implicit learning of proximal inflectional co-occurrences requires a long practice of reading and writing.

3.2.1   Method

One hundred and twelve children, regular at school and considered as normal readers by their teacher, and 28 adult students (mean age: 21;9) participated in the experiment. There were 4 different grades, and 28 children in each level. Two grades came from a same primary school: third grade (mean age: 8;6), fifth grade (10;4). Two other grades were from a junior high school: seventh grade (12;6) and ninth grade (14;7). All these participants had never been trained to orthographic revision.

Sixty-four experimental items [Noun1 + of + Noun2 + Verb] had been elaborated (see Appendix B1 and B2): 16 for each of the 4 categories obtained by varying the number (singular *vs.* plural) of Noun1 and Noun2. Noun1 and Noun2 had the same number (Singular Singular: SS; Plural Plural: PP) or differed in number (Singular Noun1 and Plural Noun2: SP; Plural Noun1 and Singular Noun2: PS). The verb was correctly agreed with the subject noun (Noun1) in one sentence out of two. In addition, Noun2 was always a plausible subject for the verb.

Eighty filler items had been inserted in the material so that participants should be unable to spot the experimental sentence structure and be only attentive to the verb agreement at the end of the sentence. Similar precautions to those used during Experiment 1 had been adopted for the elaboration of the experimental items. All the items (experimental and filler) were presented on the computer screen, one after the other and on one line, Times New Roman (size 32) being the font chosen for the experiment.

The order of presentation for the Time variable (free time *vs.* constrained time) was counterbalanced, and each experimental item was processed on these two conditions. The items were randomly assigned to different lists. Each participant received, according to the list, either the instruction to process the task rapidly or the instruction to take the time s/he needed to answer. There were pauses between each list of sentences.

The experiment was carried out individually and was preceded by a training task. The main task consisted in reading a sentence appearing on the computer screen and to indicate, by pressing one out of two joystick keys, respectively labeled "right" or "false", if the sentence contained or not an agreement error. As soon as a key was pressed, the sentence disappeared and was immediately replaced by another one. The location of the two keys (right *vs.* false) on the joystick was counterbalanced.

3.2.2   Results

The dependent variable was the percentage of "missed errors", that is the percentage of sentences with a verb agreement error that had been judged correct. These data were computed with a 5 (School grade level: third, fifth, seventh, ninth grade and university students) x 2 (Time: free *vs.* constrained) x 2 (Condition: nouns similar in number [SS – PP] or different in number [SP – PS]) x 2 (Number of subject noun: singular or plural) analysis of variance with repeated measures on the last three factors. This analysis was carried out on participants ($F1$) and on material ($F2$). Mean percentages appear in Figure 4.

The percentage of "missed errors" decreased with school level, reaching a floor effect in seventh grade (third grade: 54.7; fifth grade: 32.9; seventh grade: 12.3; ninth grade: 14.4; students: 10.4), $F1(4,864) = 100.3, p < .0001, F2(4,70) = 110.8, p < .0001$. It increased when the instruction constrained time to revise the sentence (free time: 22 *vs.* constrained time: 28), $F1(1,216) = 15.4, p < .0002, F2(1,70) = 4.15, p < .05$. It was more important when Noun1 and Noun2 differed in number (34.5) that when they had the same number (15.4), $F1(1,216) = 158.3, p < .0001, F2(1,70) = 187.3, p < .0001$. Indeed, errors were significantly more frequent when the sentence to be revised had an (incorrect) agreement by proximity.

Nevertheless, an unexpected effect also appeared and concerned the number of the subject noun: the percentage of "missed errors" was significantly higher when Noun1 was singular (30.2) than plural (19.7), $F1(1,216) = 48, p < .0001, F2(1,70) = 58.9, p < .0001$. This effect can be understood by the significant interaction between this variable and the Time factor, $F1(1,216) = 39.4, p < .0001, F2(1,70) = 49.8, p < .0001$. Indeed, there was a particularly high percentage of "missed errors" with SP sentences (44.5) compared to percentages obtained with the three other types of sentences (SS: 15.8; PP: 14.9; PS: 24.5). The planned comparison was significant, $F1(1,216) = 22.3, p < .0001, F2(1,70) = 38.4, p < .0001$. It seems that, for sentences with a proximity agreement, the presence of $-s/-ent$ inflections made it difficult for participants to detect any error.

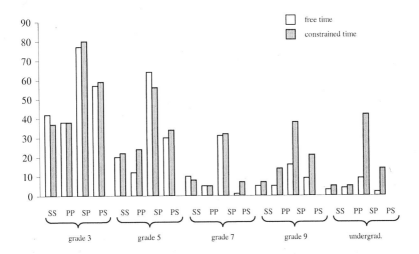

Figure 4. Percentages of missed errors according to school grade level (third, fifth, seventh, ninth grade and undergraduates), instructions (free time vs. constrained time) and sentence type (SS, PP, SP, PS).

The interaction between Time and Condition was significant, $F1(1,216) = 5.98, p < .02, F2(1,70) = 4.5, p < .04$. As predicted, the effect of the instruction relative to time was more important when Noun1 and Noun2 differed in number (free time: 29.7 vs. constrained time: 39.3) – that is when there was a proximity agreement error – than when they had the same number (respectively: 12.3 and 16.5).

The interaction between Condition and School level was also significant, $F1(4,864) = 6.2, p < .0001, F2(4,70) = 13.7, p < .0001$. To interpret this interaction, a new analysis was carried out, with the same data. This analysis was computed in order to better understand the impact of the co-occurrence of $-s/-ent$ inflections on the efficiency of the detection. It consisted in correcting percentages of "missed errors" obtained in SP and PS by removing a basis line. This basis line corresponds to the percentage of "missed errors" in comparable sentences (i.e., with a subject noun [Noun1] that has the same number) but without any proximity agreement error. Thus, the percentages of "missed errors" obtained with SS and PP sentences were removed from those obtained with SP and PS. This procedure, commonly used in such experiments, allows to study the effect of the local noun (Noun2), independently of the subject (Noun1) number (plural or singular; see Bock & Miller, 1991; Fayol et al., 1994; Largy et al., 1996).

The obtained data have been computed with a 5 (School grade level: third, fifth, seventh, ninth grade and university students) x 2 (Time: free *vs.* constrained) x 2 (Configuration of the proximity agreement: Plural [SP minus SS] or Singular [PS minus PP]) analysis of variance with repeated measures on the last two factors. Mean percentages appear in Figure 5.

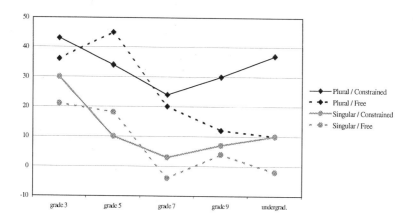

Figure 5. Net percentages of missed errors in relation with school grade level (third, fifth, seventh, ninth grade and undergraduates), instructions (free time, constrained time) and proximity concord configuration (plural [SP minus SS], singular [PS minus PP]).

Once again, the effects of grade level, $F(4,432) = 11.5$, $p < .0001$, and time instruction, $F(1,108) = 5.9$, $p < .02$, were significant. In addition, those corrected data confirmed that a plural proximity agreement was significantly less frequently detected than a singular proximity agreement (respectively: 29.1 *vs.* 9.7), $F(1,108) = 46.8$, $p < .0001$. Finally, only the interaction between the grade level and the time instruction was significant, $F(4,432) = 3.5$, $p < .01$. The net percentages of "missed errors" significantly increased under the time constraint only with ninth graders, $t(27) = 2.56$, $p < .02$, and university students, $t(27) = 4.87$, $p < .0001$; third grade: $t(27) = 1.35$, ns.; fifth grade: $t(27) = -1.4$, ns.; seventh grade: $t(27) = 1.12$, ns.

These results confirmed our hypothesis. Indeed, in a situation in which the impact of a proximity agreement was taken into account on the detection, the effect of the instruction had a belated effect and led to a fall in detection performances.

4. DISCUSSION

The purpose of this work was to study processes mobilized by beginner and expert writers during the production and the revision of the subject-verb agreement in number in French.

4.1 Interpretation of Experimental Findings

Fayol et al. (1999) have shown that two procedures led to produce correct agreements. The first one is systematically used by beginner writers. It consists in applying a "condition-action" algorithm (e.g., condition-action rules or algorithms; Anderson, 1983, 1993). For the subject-verb agreement, the rule to be applied, cognitively demanding, seeks to verify the number of the words that compose the sentence, in order to correctly agree them. The authors then explain the failure to produce the agreement by the presence of a cognitive overload that does not allow beginner writers to carry out the complete algorithm. The second procedure characterizes the expert's functioning. Due to an implicit learning, this expert procedure consists in a direct retrieval from long term memory of associations roots/inflections (Logan, 1988a, 1988b, 1992).

In brief, the frequency of subject-verb agreements, in writing as in reading, in syntactically simple sentences, would apparently lead children to go from a highly controlled algorithmic activity, to a direct, rapid and costless access in memory to the appropriate morpheme. The results obtained in production allow us to equally conceive the existence of two procedures of agreement revision, which also correspond to two levels of expertise. Beginner writers would use the systematic application of an algorithm of agreement verification (e.g., "if a word is a verb, if the subject of the verb is to the plural and if the verb has no –ent morpheme, then it is necessary to add to the verb this morpheme"). This step would be contemporary to the algorithmic step in agreement production since this procedure mobilizes the same kind of knowledge (i.e., to know the rule, to recognize a verb, to identify the subject noun, etc.). Like any algorithmic procedures, it would be cognitively expensive. Conversely, the expert would use co-occurrences between inflectional morphemes in order to revise. As in production, s/he would nevertheless preserve the possibility to use the verification algorithm. However, the frequency of agreement would allow her/him to rely on an implicit learning to revise rapidly, efficiently, and with a lower cognitive cost.

Two experiments were carried out in order to verify this idea. The first study has allowed to compare the performances of second, third and fourth graders of primary school in production and revision tasks dealing with the verb agreement. The results of the first experiment showed that, while revision performances were systematically higher to production performances in second and third graders, this difference disappeared in fourth grade. The revision activity of verb agreement seems initially easier to manage than the production of this agreement. However, how is it possible to revise an agreement (that is to say to detect and to correct an erroneous agreement) without being able to produce it in a situation of production (to write a verb and its inflection)? To revise an agreement indeed necessitates to know how it must be produced. The single possible explanation to this result is thus a problem linked to the management of the activity. The mobilization of knowledge, largely similar in revision and production, would be made in a cognitively more demanding context when the child has, in addition to look for the appropriate inflection, to manage both the spelling of the root of the word and the graphic transcription, which is not yet automated. This result would therefore verify the hypothesis formulated in terms of resources rather than confirming the hypothesis of two tasks mobilizing distinct knowledge. Largy (2001) highlighted similar results with tasks concerning noun agreement. He showed that there was a period (second and third grade of primary school) during which children were more efficient in detecting and correcting a noun agreement error than in processing this same type of agreement during word production. Nevertheless, the success in both tasks was largely more precocious in the case of noun agreements (third grade) than for verb agreements (fourth grade). This result is not really surprising since plurality is easier to conceptualize with noun than with verb agreement (a plural noun refers to multiple objects; a plural verb to replicated actions or states, which is much more abstract; Totereau et al., 1997).

The results obtained in the first experiment are thus compatible with our main hypothesis. To produce and revise a verb agreement would rely on the same set of knowledge. The application by beginner writers of a revision algorithm for the agreement is contemporary to the period during which they use a production algorithm for the same type of agreement (Fayol et al., 1999). Moreover, the revising competence for the verb agreement is demonstrated more clearly and more precociously than in writing. This advantage would be explained by the cognitive cost linked to the management of the graphic transcription, whose automation takes place later on (Bourdin & Fayol, 1994).

The second experiment aimed at comparing performances obtained by primary school and junior high school students, as well as adult students, in a task which consisted in detecting agreement errors in sentences presented on a computer screen. The results of this study revealed that the percentage of "missed errors" significantly decreased down to seventh grade, where a floor effect was observed. This early period of expertise in detection of subject-verb agreement errors corresponds to that in which children are also becoming experts in agreement production (Fayol et al., 1999). The results confirmed that the detection activity was cognitively demanding. Indeed, detection errors were more frequent when the instruction required participants to reply as quickly as possible. A great part of this cost can be attributed to the application of an algorithm of agreement verification. The precocious use of this algorithm would probably be due to the similarity between production and revision agreement rules. In both activities, the writer has to access a declarative knowledge in long term memory, to test the appropriateness of conditions and actions for the current situation and to execute the correct action.

Moreover, the effect of the instruction was even more obvious when Noun1 and Noun2 were different in number. It was therefore in the presence of a proximity agreement that the performance proved to me substantially affected by the time constraint. Finally, some results are characteristic of the application of an expert procedure. A number of sentence configurations seem to be able to delude the monitoring process. The study of these configuration shows that the revision expert founds himself on a criterion of proximity between inflections (most notably *-s/-ent*) to consider that the agreement is correct.

Indeed, these results allow us to distinguish novice from expert writers on the basis of mobilized processes. The experimental sentences were built in order to delude a monitoring system that would rely on the presence or the absence of proximal co-occurrences between verb and noun inflections to detect subject-verb agreement errors. Some sentences presented an ambiguous structure: The Noun1 (subject noun) – Verb agreement was erroneous, and the verb was agreed following a proximity agreement procedure with Noun 2 (for example: *"La tige des tulipes cassent"* [The stem of tulips break]; *"Les pavés de la route glisse"* [The cobbles of the road is slippery). An expert reviser can, like a beginner reviser, use a controlled procedure allowing her/him to look for the number of the subject with which the verb has to be agreed and thus verify the correctness of the agreement. However, the revision activity can be constrained, among others, by time and/or by the number of dimensions to be considered (meaning and formal aspects, for example). For these reasons, our hypothesis predicted that the expert had a highly automated procedure in order to revise rapidly, efficiently and economically a simple agreement such as the subject-verb agreement in number. This economy of cognitive resources, realized on a dimension such as spelling, would then allow to free resources to revise higher-level aspects, such as those linked to the meaning of the text and to the taking into account of the reader.

With the development of expertise, the monitoring system could base the detection of a possible error on the incompatibility of a proximal couple of inflections. The close presence of verb and noun singular inflections (*-e/-e*), or of verb and noun plural inflections (*-s/-ent*) would not alert the system, while an incompatibility of inflections (*-e/-ent* or *-s/-e*) would be detected. If this hypothesis is true, the expert would be deluded by erroneous sentences that locally present a compatibility of inflections (e.g., proximity agreement Noun2 – Verb). This deception should be especially manifest whenever experimental conditions force the expert to resort to this expert procedure, particularly in the case of an instruction limiting the time for revision. Indeed, the time constraint had a clear effect with erroneous sentences in which the verb agreement was made by proximity and thereby deluded the detection system. With this kind of sentences, the percentage of "missed errors" was significantly highest when the revision time was constrained.

An unexpected result, however compatible with our hypothesis, was observed. If erroneous sentences with a proximity agreement were more difficult to detect than the others, those presenting a plural proximity agreement (SP: 44.5% of "missed errors") were almost twice more difficult to detect than those with a singular proximity agreement (PS: 24.5%). The particular status of SP sentences has very often been shown in experimental studies on verb agreement, in writing (Chanquoy & Negro, 1996; Fayol et al., 1999; Largy & Fayol, 2001; Largy et al., 1996; Negro & Chanquoy, 2000) as well as in speaking (Bock & Cutting, 1992; Bock & Eberhard, 1993; Bock & Miller, 1991; Eberhard, 1999). It is now also observable during the revision of this type of agreement. Interestingly, in writing as in revision, the SP condition is only marked in adult writers and mainly when a constraint weighs on cognitive resources. This observation demonstrates that, in experts, "singular" and "plural" modalities of an agreement have not the same status and are not similarly processed. Conversely, the beginner writer, applying more systematically a binary algorithm (–e vs. –ent), would process "singular" and "plural" modalities in the same way.

A more specific analysis has confirmed that the delusion phenomenon was significantly more frequent with a couple of –s/–ent inflections. This effect is compatible with our idea about the origin of the expertise in detection tasks. Beginner writers are very frequently confronted with the co-occurrence of inflection couples, both during writing and reading activities. An implicit learning of such co-occurrences is therefore plausible. This implicit learning refers to an adaptable mode in which the behavior becomes sensitive to the structure of a situation, without this adaptation being attributable to the intentional use of the explicit knowledge of the structure (Perruchet, 1998). Several cases of implicit learning have recently been studied in the area of spelling (Pacton, Fayol, & Perruchet, 2002; Pacton, Perruchet, Fayol, & Cleeremans, 2001). For example, Pacton et al. (2001) have shown that the writing under dictation of non words by second, third and fifth graders of primary school was influenced by probabilistic regularities of French spelling, among which grapho-tactic regularities due to the graphic transcription of sounds, such as /o/, in final position.

The fact that the pair of –s/–ent inflections deludes the system of error detection in a more blatant way can be explained by the high specificity of this association of inflections. While these marks are largely the most frequent plural inflections for subject-verb (i.e., rarer occurrence of the inflections –x for nouns / –ent for verbs in French), the singular inflections for subject-verb is less regular (e.g., many singular nouns do not end with –e but with a consonant: le renard [the fox], le loup [the wolf]). The explicit learning would be applied more easily with the couple of –s/–ent inflections.

A last result tends to validate our hypothesis. When the impact of a proximity agreement is taken into account to detect an error, the effect of the time constraint was significant only from ninth graders and in adult students. This effect showed a decreasing in detecting errors when the revision time was constrained. This expert profile appears relatively late during schooling.

4.2 Implications for Instruction

These observations allow us to discuss how grammatical agreement revision should be taught and thus to establish links between cognitive processes and instructional procedures. Cognitive psychology and developmental psychology have provided models to the writing activity and have largely underlined its complexity (Alamargot & Chanquoy, 2001; Fayol, 1997). By associating the general writing process with the working memory model (Baddeley, 1986), they have described writing as a composite and cognitively costly activity (Kellogg, 1996; McCutchen, 1996). Teachers can thus find a beginning of explanation to difficulties met by children during text production. Moreover, the interpretation of writing complexity in terms of cognitive load and of the limited capacity of working memory could lead them to consider the suggestion of dividing a writing activity into several subtasks, undertaken successively, so that the cognitive load of the activity would be reduced at each stage. For example, concerning the planning process, some teachers ask children to formulate orally ideas before transcribing them graphically. In the same way, others teachers do not impose orthographic constraints during the initial production of a text (draft text), so as to decrease its cost. They thus privilege the semantic content of the text the spelling of which is only verified in a second production step.

Concerning the way to teach how to revise the subject-verb agreement in number, it is first necessary to be aware of the child's attentional resources to realize this task. The laborious application of an algorithm of agreement verification requires that young children can concentrate all their attention on this activity. In addition, since the detection of an error does not systematically lead to the appropriate correction (i.e., there are numerous erroneous corrections in –s), the teacher has to construe the revision of a grammatical agreement as a composite activity. Thereby, s/he would, on the one hand, be sure that children are able to notice the "conditions" that rule the releasing of an "action" and, on the other hand, to control the appropriate coupling condition(s)/action(s).

More specifically, such research raises questions on the way plural morphology could be effectively taught to children. Indeed, the cognitive system seems rapidly able to move away from the binary logic of grammatical rules allowing to distinguish between the singular from the plural. In the case of the revision of subject-verb agreement, our results tend to confirm that the cognitive system bases its expertise on the research of known configurations. In the same way, for agreement production, Fayol, Largy, and Ganier (1997) and Fayol et al. (1999) have shown that the expert directly accesses root-inflection association in memory. Furthermore, Largy et al. (1996) have shown that the access to these associations is sensitive to their linguistic frequency. This sensitivity to the recurrent character of an information is one of the bases of implicit learning (Perruchet, 1998). The singular and the plural have not the same status during acquisition. Indeed, the storing in long term memory of recurrent configurations is realized from written clues. The written morphology would therefore interact with this form of learning. In French, the plural morphemes are salient: –s added to nouns and to adjectives; –ent added to verbs. They are thus useful clues for implicit learning. Conversely, the singular morphology is largely less propitious to this type of acquisition, mainly because, in French, it is not based on specific morphemes.

Without claiming that it is possible to provide solutions, we hope that this kind of research could be stimulating to teachers' reflection. Until now, teachers have often had trouble understanding why pupils fail to apply grammatical rules which have been repeatedly taught. Today, we can show that errors arise in part from what pupils have in fact implicitly learned in school. This paradox merits further investigation.

APPENDIX A. ITEMS OF EXPERIMENT 1

bague / briller	ring / to shine
singe / grimper	monkey / to climb
vache / brouter	cow / to graze
Garcon / ranger	boy / to tidy
poule / picorer	chicken / to peck
Robinet / couler	faucet / to flow
dame / discuter	lady / to discuss
Briquette / brûler	lighter / to burn
chatte / trembler	cat / to tremble
cuisinier / déguster	cook / to taste
Mule / trotter	mule / to trot
Lapin / grignoter	rabbit / to nibble
Mère / chanter	mother / to sing
comédien / réciter	actor / to recite
Bête / reculer	beast / to retreat
Chemin / monter	path / to climb
feuille / voltiger	leaf / to hover
coiffeur / parler	barber / to speak
couverture / chauffer	cover / to heat
Train / circuler	train / to circulate
cheminée / fumer	chimney / to smoke
lit / craquer	bed / to crack
cheville / saigner	ankle / to bleed
Gardien / siffler	guardian / to whistle
Bulle / voler	bubble / to fly
monstre / dévorer	monster / to devour
Roue / tourner	wheel / to turn
soldat / rentrer	soldier / to come back
Voiture / freiner	car / to brake
ballon / rouler	balloon / to roll
Cloche / sonner	bell / to ring
crapaud / sauter	toad / to jump

APPENDIX B1. CORRECT ITEMS OF EXPERIMENT 2

The translation of the following items does not respect the rules of English syntax. It is supposed to reproduce the syntactical structure of the items in French so as to emphasize proximity agreements.

Singular - Singular

Le chien du facteur grogne	The dog of the factor grumbles
Le bouchon de la carafe saute	The cork of the carafe jumps
La manche de la veste dépasse	The sleeve of the jacket exceeds
La lame du couteau coupe	The blade of the knife cuts

Le voisin du docteur ronfle	The neighbor of the doctor snores
Le moment de la récolte arrive	The moment of the crop arrives
La date de la fête approche	The date of the feast approaches
La barque du marin chavire	The boat of the sailor overturns

Plural- Plural

Les parents des canards barbotent	The parents of ducks paddle
Les maris des fermières travaillent	The husbands of farm women work
Les planches des baraques abritent	The boards of huts shelter
Les pattes des crabes pincent	The paws of crabs pinch
Les camions des pompiers circulent	The trucks of firemen run
Les rires des gamines résonnent	The laughter of little girls resonate
Les réserves des fourmis diminuent	The reserves of ants decrease
Les chaînes des vélos rouillent	The chains of bikes rust

Singular - Plural

Le papa des poussins picore	The daddy of chicks pecks
Le chargement des remorques bascule	The loading of trailers rocks
La laine des chaussettes réchauffe	The wool of socks warms up
La famille des lapins tremble	The family of rabbits trembles
Le spectacle des tigres continue	The spectacle of tigers continues
Le tissu des voiles résiste	The cloth of sails resists
La ceinture des jupes éclate	The belt of skirts bursts
La baguette des magiciens dirige	The stick of magicians manages

Plural - Singular

Les clients du marchand achètent	The clients of the merchant buy
Les canons de la guerre bombardent	The canons of the war bomb
Les bougies de la chambre éclairent	The candles of the bedroom illuminate
Les pages du livre tournent	The pages of the book turn
Les meubles du grenier brûlent	The furniture of the granary burn
Les singes de la forêt existent	The monkeys of the forest exist
Les journées de la semaine passent	The days of the week pass
Les billes du garçon roulent	The marbles of the boy roll

APPENDIX B2. ERRONEOUS ITEMS OF EXPERIMENT 2

SS

Le bouton du placard manquent	The button of the cupboard lack
Le bouillon de la marmite débordent	The soup of the pot overflow
La tante de la danseuse louchent	The aunt of the dancer squint
La bouée du navire flottent	The buoy of the ship float
Le frère du chasseur tirent	The brother of the hunter pull
Le carton de la boîte craquent	The cardboard of the box crack
La couronne de la reine penchent	The crown of the queen lean
La bouche du bébé bavent	The mouth of the baby drool

PP

Les dessins des nuages change	The drawings of clouds changes
Les soldats des casernes défile	The soldiers of barracks parades
Les poignées des portes bouge	The handles of carry them moves
Les feuilles des chênes respire	The leaves of oaks breathes
Les patrons des cafés fume	The owners of cafes smokes
Les volets des cabanes grince	The shutters of huts grates
Les sorcières des tribus chante	The witches of tribes sings
Les mamans des gagnants soupire	The mummies of winners sighs

SP

Le marteau des forgerons frappent	The hammer of blacksmiths knock
Le miel des tartines coulent	The honey of sandwiches flow
La tige des tulipes cassent	The stem of tulips break
La sirène des policiers hurlent	The siren of policemen howl
Le gardien des prisons surveillent	The guardian of prisons watch
Le sommet des collines brillent	The summit of hills shine
La copine des vendeuses rêvent	The friend of saleswomen dream
La voiture des mariés reculent	The car of the bride move back

PS

Les miettes du biscuit tombe	The crumbs of the cookie falls
Les pavés de la route glisse	The cobbles of the road slips
Les robes de la poupée sèche	The dresses of the doll dries
Les salades du jardin pousse	The salads of the garden grows
Les gendarmes du village cherche	The policemen of the village seeks
Les coffres de la banque ferme	The chests of the bank closes
Les filles de la maîtresse patine	The daughters of the teacher skates
Les plumes du pigeon vole	The feathers of the pigeon flies

REVISION IN THE CONTEXT OF DIFFERENT DRAFTING STRATEGIES

DAVID GALBRAITH & MARK TORRANCE

Staffordshire University, United Kingdom

Abstract. Our position in this chapter is that revision cannot be understood independently of the writing strategies in which it is embedded. Some authors have promoted an interactive writing strategy (e.g., Elbow, 1998) which relies on multiple rewriting as a means of developing text content in lieu of producing a structured outline. Galbraith's (1999) dual-process model, which describes writing processes as an interleaving of dispositional content generation and rhetorical structuring, provides some basis for understanding why this kind of strategy might be successful. We review existing research exploring the efficacy of outlining and rough-drafting strategies. This suggests a clear benefit for outline-based strategies over various forms of rough-drafting strategies, but has not, we argue, included an appropriate form of interactive writing strategy. We then discuss research exploring the writing processes of writers performing non-laboratory real-world writing tasks and find that a minority of writers, and particularly more experienced writers, appear to habitually adopt a non-outline multiple-drafting strategy similar in form to that specified by the dual-process model. Finally, we describe an experiment in which we found (a) that this form of interactive strategy was more effective than the forms of rough drafting strategy which have been investigated in previous research, (b) that, consistent with previous research, outlining also has clear text-quality advantages, and (c) that the effectiveness of revision depends on the form of initial draft to which it is applied.

Keywords: Text production, outlining, multiple drafting, self-monitoring, dual-process model

1. INTRODUCTION

For many people, rewriting and revision are the key characteristics distinguishing the expert from the novice writer. Murray (1978), for example, claims that "Writing is rewriting... Rewriting is the difference between the dilettante and the artist, the amateur and the professional, the unpublished and the published" (p. 85). His observations are supported by a growing body of empirical research demonstrating that more experienced writers revise more globally, and to a greater extent, than less experienced writers (e.g., Faigley & Witte, 1981).

There is a range of possible explanations for this difference. It could, for example, be a consequence of a difference in basic revision skills. Maybe less experienced writers are less able to detect problems in their texts, or less able to think of alternative ways of expressing unsatisfactory text. If this were the case, then it would suggest that writing instruction should focus on improving novice writers' basic skills. Or, it could be a consequence of differences in the two groups' definition of revision. Perhaps it is not so much that novices cannot revise as that they do not realize what is involved in revision. Wallace, Hayes, Hatch, Miller, Moser, and Silk (1996), for example, found that a simple, 8 minute demonstration of global revision was sufficient to improve the quality of undergraduate revision, and reasoned that this was a consequence of a change in their task definition rather than any change in basic revision skills. These explanations are not mutually exclusive, but clearly it is important to establish which of these possibilities is more relevant in any given context, if one is to provide the right kind of support. Training in basic revision skills might not be much help if the basic problem is the writers' definition of the goals of revision. Equally, changing their task definition would not be much help if the writers lacked the basic skills required to implement their goals.

In this chapter we argue that differences between writers in the amount of revision they carry out are not just a consequence of differences in basic revision skills, or in how revision itself is defined, but also of higher-level differences in writers' overall drafting strategies. We also suggest that, in order to have maximum effect, the teaching of revision needs to be carried out in the context of an overall drafting strategy.

The observation that there are wide individual differences in the overall drafting strategies employed by writers has been a staple of discussions of writing (see, for example, review by Chandler, 1992). Underlying the variety of ways in which these differences have been characterized there is a general contrast between two different approaches to writing. On the one hand there is what might be broadly described as a *planning* approach in which writers concentrate on working out what they want to say before setting pen to paper, and only start to produce full text once they have worked out what they want to say. On the other hand there is, again very broadly, what might be described as an *interactive* approach in which writers work out what they want to say in the course of writing and in which content evolves over a series of drafts. The contrast is summed up forcefully by Elbow in his, now classic, *Writing without teachers* (Elbow, 1973, second edition, 1998):

> The commonsense, conventional understanding of writing is as follows. Writing is a two-step process. First you figure out your meaning, then you put it into language. Most advice we get either from others or from ourselves follows this model: first try to figure out what you want to say; don't start writing till you do; make a plan; use an outline; begin writing only afterward . . . This idea of writing is backwards. That's why it causes so much trouble. Instead of a two-step translation of meaning-into-language, think of writing as an organic, developmental process in which you start writing at the very beginning – before you know your meaning at all – and encourage your words gradually to change and evolve. (pp. 14-15)

For present purposes, the crucial feature of these two conceptions of writing is that they involve a different role for revision. In the planning approach, the writer's goal is to work out what to say first, and then to work on expressing their meaning as effectively as possible. Revision in this context is intrinsically reactive: it is about evaluating the extent to which the text satisfies the writer's pre-established goals and modifying the text so as to better achieve these goals. In the interactive approach, the writer's goal is not to produce a text that satisfies rhetorical constraints, but rather to produce an initial draft freely expressing their thoughts about the topic. Revision in this context is intrinsically proactive: it is about identifying potential ideas in the initial draft with a view to developing these further in subsequent drafts. The crucial point being that these differences in the role of revision are a function of the writer's overall drafting strategy rather than differences in writer's definitions of revision or their basic revision skills.

Murray (1978) makes a similar point when he distinguishes between two different types of revision. In his view (italics in the original):

> There are two principal and quite separate editorial acts in revision.
>
> *Internal revision.* Under this term, I include everything writers do to discover and develop what they have to say, beginning with the reading of a completed first draft. They read to discover where their content, form, language, and voice have led them. They use language, structure, and information to find out what they have to say or hope to say. The audience is one person: the writer.
>
> *External revision.* This is what writers do to communicate what they have found they have written to another audience. It is editing, and proofreading, and much more. Writers now pay attention to the conventions of form and language, mechanics and style. They eye their audience and may choose to appeal to it. They read as an outsider, and it is significant that such terms as *polish* are used by professionals: They dramatize the fact that the writer at this stage in the process may, appropriately, be concerned with exterior appearance. (p. 91)

Our addition to this distinction is the suggestion that they are not just different kinds of revision but that they may be intrinsically related to different drafting strategies. In our view, a planned initial draft is intrinsically less revisable than an unplanned draft. Differences in the amount inexperienced writers revise their texts may partly, therefore, be a consequence of differences in the way they produce their initial drafts, and their overall conception of writing, rather than just in their basic revision abilities.

In what follows, we will explore this distinction as it applies to: (i) previous experimental research on drafting strategies; (ii) some of our own studies of individual differences in drafting strategies; and (iii) a recently completed experimental study of the effects of revision in the context of different drafting strategies. We will conclude by examining the implications for the teaching of revision.

2. WHAT IS AN INTERACTIVE DRAFTING STRATEGY?

Previous research on drafting strategies has overwhelmingly favored planning strategies over interactive strategies. We think, however, that this reflects the way the interactive strategy has been operationalized in this research rather than a genuine difference in their effectiveness. One of the difficulties that arises in considering the interactive approach is that it tends to be described in terms of its proponents' own practice rather than in terms of models of the cognitive processes involved.

This means that there is considerable room for interpretation when it comes to characterizing these processes. In this section we first describe how the interactive approach has been characterized in previous research on drafting strategies. We then describe an alternative conception of the approach, derived from Elbow's description of the process and Galbraith's (1999) dual-process model of writing. We conclude by summing up the key features of the interactive approach under this conception.

2.1 *The Interactive Strategy as Rough Drafting*

Research on this topic has been based largely on Hayes and Flower's (1980) model of writing. In this model, the writing process has 3 basic components: planning, which involves goal-setting, and generating and organizing ideas to satisfy goals; translating, which involves expressing ideas in text; and reviewing, which involves reading and editing the text already produced. In later research, more elaborate models of revision were developed, in which it was not just a matter of editing text, but involve more elaborate evaluation and modification of text and plans in order to satisfy the writer's goals (Hayes, Flower, Schriver, Stratman, & Carey, 1987; Scardamalia & Bereiter, 1983). In recognition of the more elaborate nature of revision in these models, Hayes (1996) has suggested that revision should no longer be treated as a basic component of the writing process, but should instead be treated as a composite of the more basic processes of reflection (equivalent to planning in the original Hayes and Flower model), text production (equivalent to translation in the original model) and text interpretation (replacing the revision component of the original model). The key feature of text interpretation during revision in these models is that it is not just a matter of reading-to-comprehend, but is actively concerned with identifying problems in the text. Revision, in these models, then, is a matter of identifying problems with already formulated text, and with modifying text or plans in order to remedy these problems. And research on drafting strategies has been based on the assumption that different drafting strategies represent different ways of combining the basic processes involved in writing, in particular, that the interactive approach involves postponing evaluation and revision until after a draft has been completed.

The first major study of different drafting strategies was carried out by Glynn, Britton, Muth, and Dogan (1982). Following Hayes and Flower (1980), they identified four distinct operations in writing: (a) generating ideas, (b) sequencing or organizing ideas, (c) expressing ideas in sentences, and (d) complying with spelling and grammatical conventions. The extent to which these operations had to be carried out at the same time was manipulated by instructing writers to divide the writing of a brief letter into two separate ten-minute sessions and varying the number of operations which had to be carried out during the preliminary draft. The resulting four preliminary draft formats successively removed one of the operations. In the polished sentences condition, writers had to write a complete, polished version of the letter on the first draft. In the mechanics-free sentences condition, they had to write the complete text, but without worrying about mechanics (spelling and punctuation). In the ordered notes condition, they were instructed to write their ideas down in brief three or four word notes, and to ensure these were organized into a logical order. Finally, in the unordered notes condition, they were instructed to jot their ideas down in note-form as before, but not to worry about the order in which they were expressed. After a short break, all the groups were then asked to produce a final version of the text, writing the "best letter they could" and making "any changes (additions, deletions and substitutions) that you think will improve this final version" (Glynn et al., 1982, p. 559). Glynn et al. found that the number of ideas generated in the preliminary drafts was progressively lower as the number of constraints present increased, with the fewest ideas being generated in the polished sentences conditions and the most ideas being generated in the unordered notes condition. They concluded that generating ideas was more productive when it was carried out in note-from prior to the production of text than when it was carried out at the same time as producing the text.

For present purposes, we want to highlight two features of this study. First, it reflects a particular interpretation of the interactive strategy, in which it is regarded as a matter of separating evaluation of expression from the production of the text, and revision is treated as essentially reactive in form, as a matter of polishing the expression of previously produced text. Second, although there were clear differences in the number of ideas generated in the different conditions, no measures of how this related to text quality were made.

The most thorough investigation of the effectiveness of different kinds of pre-writing or first-draft strategy was carried out by Kellogg in a series of experiments (Kellogg, 1988, 1990; see Kellogg, 1994, for a review). Kellogg (1988) distinguished two different ways in which writers might reduce cognitive load during writing. The outline strategy minimizes the attention paid to translation during planning, by getting writers to generate and organize their ideas prior to writing, before focusing their attention on the translation and revision processes. The rough-drafting strategy on the other hand involves translating text without worrying about how well expressed it is, leaving monitoring of expression to revision of the draft after writing. In effect, this separates the process of translation and revision. In combination, outlining followed by rough drafting should in theory provide for the most efficient distribution of resources during writing since it will separate both planning from translation and translation from revision. Kellogg (1988) tested this by manipulating two variables. Writers were instructed either to make a hierarchical outline before writing, or to start writing immediately. Then, when they produced the text itself, they were instructed either to write the text freely, without worrying about how well it was expressed, returning later to revise, or to attempt to produce a polished text on the first draft. The effect on the distribution of processes during writing (as indicated through directed retrospection) and the quality of the final text were measured.

The results were very clear. First, the manipulations did indeed lead to a redistribution of processing during writing. In the outline conditions, writers showed much less evidence of planning during text production, presumably because this had largely been completed prior to writing. In the rough draft conditions, revision was reduced during the initial draft and postponed until later. Second, outlining was associated with higher quality final drafts but rough drafting showed no effect, despite the fact that revision had been postponed and should, therefore, have been able to draw on more attentional resources. This experiment appears to contradict two of the main claims made by proponents of the interactive strategy. First, it suggests that it makes no difference whether or not revision is carried out at the same time as translation, and so contradicts the basic assumption that rewriting is a crucial part of the writing process. Second, it suggests that, far from being the cause of "trouble" in writing, as claimed by Elbow in the quote above, outlining is actively helpful.

Overall, then, these studies suggest that an outlining strategy, in which ideas are generated and organized in note-form prior to writing the text, is more effective than a rough drafting strategy, in which full text is produced without pre-planning, but with revision postponed until after writing. Although there has been debate over whether the initial notes should be in an unorganized form (Glynn et al., 1982) or in an organized form (Kellogg, 1988), more recent research by Kellogg (1990) has shown that the construction of a hierarchically organized outline prior to writing is associated with a higher quality final product than is the construction of an ordered list of ideas, and that this in turn is associated with higher quality final text than a simple clustering strategy. Furthermore, this is true despite the fact that more ideas tend to be generated using a clustering strategy than when an outline is constructed. Kellogg's (1994) general conclusion is that the effectiveness of the outlining strategy is a consequence of the fact that it enables writers to organize their ideas better prior to writing, as well as that it then enables them to devote more resources to formulating these ideas effectively in text.

2.2 The Interactive Strategy as Multiple Drafting

As Kellogg (1994) himself emphasizes, these studies have only tested relatively weak versions of the rough drafting strategy, and have only used relatively short tasks. Conceivably the kinds of rough drafting strategy implemented in these experiments might be more effective if participants had to engage in longer and more complex writing tasks, and if they were allowed to revise initial drafts over a series of separate sessions. Alternatively, it could be that the relatively inexperienced writers studied by Kellogg lacked the basic revision skills required to take advantage of the attentional resources made available by postponing revision until after the production of the initial draft. These possibilities could be tested in a variety of ways: by setting more complex tasks, or by explicitly teaching revision skills, or by studying more experienced writers. We believe, however, that the problem goes deeper than that, and lies in the way the rough draft strategy is defined in these experiments.

The rough drafting strategies implemented in these studies share three particular features. First, the interactive strategy is assumed to be essentially a matter of separating revision from other processes, with potential benefits for the efficiency with which both revision and these other processes can be carried out. Second, all the rough drafting conditions have involved the production of an organized first draft of text, either though pre-planning or through concurrent organizing of the text. Finally, revision has been treated as a fixed process varying only in the point at which is carried out, and as an intrinsically reactive process, in which an already organized text is evaluated with respect to the writer's goals. Typically, therefore, it is treated as a relatively low-level process concerned with evaluating how well the text is expressed, rather than with more radical development of content. There are two problems with this.

First, it does not correspond well with the interactive strategy as it has been described by its proponents. The key characteristics of the interactive strategy as described by Elbow (1981, 1998), for example, are: (i) that the initial draft is an unplanned, spontaneous exteriorization of thought on paper, and (ii) that subsequent drafts should be written in the light of conclusions reached in the first draft, and following a systematic extraction of ideas from the first draft, rather than simply a revision of the text into a better organized and better expressed form. This conflicts with each of the basic features of the rough drafting strategy as it has been implemented in previous research. It involves a different way of separating the basic cognitive processes, one in which text production is separated from organization as well as from revision, and in which is organization is postponed to after writing, rather than being applied before writing, as in the outline planning strategy. It therefore involves the production of an unorganized initial draft rather than an organized one. Furthermore, revision is not a fixed process which is shifted in location within the different strategies, but is a different process in the two contexts. In the context of the outline planning strategy and the rough drafting strategies as implemented in previous research, revision is about evaluating text that has already been organized. In the interactive strategy as described by Elbow (and see Murray, above), it is about building an organization from the text which has been produced, as well as, in later stages, evaluating text with respect to goals.

Second, we also think that the basic assumptions which previous research has made about the cognitive processes involved in writing can be questioned, and that this casts a different light on the nature of different drafting strategies. In a recently developed dual process model of writing, Galbraith (1999) questions how full an account current cognitive models provide of the writing process. Specifically, he claims that they share a flawed assumption about the way knowledge is represented. In the classic cognitive models of writing (e.g., Bereiter & Scardamalia, 1987; Hayes & Flower, 1980), knowledge is represented explicitly as an interrelated network of fixed, independent ideas, and retrieval of knowledge is treated as an independent component of the writing process. In consequence the process of generating content is treated as a single process which takes the same form during planning and during text production. Galbraith claims that, although this does capture the way content is generated during the higher problem-solving processes in writing, it neglects the more implicit processes involved in some forms of text production. The dual process model, therefore, claims that different types of process are involved in the generation of content during planning and during text production.

For present purposes, the model has two crucial features. The first is that text production is assumed to operate on an implicit representation of knowledge, which Galbraith (1999) calls the writer's disposition towards the topic, and in which knowledge is represented as a distributed conceptual network operating according to connectionist principles (see Rumelhart, McClelland, Smolensky, & Hinton, 1986). In this form of representation, ideas are not represented in a fixed, independent form, but rather as different patterns of activation across the same set of conceptual units, and ideas are seen as being constructed in the course of text production rather than as existing prior to it. In order to gain access to this content, writers have to constitute their ideas in connected prose, and this has to follow the path of thought as it unfolds, spontaneously, according to the implicit organization of the writer's disposition towards the topic. In other words, text production is not necessarily a matter of translating already formed ideas into text, but can be an active knowledge-constituting process in its own right, in which implicit knowledge is constituted as distinct ideas during unorganized (or dispositionally organized) text production, just as proponents of the interactive strategy claim. The second crucial feature is that, although higher-level planning and problem-solving processes are assumed to operate in much the same way as described by traditional cognitive models, they are assumed to operate on a separate, episodic store of knowledge, consisting of explicitly represented and independent ideas which the writer has previously formulated. In other words, these processes only have access to what the writer already explicitly knows about the topic, including the results of previous knowledge-constituting processes, but do not have access to the implicit knowledge which makes up the writer's disposition towards the topic. Thus, although these processes play a vital role in reorganizing existing knowledge to satisfy the external constraints present in specific rhetorical contexts, they are not responsible for developments in the writer's understanding of the topic. Instead, this depends on the dispositionally organized knowledge-constituting process in which implicit thought is formulated as distinct ideas during the course of text production.

According to the dual process model, then, both dispositional text production and rhetorical planning are necessary for effective writing. Dispositional text production is necessary to allow the writer to constitute their implicit knowledge of the topic, and rhetorical planning is necessary in order to create a coherent mental model of the global structure of thought and to adapt this to rhetorical goals. The problem for the writer is that these two processes operate best under diametrically opposed conditions. Knowledge constituting during text production depends on the text being formulated in connected sentences and on the writer following the path of their thought as it unfolds. Organization of ideas into a coherent mental model depends on the writer representing ideas in a fixed abbreviated form and on the extent to which these are deliberately adapted to satisfy external goals. The result is a fundamental conflict between two distinct kinds of processing, and different drafting strategies represent different ways of resolving this conflict.

To date, the empirical research on which the dual process model is based has been concerned with investigating the conditions under which writers develop their understanding of a topic while writing various forms of single draft (Alamargot, Favart & Galbraith, 2000; Galbraith, 1992, 1996, 1999). This research is broadly supportive of the first assumption of the interactive strategy in that it suggests that, dispositionally-driven text production is associated with developments of understanding, whereas planning in note-form and rhetorically organized text production are not (Galbraith, 1992, 1999). At the same time, it also provides support for the effectiveness of outlining in that it suggests that, although planning in note-form may not lead to development of the writer's understanding, it does enable the writer to organize their existing ideas more effectively than when planning is carried out at the same time as text production or when notes are dispositionally produced rather than rhetorically organized (Galbraith, 1992, 1999).

According to the dual process model, then, the empirical findings of previous research on drafting strategies are not in dispute, but they are restricted in scope and have not tested a full version of the interactive strategy. What they do show is that outline planning, involving as it does the manipulation of ideas in note-form separate from full text production, is a more effective form of organizing ideas than when planning is carried out at the same time as text production. What they do not show, because they have not included conditions in which initial drafts of unorganized but connected text are produced, is how effective the interactive strategy is relative to other forms of drafting. In order to test this properly a fuller implementation of the interactive strategy is required. According to the dual process model this should take the following form.

First, as we have already emphasized, it should include an unorganized first draft of text. By itself, however, this will only produce an unorganized exteriorization of the unfolding of the writer's disposition, which will be neither rhetorically well-formed nor fully explicit. As it is conceived in the model, this process produces an undifferentiated mass of content, which may include novel ideas, and hence contribute towards increased understanding, but it does not produce a fully explicit representation of the distinct ideas and their interrelationships. In order for writers to fully develop their understanding, therefore, the second phase of the interactive strategy should focus on identifying the individual ideas contained in the text and organizing them into a coherent mental model. This is broadly similar to revision as it is conceived in traditional cognitive models of writing in that it involves reading over of the initial draft (or text interpretation as Hayes (1996) describes it in his new model). However, unlike these models, this is not a matter of reading to identify problems, but is instead a matter of actively constructing the gist or macrostructure of the text. It is this which leads us to describe this as proactive, rather than reactive, revision. The aim of the process is to construct a model from the text, rather than to modify the text in order to satisfy rhetorical goals. The third phase of the strategy involves using this more explicit understanding to guide the production of a new draft. The precise form this takes depends on the state of the initial draft. In cases where it is relatively well formed and corresponds to a relatively full understanding of the topic, it may only involve modifying elements within the existing text. In cases where the text is extremely disorganized or where the writer's understanding remains relatively undeveloped, it may involve the production of a completely new draft. And this may still be a relatively unorganized draft, in that the aim may still be to further develop the writer's understanding, rather than to produce a rhetorically well-formed text. In principle, then, the writer may continue alternating between knowledge-constituting text production and proactive revision over several drafts of text.

To sum up, the dual process model claims that different drafting strategies represent different ways of resolving the conflict that arises between two different types of processing, both of which are necessary for effective writing. In this view, the aim of the interactive strategy is to focus first on the knowledge-constituting properties of text production, and then on applying higher-level reflective processes, with the aim of extracting a coherent mental model from the resulting text. This involves producing an unorganized initial draft of text followed by a different, more proactive, form of revision. And, given the empirical support for the beneficial effects of a dispositionally organized initial draft on the writer's understanding of a topic (Galbraith, 1992, 1999), the key question about this strategy is whether writers can revise and rewrite such an initial draft into a rhetorically appropriate final text. By contrast, the aim of the outline planning strategy is to focus first on the organizational benefits of planning in note form, and then on formulating thought in text. This involves producing organized drafts of text accompanied by a relatively reactive form of revision. And the key question, from the dual-process point of view, is how the writer can implement the global structure derived during planning as a text, which captures their implicit disposition towards the topic.

3.   INDIVIDUAL DIFFERENCES IN DRAFTING STRATEGIES

In this section we re-examine some of our earlier work on drafting strategies, as revealed in self-report studies, to determine whether there is evidence of an interactive strategy consisting of an unorganized initial draft followed by substantial revision devoted to reorganization of text, as opposed to the kind of rough drafting strategy implemented in the experimental studies we have described. We describe several questionnaire and diary-based studies exploring the writing strategies of academic writers, ranging from undergraduates to publishing academics. We have two specific aims. The first is to identify whether higher-level revision is specifically associated with the production of an unorganized initial draft (as is predicted by the dual-process model), rather than being equally associated with both planned and unplanned initial drafts (as is predicted by models in which revision is treated as an independent process). The second is to evaluate whether the effectiveness of revision depends on the form of initial draft it is combined with.

Looking first at undergraduate writers, Torrance, Thomas, and Robinson (1999) conducted what can be seen as a naturalistic equivalent of Kellogg's (1988) directed retrospection study of drafting strategies. In Torrance et al.'s study, undergraduates writing coursework essays were prompted (by a bleep on a portable tape recorder, occurring on average every 110 seconds) to complete a log indicating the activity they were currently engaged in. The students' responses were categorized as one of collecting (reading/making notes from reference materials), planning, translating, revising, or neat copying. These were then cluster analyzed to identify systematic differences among students in the distribution of activities over time. Three distinct patterns of activity were identified.

The first of these writing procedures corresponded very directly to a planning strategy. It involved an extended initial period of collecting accompanied by planning. This was then followed by a period of planning on its own. Overall, these two activities occupied the first 45% of total writing time. The next period (occupying about 30% of writing time) was devoted exclusively to translation. The final 25% of writing time was devoted to neat copying, and, to a lesser extent, to revision. This strategy bears a striking resemblance to the outline-planned, rough-drafting condition of Kellogg's (1988) experiment: Planning is shifted to before the production of text; translation is the exclusive focus of text production, and revision is postponed until after text production, but is only present to a relatively minor extent. A substantial minority of undergraduates (30% in this sample) therefore appear to divide up the writing process in a way that, in Kellogg's account, optimally reduces the probability of cognitive overload.

The second grouping corresponded fairly directly to a single draft strategy. The first 30% of total writing time was occupied exclusively in collecting. This was followed by a period in which planning, translating and revising were carried out together (40% of total time), and this, in turn, was followed by an extended period of neat copying and some revision (the remaining 30% of total time). This corresponds closely to the distribution of processing in the non-outline-planned, polished draft condition of Kellogg's (1988) experiment. It was the most frequently employed strategy, representing the writing procedure for 50% of the essays in the sample.

The final grouping appeared to correspond most closely to an unplanned drafting strategy. It consisted of an initial, relatively brief period (about 20% of total time) devoted almost exclusively to collecting, but including a small amount of planning. Translation (about 40% of the total time) then began very early, while collecting was still being carried out, and continued, on its own, with almost no accompanying planning or revision. The final 40% of the writing time was then devoted to revision (about twice as much as in the other clusters) and neat copying. This strategy has no direct equivalent in Kellogg's (1988) study, involving as it does unplanned translation, starting very early during writing, and followed by an extended period of revision. It does, however, contain many of the features of a multiple drafting strategy, without, perhaps, involving as much revision of text. This strategy was employed for 20% of the essays in the sample.

Overall, then, we think this study provides direct evidence for the existence of a multiple drafting strategy of the form specified by the dual process model. Furthermore, there is little evidence of a strategy in which high levels of revision are combined with the production of a planned initial draft, as would be predicted if revision was an independent component of the writing process. There was, however, no evidence that any of these strategies was more effective than the others. We suspect that this was a consequence of low statistical power (the study had a sample size of 25 students and 42 essays). In a more recent study, using a brief questionnaire about writing processes completed after writing coursework essays (term papers), Torrance, Thomas, and Robinson (2000) found evidence for a similar set of strategies but also that these differed in their relative effectiveness. Specifically, within the planning strategies they identified, a "detailed-planning" strategy was associated with higher marks than other less elaborate forms of planning or single draft strategies. Strikingly, however, the remaining strategy, in which an unplanned initial draft was followed by a relatively high amount of revision, was also associated with the same level of high marks as the "detailed-planning" strategy. In other words, there is some evidence that both the kind of detailed planning strategy identified by Kellogg and the kind of multiple drafting strategy we are proposing may be more effective than other less detailed planning or single draft strategies.

In both these studies of relatively inexperienced undergraduate writers, there was evidence of either a planning strategy or an interactive strategy but no evidence of writers combining planning with extensive revision. This may in part be a consequence of the relatively inexperienced nature of the sample. A questionnaire study of a sample of 110 postgraduate research students by Torrance, Thomas, and Robinson (1994) suggests that this may be the case. This study identified three strategy clusters. The first of these – the "planners" – tended to make detailed plans for their text but then write only one, or at most, two drafts. They corresponded well, therefore with the planning strategy identified in other research. The remainder of the group (about 50% of the sample) reported engaging in more extensive revision. Within this group two clusters could be identified. "Revisers" wrote more drafts than "planners", and were much more likely to report that they could not think without writing and that it was only after writing something down that they felt that they understood their own arguments. This group, therefore, appeared to be strategically adopting a multiple-drafting strategy to explore their understanding of their topic. By contrast, the other group, whom Torrance et al. described as "mixed-strategy-writers", both planned and wrote multiple drafts. This group, however, were no more likely to report seeing the writing process as functioning to develop their ideas than were the planners.

This study, therefore, does provide some evidence for a strategy in which planning and revision are combined, and hence some support for the claim that planning and revision are independent components of the writing process. However, it should also be noted that this mixed strategy was not associated with the use of writing as a means of developing ideas, whereas the strategy in which revision was combined with an unorganized initial draft, was associated with the development of the writers' ideas. This is consistent with the dual process model's claim that revision in the context of a planned initial draft is relatively reactive in form, whereas revision in the context of an unplanned initial draft is more proactive in form. Furthermore, there was some evidence in this study that the mixed strategy writers were less productive than the other writers, with the implication that their higher level of revision may reflect a higher level of problems in writing. One possible interpretation of this is that the mixed-strategy group represent a half way house between a planning strategy and a multiple-drafting strategy. They have begun to develop more extensive revision than the typical undergraduate, but this is still relatively reactive in form, and has not been incorporated into a deliberate multiple-drafting strategy.

Stronger evidence that a strategy in which revision is combined with planning may be less effective than one in which it is combined with an unorganized initial draft comes from a study of individual differences in drafting strategies by Galbraith (1996). This study compared the drafting strategies employed by low and high self-monitors and was designed as a follow up to a study by Galbraith (1992). Self-monitoring is an individual difference variable measuring the extent to which individuals control their expressive behavior in order to satisfy social goals (Snyder, 1986), and Galbraith (1992) used it to distinguish between individuals whose writing is directed towards dispositional goals (low self-monitors) and writers whose writing is directed towards rhetorical goals (high self-monitors). Consistent with the claims of the dual process model, he found that low self-monitors tended to discover new ideas as a function of writing full text, whereas high self-monitors tended to discover new ideas as a function of planning in note-form. The later study (Galbraith, 1996) was designed to test the prediction that the low self-monitors would be more likely to employ a multiple-drafting strategy, whereas the high self-monitors would be more likely to employ a planning strategy. A 55-item questionnaire about the writing processes employed in coursework essays was administered to a sample of 186 undergraduate psychology students. Following a principal components analysis of the responses, the low and high self-monitors were compared on 8 scales corresponding to different components of the writing process. Consistent with the prediction, it was found that low self-monitors reported a greater tendency to write multiple drafts and to generate ideas during text production, and a lower tendency to engage in detailed planning prior to writing. Furthermore, the two groups combined the two main factors identified in the principal components analysis in different ways: Low self-monitors were more likely to write multiple drafts the *less* they planned and controlled text production, whereas high self-monitors were more likely to write multiple drafts the *more* they planned and controlled text production. In other words, there was evidence that higher levels of revision were associated with both an unorganized initial draft (for the low self-monitors) and with a planned initial draft (the high self-monitors). Crucially, however, there was also evidence that this difference was associated with differences in performance: The low self-monitors who wrote multiple drafts achieved significantly higher marks for their essays than the high self-monitors who wrote multiple drafts. Although their could be a number of explanations for this, including differences in effort, it is consistent with the general claim that the effectiveness of multiple drafting depends on it being combined with dispositional text production. More generally, the results as a whole provide further evidence of the existence of a multiple-drafting strategy similar to that described by Elbow and consistent with the predictions of the dual-process model.

To sum up, we think that these studies confirm the existence of a planning strategy of the form described by Kellogg (1988), in which writers seek to reduce cognitive load by reorganizing the distribution of writing processes. This strategy appears to be used more frequently and, when carried out appropriately, to be effective in terms both of productivity and performance. However, we think that there is also support for the existence of a multiple drafting strategy of the form described by Elbow (1973), and as specified by Galbraith's (1999) dual-process model, but different to that implemented in the experimental studies of Kellogg (1988) and Glynn et al. (1982). This appears to be a less frequently adopted strategy, but, in the few cases where evidence is available, to be equally effective in its effects on performance. Although there is also some evidence that planning and revision can be combined, as would be predicted if revision is an independent component of the writing process, this appears to be less prevalent, and, possibly, to be less effective than when revision is combined with an unorganized initial draft. It also appears to be less associated with the development of the writers' ideas and this is consistent with the dual-process model's claim that it involves reactive revision, in contrast to the proactive form of revision associated with the production of an unorganized initial draft. Clearly, however, these conclusions should be treated with some caution given the indirect nature of self-report measures and the correlational nature of the data upon which they are based.

4. EVALUATING A STRONG VERSION OF THE MULTIPLE-DRAFTING STRATEGY

In this section, we briefly describe some of the results of a recent experimental study comparing the effects of different drafting strategies on the generation and organization of ideas during preliminary drafts, and the overall effects of this on the quality of the final text. Our overall aim in this study was to create the conditions for an interactive strategy – defined as the production of an unorganized (or dispositional) draft in connected sentences followed by a redrafting of the text – and compare it to the kinds of strategies implemented in previous research (rough drafting, outlining and free generation of notes). As part of the study, we also manipulated the way revision of the initial draft was carried out, and evaluated whether this manipulation had the same effect in the context of the different drafting strategies. Our initial broad expectations were that: (i) the form of interactive strategy implemented in this study would have beneficial effects on the quality of the final texts, and (ii) that the manipulation of revision would only be effective in the context of this interactive drafting strategy.

4.1 *Task, Experimental Design and Participants*

Participants were asked to write an article for the university magazine discussing the pros and cons of legalizing cannabis and justifying their own opinion of the matter. It was stressed that they should be careful to consider both sides of the issue. They were informed that they would have approximately 50 minutes to do this in and that the time would be divided into two equal length phases consisting of time to write a preliminary draft or plan, and time to write the final version of the article.

In the first phase, we manipulated two variables to create four different preliminary draft formats. The organization variable manipulated the extent to which what the students wrote had to be explicitly organized to satisfy rhetorical goals. In the unorganized (or "dispositionally guided") conditions, writers were instructed to think about the topic, discussing the issues with themselves, and writing down their thoughts as they unfolded, without worrying about how well organized or well-expressed the text was. In the organized conditions, writers were instructed to aim for a well-organized article, with the structure of the final text, but without worrying about how well expressed the text was. The mode of writing variable manipulated whether the ideas had to be expressed in connected sentences or in note-form. In the sentences conditions, participants were instructed to write the text in connected sentences. In the notes condition, they were instructed to express their ideas in three or four word notes. In all conditions participants were also told that they would have the opportunity to turn their initial draft or notes into an organized and properly expressed article on the second draft.

The resulting four conditions were designed to correspond to four preliminary drafting strategies. The organized sentences condition, in which participants were required to produce well-organized text, but without worrying about how well-expressed the text was, was designed to correspond to the rough drafting strategy implemented in Kellogg's (1988) and Glynn et al.'s (1982) studies. The unorganized sentences condition was designed to correspond to the initial draft as specified in Elbow and Galbraith's description of the multiple drafting strategy. The organized notes condition was designed to correspond to the outlining condition implemented in Kellogg's (1988) study. The unorganized notes condition was designed to correspond to the unordered notes condition implemented in Glynn et al.'s (1982) study.

After writing the preliminary draft all participants were given 5 minutes to read over their initial draft. They were asked to note down the main changes in content they would make to the initial draft, and to write a single sentence summing up the main point they wanted to make. This was designed to focus all participants' attention on the global content of the preliminary draft and on their goal for the final text. It was also designed to be relatively neutral with respective to different forms of revision in that it included elements designed to promote identification of ideas in the text, as well as elements designed to promote evaluation of ideas with respect to goals.

In the second, final-draft, phase all participants were instructed to produce the best article they could, were reminded of the initial specification for the article, and were told to budget their time for the 20 minutes available. In addition, in an attempt to influence the extent to which the writers were able to reorganize the global structure of the initial draft, the conditions under which the final draft was to be produced were manipulated. For half of the participants in each of the preliminary draft conditions, the participants were allowed to consult their initial drafts, but were not allowed to write anything on it. Thus, in this "text-available" condition, the participants were free to make as few or as many changes to the initial text as they wished, but would nevertheless have to incorporate these in a fresh copy of the text rather than by making modifications to the existing text. For the other half of the participants in each condition, the initial draft was removed, and the participants had to produce a completely new draft. Our expectation was that the removal of the initial draft in this "text-unavailable" condition, would prompt a more global reorganization of the ideas contained in the initial text. This manipulation, therefore, was designed to create conditions in which it was easier (text unavailable condition) or harder (text available condition) for these relatively inexperienced writers to implement any changes they had identified while re-reading the first draft. Our hypothesis was that removing the text would have a beneficial effect on the quality of the final draft, but that this would only apply when the initial draft was unorganized in form, because it would only be in this condition that more proactive changes to the text would be suggested during re-reading. When the initial draft was organized, we expected writers to be more likely to focus on expressing this organization more effectively (reactive revision), and hence would not take advantage of the opportunity to make more radical changes to the text.

In summary, then, we manipulated three factors: organization of initial draft (organized versus unorganized), mode of writing for initial draft (sentences versus notes), and whether or not the initial draft was available during the production of the final draft. All three factors were manipulated between participants.

The findings that we report below deal with three dependent variables: (1) We counted the number of ideas for or against drug legalization in the students' preliminary drafts. For this analysis, two judges divided the texts into idea units – defined as a distinct argument either for or against the proposal, and including the main proposition and its associated explications. The interrater agreement was statistically significant though relatively low, ranging between 0.60 and 0.74 within the conditions. (2) In order to measure the extent to which the writers changed their opinion of the topic during the preliminary draft, participants in all conditions were asked to rate on a seven point scale the extent to which they agreed with the proposal before and after producing this draft. (3) Two judges rated the overall quality of the final drafts on a nine-point scale. They were instructed to keep in mind the following features – fluency of language, coherence of the overall argument, originality, and the appropriateness of the tone and relation to audience for an article in the university magazine. As an overall orientation the judges were instructed to imagine they were the editor of the magazine and to consider the extent to which they would publish the relevant article. Interrater agreement between the two judges was 0.76.

One hundred and two undergraduate students, studying a variety of disciplines at Staffordshire University, were paid to participate in the experiment.

4.2 *Results and Discussion*

For present purposes, we will explore just the following predictions. First, on the basis of Galbraith's (1992, 1999) previous research, we expected different conditions to be associated with different output during the first phase of the experiment. Specifically, we anticipated that students writing unorganized sentences in the prewriting phase would be better able to constitute their implicit disposition towards the topic in the text. Hence, they would generate ideas corresponding more directly with their opinion of the topic, and would tend to shift towards stronger opinions of the topic. At the opposite extreme, we anticipated that students writing organized notes would generate and structure ideas so as to meet rhetorical goals, which in this experiment involved considering both sides of the drug-legalization argument. Hence the ideas they generated should correspond less directly with their personal opinion of the topic, and they would tend to shift towards weaker opinions of the topic.

Second, we expected the different conditions to be associated with differences in the quality of the final text. In line with Kellogg's (1988, 1990) previous research, we expected the organized notes conditions (outline planning) to produce higher quality text than the organized sentences conditions (rough drafting) or the unorganized notes conditions. In line with Galbraith's (1999) dual-process model, we expected that the unorganized sentences conditions would produce higher quality text than these conditions as well, because it should only be in these unorganized sentences conditions that writers would develop their understanding of the topic thorough formulating and re-reading the initial draft. We expected that this would be more pronounced in the condition where the initial draft was removed, because writers should be better able to articulate their more developed understanding of the topic in a fresh draft, as opposed to when they have to modify their initial draft. No such difference should be present for the organized initial drafts, where we expected revision to be concerned with improving the expression of the already organized text, and to be unaffected by the opportunity for making more radical changes to content.

All of the effects that we report in the discussion that follows were statistically significant ($p < .05$).

4.2.1 Ideas Generated during the Preliminary Drafts

Figure 1 shows the pattern of idea generation in the preliminary notes / drafts phase across the different groups. Ideas were classified according to whether they were consistent with the opinion of the essay topic that the writer expressed prior to the start of the experiment.

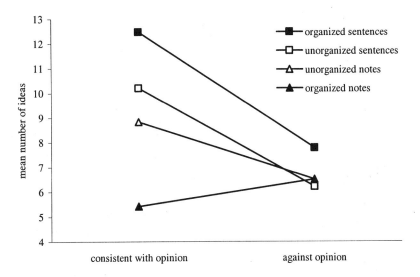

Figure 1. Mean number of ideas produced in the first, pre-writing phase by experimental condition and by whether the ideas were consistent with or contrary to the writer's previously expressed opinion of the writing topic (drug legalization).

The first important feature of these results is the marked contrast between the organized notes (outline) condition and the unorganized sentences condition. In the organized notes initial draft, the writers generated a similar number of ideas both for and against their opinion. Given that the instructions specified the rhetorical goal of providing a balanced argument about the issue, this pattern is compatible with the assumption that ideas were generated in order to satisfy rhetorical goals in this condition. By contrast, in the unorganized sentences condition, the writers generated a greater number of ideas in favor of their opinion than against their opinion. In other words, the ideas in their texts corresponded more directly with their opinion or disposition towards the topic. In this respect, the findings are consistent with the dual-process model's predictions.

However, two other features of the data are less consistent with its predictions. First, although the contrast between the number of ideas for and against the writer's opinion is less pronounced in the unorganized notes condition, as would be expected if notes provide less access than continuous prose to the writer's implicit disposition towards the topic, this difference was not statistically significant. Second, and much more problematic, the highest number of ideas in the whole experiment were produced in the organized sentences condition. This contradicts, not just the dual-process model, but also Glynn et al.'s (1982) findings, which were that the equivalent condition produced many fewer ideas than other forms of initial draft.

We suspect that this may be a consequence of the coding system we used for the analysis, which was relatively fine-grained, and which may have counted as separate ideas, ideas which were in fact elaborations of the same main point. This would be expected to particularly affect the organized sentences condition because this was the only condition in which the writers were trying to produce a full, communicative text. It therefore included more "signposting"– introductory sentences, linking sentences, and summary sentences – designed to guide the reader through the text. We are currently re-analyzing the texts using a coding scheme which distinguishes between content and "signposting" sentences and which includes associated elaborative material as part of higher level units of content.

If we are right in this assumption about the data for the organized sentences condition, then we would expect there to be other evidence that this was different to the unorganized conditions and similar to the organized notes condition. There was in fact evidence of just such a difference in the way the writers changed their opinions as a function of their initial drafts. In both the unorganized conditions, the writers' opinions shifted further in favor of their opinion (from a mean of 4.4 before writing to a mean of 4.6 after writing the initial draft). This is consistent with the dual-process model's claim that an unorganized initial draft should enable greater access to the writer's implicit disposition towards the topic (though note again that there is no difference between the notes and sentences conditions in this respect). In both the organized conditions, the shift was in the opposite direction, against their initial opinion of the topic (from a mean of 4.4 before writing to a mean of 4.1 after writing). This is consistent with the dual process model's claim that rhetorical organization should obscure the writer's implicit disposition towards the topic, and applies equally to the notes and sentences conditions, despite the apparent difference in the way ideas were generated in these conditions.

4.2.2   Quality of Final Draft

Figure 2 below shows the mean ratings of the quality of the final draft as a function of the different preliminary draft formats and of whether the initial draft was available to the writer during the production of the final draft.

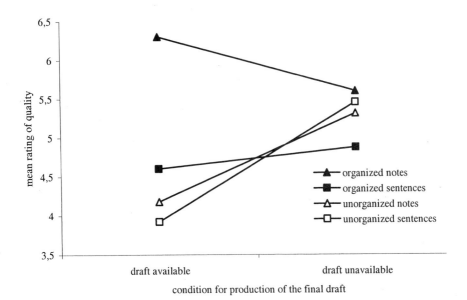

Figure 2. Mean ratings of quality of completed text by pre-writing condition and whether the products of pre-writing were available to the writer or not available to the writer during the production of the final draft.

The first important feature we want to draw attention to is the differences in quality when the writers had their initial drafts in front of them while they wrote the second draft. In this condition there was a clear advantage for the organized notes or outline planned condition over all the other conditions. This result corresponds directly with Kellogg's (1988) finding that outline planning is superior to a concurrently planned initial draft which the writer then has the opportunity to revise (organized sentences). It extends this result to show that outline planning is also superior to unorganized initial drafts which the writer can then revise.

However, as can be seen on the right hand side of Figure 2, there was a markedly different pattern for the quality of the final drafts produced when the initial draft was unavailable.

First, the unorganized conditions showed a very pronounced increase in quality, sufficiently large in fact, for the difference in quality between these texts and the outline planned texts, even when the initial draft was available, to be statistically non-significant. This is consistent with the dual-process model's prediction that an unorganized initial draft combined with proactive revision (enabled in this instance by the removal of the first draft) should lead to higher quality text. Note, though: (i) that this applies to both the notes and sentences conditions, contrary to the dual-process model's predictions, but in line with the fact that both initial draft formats appear to have had the same effect on the way ideas were initially generated; and (ii) that, although the difference is not statistically significant, the outline planning condition in which the initial draft remained available does still appear to produce a larger effect.

Second, there was no corresponding effect of removing the initial draft on the quality of the text produced in the organized conditions. This is consistent with the dual-process model's claim that, when a text has already been organized, revision is relatively reactive in form, and hence writers do not make radical changes in content, even when this facilitated by the removal of the initial draft. Revision has different effects depending on whether it is combined with an unorganized or an organized initial draft.

4.2.3   Conclusions

We want to draw two main conclusions from the results of this experiment. First, although it is clear that the most effective strategy in this experiment was the outline planning strategy (as in the earlier research by Kellogg, 1988, 1990), we think that the form of interactive strategy implemented in the "text unavailable" conditions is much closer in effectiveness to the outline planning strategy than the forms implemented in earlier research, and that the broad form of interactive strategy that we have described here has potential for further development. Our main caveat about this conclusion stems from the fact that there were no differences between the unorganized notes conditions and the unorganized sentences condition, either in the way ideas were generated or in the quality of the final text. This directly contradicts one of the main assumptions of the dual-process model. We suspect, however, that this may be because there was only a relatively weak compliance with this aspect of the instructions in this experiment. Our impression of the texts produced in the unorganized sentences condition was that, although they were written in sentences, they were nevertheless relatively list-like in character, rather than being fully connected prose. If this impression is correct, then it implies that the unorganized sentences condition was a relatively weak form of dispositionally-guided writing, and suggests, therefore that a fuller implementation of this in future research might lead to higher levels of text quality than in this experiment. One reason for favoring this interpretation is the fact that in Galbraith's (1992) experiment, where dispositionally-guided writing was operationalized by selecting appropriate participants (low self-monitors) rather than by instructions about the writing process, there were pronounced differences in the extent to which writers clarified their thought as a function of writing notes or prose. We plan, therefore, to explore this possibility in future research by examining the effects of both individual differences and different instructions on this variable.

A second reason for thinking that these results may underestimate the effectiveness of the interactive strategy is that this experiment did not include any specific revision strategy, other than asking all the writers to read over their initial draft, noting the main changes they would make to it, and summing up their main point. Indeed, these instructions were deliberately intended to be relatively neutral so that they would be compatible with both reactive and proactive forms of revision. In future research, we plan to give more explicit instructions about how to extract ideas from the initial text and how to produce a fresh draft.

The second important implication of this experiment comes from the fact that removing the initial draft only had an effect on the quality of the final texts in the unorganized conditions. This provides strong support for our general contention that the effectiveness of revision depends crucially on its role within an overall drafting strategy. Our assumption here is that the writers in the different conditions have the same basic revision skills, and that removing the initial draft offers the same opportunity for writers to make more radical changes to content. If revision were a fixed process, therefore, one would expect removing the initial draft to have the same effect for both organized and unorganized initial drafts. The fact that it does not suggests that the ability to revise text depends, not just on the writers' basic skills or the opportunity they have for revision, but on the form of the initial draft.

According to the dual process model, there are two fundamental differences between organized and unorganized initial drafts in this respect. The first is that unorganized text production followed by active extraction of ideas leads to developments of the writers' understanding, whereas organized text production, because it involves imposing an organization based on existing ideas on the production of text, does not. The two forms of initial draft do not, therefore, afford the same opportunity for identifying ideas corresponding to the writer's implicit disposition towards the topic. The second difference stems from the fact that in an organized draft the text already has an explicit organization and this makes it more difficult for the writer to construct an alternative organization for the second draft. By contrast, when the initial draft is unorganized, there is no explicit organization in the initial draft, and it is therefore easier to construct an organization based on the writers' more fully developed understanding of the topic. This difference is similar to the difference within the unorganized conditions between those where the text remains in front of the writer and those where it is removed. When the initial draft is retained, even though it is unorganized, the presence of the text itself makes it harder to make radical changes, with the result that the text is more likely to remain in its initial unorganized state, and to be judged to be of relatively low quality. By contrast, when the initial draft is removed, the writer has to produce a fresh text, and this can be based on the writers' more fully developed understanding of the topic, free from interference by the presence of the initial text.

The dual process model, therefore, makes two predictions about the effects of an interactive strategy. The first is that the initial unorganized draft should be associated with a greater development of understanding than organized text production. Given the problematic nature of the results comparing the patterns of idea generation in this experiment, this is clearly in need of further research. The second prediction is that the higher quality of the texts produced after an unorganized initial draft (with the initial draft removed) should be associated with a greater change in content between the first and second drafts than other conditions. We plan to carry out this analysis once we have developed a more reliable system for coding the ideas contained in the texts.

5.   GENERAL CONCLUSIONS

Our central claim in this chapter has been that revision is not a fixed component of the writing process, varying in the effectiveness with which it is carried out, and in the extent to which it is carried out at the same time as other components of the writing process or is separated from them. Instead, we have argued that revision takes a different form in the context of different drafting strategies. In the context of a planning strategy, it is essentially reactive in form, and involves evaluating and modifying text in order to satisfy rhetorical goals. In the context of an interactive strategy, it is essentially proactive in form, and involves identifying plans and goals in a spontaneously produced draft of text, with a view to using these to guide the production of further drafts of text.

We have argued that this characterization of the interactive strategy and of the form of revision it involves, corresponds more directly with the way the strategy is described by its proponents, and that it is compatible with Galbraith's (1999) dual-process model of writing. We concluded from a review of our previous research on drafting strategies that there was evidence for the existence of this strategy, even among relatively inexperienced undergraduates. There was also some less clear evidence that revision was more proactive, and more effective in the context of this strategy than when it was combined with planned initial drafts. These conclusions were supported by the preliminary findings of a recently completed experiment, which suggested that, when implemented in the form advocated here, the interactive strategy was more effective than the forms that have been implemented in previous research. There was also further evidence to support the claim that revision is less effective following a planned initial draft than it is following an unplanned initial draft. This evidence is sufficient, in our view, to suggest that further research would be productive.

The fact remains, however, that, in the research reported here, as well as in most previous research, there is clear evidence that an outline planning strategy is equally, if not more effective, than the interactive strategy. This being so, one might ask why an interactive strategy is necessary at all. One answer is that there seem to be clear individual differences in preferences for the two strategies, and that they may therefore be necessary to accommodate different cognitive styles. Another possibility is that the apparent equivalence of the two strategies is a consequence of measuring the quality of text on a single overall scale. It may be that the interactive strategy produces more discursive, less coherently organized texts, while the planning strategy produces less discursive, but more coherently organized texts. If both these properties are necessary for effective writing then overall judgements of quality may be actually be a combination of these two ingredients, and more sophisticated measures of different aspects of the text might reveal differences in the properties of the text produced by the two strategies.

Although we have focused in this chapter on differences in global drafting strategy, we suspect that in fact most writers employ both strategies at different points within the writing process, both within and across drafts. Which strategy is used when may depend, therefore, on whether the writer needs to further develop their understanding of the ideas contained in a particular section of text, or whether they need to integrate different sections of text into a more coherent global structure. The crucial point is that in order to do this writers need to understand the functions of different forms of revision, and how revision relates to other components of the writing process. In particular, given the relative rarity of the interactive strategy, we would advocate that writing instruction should include explicit teaching of strategies for extracting ideas from spontaneously formulated text.

AUDIENCE PERSPECTIVE IN YOUNG WRITERS' COMPOSING AND REVISING

Reading as the Reader

DAVID R. HOLLIWAY* & DEBORAH MCCUTCHEN**

*Marshall University, USA, **University of Washington, USA*

Abstract. In this study we examined how young writers (5th and 9th grade US students) benefited from perspective-taking experiences as they composed and revised descriptive essays. We investigated the contrasting benefits of three revision conditions that varied in the amount of reader insight they offered. The three conditions were a "feedback only" condition, a "rating-other" condition, and a "reading-as-the-reader" condition. Both the 9th and the 5th graders showed consistent significant improvement under the "reading-as-the-reader" condition, both when revising their essays and when drafting anew. Results suggested that when young writers engage in a task that duplicates their readers' experiences, they could more accurately revise their descriptive writing to meet their readers' informational needs.

Keywords: Reader perspective, revision, children's writing, descriptive writing

1. INTRODUCTION

Writing requires both cognitive and social processes (Dyson & Feldman, 1991; Fitzgerald, 1992; Flower, 1994; Rafoth & Rubin, 1988). Writers are faced with the cognitive task of deciding what information to communicate and how they will communicate it. Additionally, writers must consider the context of their writing and for whom their writing is intended. Traxler and Gernsbacher (1992, 1993; see also Fitzgerald, 1987, 1992) theorized that to meet the informational needs of readers, a writer must coordinate three overlapping mental representations: a representation of personal communicative intent (what do I want to say?), a representation of the text produced (what have I written?), and a representation of the reader's perspective (how will the reader interpret my writing?).

Protocols of skilled writers at work are replete with interactions among writer, reader and text (Hayes & Flower, 1980; Hayes, Flower, Schriver, Stratman, & Carey, 1987; McCutchen, 1984, 1988), but the skill of managing such interactions is not easily learned (Witte, 1992). Coordinating the mental representations for communicative intent, written text, and reader perspective is a socio-cognitive accomplishment that builds on multiple sources of interpersonal, cognitive, and textual competencies (Berkenkotter, 1981; Cameron, Hunt, & Linton, 1996; Fitzgerald, 1992; Littleton, 1998; Rafoth & Rubin, 1988). Such socio-cognitive coordination is especially challenging for young writers (Bereiter & Scardamalia, 1987) and may account for much of children's difficulty with revision. Indeed, Beal (1996) concluded that the biggest developmental hurdle for young writers is learning to focus "on the literal meaning of their own text which is all that will be available to the prospective reader" (p. 223). Within supportive environments children show the potential for sophisticated rhetorical thinking about text and audience (Cameron et al., 1998); however, in many classrooms young writers still struggle. Conditions that foster "comprehension monitoring" (Beal, 1990; Fitzgerald & Markham, 1987) and "knowledge-transforming" (Bereiter & Scardamalia, 1987) can help young writers differentiate their intended message from the text they have created. The research literature is less clear, however, about conditions that help young writers view their text from the perspective of their readers, and thus improve the communicative quality of their writing.

The ability to take the reader's perspective draws on many competencies – competencies that have been studied within a number of research traditions. Before describing our study, we briefly ground our discussion of audience perspective (and our methodology) within research on cognitive development and rhetoric, and we then situate the study within cognitive approaches to revision.

2.   LITERATURE REVIEW

2.1 *Perspective Taking in Written Referential Communication*

Perspective taking is the ability to think about another person's thinking. This socio-cognitive ability includes thought about others' social, emotional, and physical experiences. Crucial in perspective taking are the metacognitive processes needed to reflect on one's own thoughts and world experiences. This "wheels within wheels" thinking is a context dependent, developmental accomplishment (e.g., Miller, Kessel, & Flavell, 1970; Olson, 1994).

Many psychologists have used "egocentrism" and "decentering" to define opposite ends on this socio-cognitive spectrum. Flavell (1992) characterized egocentrism as children's limited ability to understand that "their own perspective may differ from those of others" (p. 107). Chandler (1977) suggested decentering is a socio-cognitive achievement that enables children to "transport themselves into the role or vantage of someone else" (p. 110).

Such socio-cognitive processes, however, are highly complex. According to Rubin (1984), "it is not possible to pinpoint a single age of onset of social decentration because different types of social cognitive processes become operative at different ages" (p. 218). The development of literacy skills, for example, requires a decentering ability to distinguish "the said" from "the intended" (Olson, 1994). Jokes, lies, and tall tales are great fun for children as they learn that what is said is not always what is meant. "Children understand that someone may misunderstand as long as the judgment is made from their own perspective. . . . [T]hey have yet to come to understand the possibility of another's beliefs about understanding and misunderstanding" (Olson, 1994, p. 129). Between the ages of four and five children acquire the rudimentary socio-cognitive ability to distinguish discrepancies between a speaker's communicative intent and his or her spoken words (e.g., Demorest, Silberstein, Gardner, & Winner, 1983).

The study of these socio-cognitive skills in communication (also labeled "perspective-taking skills") has a detailed history (Chandler, 1977; Flavell, 1992). The "referential communicative task" is one of the most fruitful research designs in studying the development of perspective taking (e.g., Bonitatibus & Flavell, 1985; Chandler, 1977). The referential communicative task requires participants to communicate clearly the critical distinguishing properties of some object or complex stimulus array so that another person can recognize it (see Chandler, 1977). In such tasks the informational needs of the audience are usually constrained by the content of the experiment.

The referential communication paradigm has been primarily used in studies of spoken communication. Glucksberg and Krauss (1967), for example, found that older children were more informationally accurate (i.e., socially appropriate) in orally describing abstract figures than younger children. Younger children, "in addition to displaying limited response repertoires, failed to edit, i.e., they did not modify their message in socially appropriate ways" (p. 313). The authors concluded that perspective taking in oral referential communication is a developmental achievement in which egocentric language is replaced by more decentered language that includes listener-useful descriptions. The referential communication paradigm has also been used extensively in non-developmental studies to investigate the spatial and communicative perspectives that speakers take when they orally describe different environments represented by maps (e.g., Schober, 1993; Taylor & Tversky, 1996).

Although Littleton (1998) used an oral referential communication task to make inferences about children's emergent writing competence, written communication per se has received limited attention in the literature on the development of perspective taking. Kroll (1978) investigated differences between oral and written modes of discourse by having fourth-graders describe the rules of a game to an experimenter. Fourth-graders were more successful at explaining and describing the rules in speaking than they were in writing. Kroll concluded that decentered language emerged earlier in children's speaking than in their writing. Speaking may facilitate children's social cognition because oral communication allows speakers and listeners to coordinate their interpretive perspectives based on facial gestures, intonation, pauses, and on an assumed contextual familiarity. Writers, however, have no immediate feedback. Decentering in written communication requires a writer to develop a representation of the readers' possible interpretation, a socio-cognitive achievement that is challenging for young writers (Bonk, 1990; Olson, 1994).

The literature in the development of perspective taking in written communication reflects varied methodologies, but remains unclear in terms of conditions that can facilitate socio-cognitive development for young writers (e.g., Bonk, 1990). For example, Frank (1992) found that subtle manipulation of audience specification in writing prompts led fifth-grade writers to compose newspaper advertisements differently for two audiences. Similarly, Cameron, Hunt, and Linton (1996) reviewed a study where second-, fourth-, and sixth-graders in a highly supportive writing environment were able to adapt the content of their writing for multiple audiences. However, other studies that varied audience specifications (e.g., older vs. younger, fictional vs. actual world, teacher vs. other students) offered mixed results on college students' ability to take the reader's perspective (e.g., Oliver, 1995).

Being sensitive to audience perspectives, however, does not guarantee effective revision. Bracewell, Scardamalia, and Bereiter (1978) concluded from two studies combining audience prompting with referential communication tasks that twelfth-graders' revisions improved the communicative quality of their descriptions, whereas fourth- and eighth-graders' revisions actually decreased the communicative quality of their writing. The referential communicative task, although underused in research on writing development, seems especially sensitive to the communicative effectiveness of texts. Thus, the task may provide a useful experimental window on children's ability to take the perspective of their readers.

2.2 Audience and the "Reader's Perspective"

Issues of reader perspective are related to those known variously as "audience awareness" and "sense of audience" and have deep historical roots (e.g., Ede, 1984; Elbow, 1987; Park, 1982; Rafoth, 1989). Kroll (1984), for example, attempted to summarize three overlapping views of audience: *the rhetorical, the informational,* and *the social.* The rhetorical perspective is based on Platonic and Aristotelian notions that teach students "methods of analyzing the knowledge, traits, and beliefs of their readers, so that the students will be able to identify their audience with realistic detail" (p. 175). In contrast, the informational perspective is grounded in the cognitive model of human information processing that suggests "the writer aims to get information into the reader's head" (p. 176). The social perspective views writing as a "social activity, entailing processes of inferring the thoughts and feelings of the other persons involved in the act of communication" (p. 179). The writer uses written language here, not to persuade or inform, but to induce dialogue, reflection and imagination. It is clear that rhetorical, informational, and social perspectives of audience assume different relationships among writer, reader, and text, and they require different inferences on the part of the writer.

Integrated within the study of audience are issues of the functional purposes that writing serves. Britton, Burgess, Martin, McLeod, and Rosen (1975) argued that texts are embedded within larger discourse functions that relate both to the writer's intentions and to the reader's response. They characterized three main functions in writing that are interdependent with reader perspectives: *transactional writing, expressive writing,* and *poetic writing.* Transactional writing functions to inform, ad-vise, persuade, and/or instruct the reader. It requires "accurate and specific reference to what is known about reality" (p. 88). Expressive writing functions "close to the self" (p. 90) with little concern for a reader beyond the self. The meaning encoded in expressive language is not made explicit because the writer assumes that the content can be immediately known. The poetic function of language is "an art medium" (p. 90), and results in "patterned verbalizations" of emotions and concepts that may evoke emotional responses from the reader. As the function of writing changes (from transactional to poetic or expressive), so too must the writer's conceptualization of the reader.

Rubin (1984) offered a socio-cognitive theory within which he integrated the multiple roles of audience with the multiple functions that writing can serve. According to Rubin, a writer's social cognition is implicated in (a) her ability to represent a reader's perspective as different from her own, (b) to coordinate her own perspective with that of the reader (either a single determinate other or a generalized other), and (c) to make inferences about the nature and stability of the readers' mental states.

Thus, writing tasks can differ in the audience demands they impose, due to different writing functions, and writers can differ in the aspects of social cognition in which they need support. Such factors should be considered in studies of reader perspective.

2.3 *Reading as the Reader: A Representational Strategy for Revision*

In addition to its pervasive role in general models of composition, reader perspective plays a central role in models of revision. Not only do skilled writers revise more than less experienced writers (Faigley & Witte, 1981; Flower, Hayes, Carey, Schriver, & Stratman, 1986), skilled writers attend more explicitly to their potential readers (Hayes et al., 1987; Sommers, 1980). Protocols of skilled writers reveal that they revise on multiple levels (Hayes et al., 1987). Skilled revisers evaluate texts against general standards of correct spelling and grammar and against the writer's intention. These two levels of evaluation form the basis of Bereiter and Scardamalia's (1987) well-known C.D.O. (compare, diagnose, and operate) model of revision, and novice writers' emphasis on the first over the second is probably responsible for their well-documented tendency to attend to surface features at the expense of meaning during revision (Bridwell, 1980; Butterfield, Hacker, & Plumb, 1994; Chanquoy, 2001; Daneman & Stainton, 1993; Fitzgerald, 1987; McCutchen, Francis, & Kerr, 1997; Wallace et al., 1996). Hayes et al. (1987) argued, however, that skilled writers go beyond evaluating whether a text instantiates a writer's intentions to evaluate the adequacy of the intentions themselves in terms of higher-level goals that include a representation of the reader.

Revising for the readers' informational needs also requires that a writer be a skilled and strategic reader (Hayes, 1996; McCutchen et al., 1997). Olson (1994) theorized that learning to differentiate one's own perspective in reading from another's perspective is a benchmark in the acquisition of literacy: "Readers frequently fail to consider how texts could be understood or misunderstood by readers other than themselves" (p. 135). A major accomplishment for the developing writer is recognizing that "text is a representation for meaning, not meaning itself" (Beal, 1996, p. 221). The ability to "decenter" from one's privileged knowledge as author and reread from the perspective of a reader is a key element of revision, one that no doubt contributes to writers increased difficulties editing their own texts compared to others' texts (Bartlett, 1982; Daneman & Stainton, 1993).

Past research has found that, in some revision circumstances, adults will modify their internal representations of text and readers' perspective, and, ultimately, revise their writing in closer accordance with their readers' informational needs. In a series of five written referential communicative experiments (Traxler & Gernsbacher, 1992, 1993), first- and second-year college students wrote and revised descriptions of geometric figures (tangrams). The dependent measure in these studies was the number of readers who successfully matched tangram descriptions with the appropriate target-tangrams. This measure thus gave a direct index of the informational needs of the reader (i.e., the readers required enough descriptive information to distinguish one tangram from similar looking tangrams).

In their initial experiment, Traxler and Gernsbacher (1992) compared two groups of writers: One group received minimal feedback (a number indicating the number of readers who successfully matched their descriptions with the appropriate figures), and one group received no feedback. Compared with writers receiving no feedback, writers receiving feedback revised their descriptions in a way that led readers to make more accurate judgments in a second scoring session. Traxler and Gernsbacher concluded that even minimal feedback can help writers envision how readers interpret their texts by forming a representation of their readers' informational needs.

In a subsequent study, Traxler and Gernsbacher (1993) investigated the differences between two feedback conditions and their influence on revision. After writing descriptions of tangrams in an initial session, writers were randomly assigned to either a "readers' task" or a "rating task." Before they revised, one group of writers read descriptions and then matched them with tangrams (just as their readers did), whereas the other group rated texts in terms of informational adequacy and clarity (e.g., how clear was the description?; how much information did the description contain?). Those writers who matched descriptions to tangrams revised their descriptions more effectively than those who only rated texts on their informational adequacy. Reading-as-the-reader, Traxler and Gernsbacher concluded, helped "writers communicate more clearly because perspective-taking helps the writers form a mental representation of how readers interpret their texts" (p. 311).

For the writers in the Traxler and Gernsbacher studies, reading-as-the-reader provided the revision experience needed to create, modify and coordinate informational representations of their readers. Other minimal instructional interventions have proven sufficient to change the revision strategies of relatively skilled writers, but the strategies of less-skilled writers have proven more resistant to change (Wallace & Hayes, 1991; Wallace et al., 1996). It remains to be seen whether young writers would benefit as much from stepping "in their readers' shoes" (Traxler & Gernsbacher, 1993, p. 311).

In the present study, we adapted the referential communication task of Traxler and Gernsbacher (1992, 1993) to explore whether young writers would benefit from reading as the reader, as had the college undergraduates whom Traxler and Gerns-bacher studied. The writing task was thus limited to transactional writing (Britton et al., 1975) and involved an informational perspective on audience (Kroll, 1984). Although limited within a specific discourse function, such concrete experiences like reading as the reader may help young writers begin to coordinate "what I want to say" and "what I have written" with "how my reader interprets my writing."

3.   METHOD

3.1 *Participants*

The fifth-grade and ninth-grade participants for this study came from four school districts in a large North American metropolitan area. There were two groups of participants: the writers and the readers. The writers consisted of 78 fifth-graders and 76 ninth-graders. The readers were a separate group of 52 ninth-grade readers in advanced placement English classes.

3.2 *Design*

A written referential communicative paradigm was adapted from Traxler and Gerns-bacher (1993). Each of three writing sessions was followed by a reading session. Writing sessions were separated by one-week intervals (see Table 1).

3.2.1   Writers

Writers participated in three 30-45 minute writing sessions. In the first writing session, all writers were given a notebook with written instructions and three tangram figures to be described (hereafter referred to as "targetgrams"). Each targetgram was presented on a separate page with ample space to write.

In the second session, each writer received a typed version of the descriptions they composed in the first session. During the second session, writers were randomly assigned to one of three perspective-taking conditions:

Condition 1 - Feedback only. Writers received a sentence for each description indicating whether their reader successfully matched their descriptions with the targetgrams. Writers were then asked to revise their original descriptions.

Condition 2 - Feedback + rating. Like condition one, all writers received feedback sentences indicating whether their reader successfully matched each description with the targetgram. Then, writers in this condition received three descriptions written by another student and rated the descriptions by considering the informational adequacy of each description. They then revised their own original descriptions.

Condition 3 - Feedback + read-as-the-reader. Like conditions one and two, writers received feedback sentences indicating whether their reader successfully matched their descriptions with the targetgrams. Then, writers in this condition were asked to read three descriptions written by another student and match descriptions with tangrams (a task identical to their readers' task). Writers then revised their original descriptions.

In the third writing session, writers remained in their assigned experimental conditions and received condition-appropriate feedback about their revised descriptions. Writers then composed new descriptions for tangrams they had not previously seen. In addition, after students had completed their descriptions, students were encouraged to describe, in writing, their perceptions of the value of the writing experiences they had as participants in the study.

3.2.2   Readers

For the entirety of the experiment, each writer was assigned to a specific reader. Each reader read nine tangram descriptions per session; three from each of three wripters, with one writer representing each of the three perspective conditions. For each description, readers saw four similar tangrams and decided which one of the four tangrams was described (see Figure 1). This reading process was repeated across three reading sessions: once for the original draft descriptions from session 1, once for revisions from session 2, and once for the new descriptions written in session 3.

Table 1. Sequence of weekly experimental sessions

	Writers	Readers
Week One	Writers are given notebook of three tangrams to describe.	Readers read descriptions and make description-to-tangram matches.
Week Two	Writers are randomly assigned to one of three conditions. After task is completed, they revise their original descriptions.	Readers read and make new description-to-targetgram matches.
Week Three	Writers remain in assigned condition and describe a new group of three tangrams.	Readers read new descriptions and make targetgram matches.

3.3 Materials

The stimulus materials consisted of 72 different tangram figures (similar to those used by Traxler and Gernsbacher, 1992 and 1993). The tangrams were divided into 6 sets, with sets counterbalanced across conditions and sessions. Each set contained three separate groups of four similar looking tangrams (see Figure 1). Each group contained one targetgram and three distracters.

Tangrams

Groups of Similar-looking Tangrams

Figure 1. Groups and sets of similar-looking Tangrams.

During each writing session, each writer received a notebook with a cover page of written instructions and three separate pages containing one targetgram (again, see Figure 1 for examples of tangram sets). If additional writing space was needed, writers were invited to continue on the back of the page.

During each reading session, readers received a notebook and a scorebook. The notebook contained nine student-generated descriptions that had been typed by the first researcher to eliminate handwriting differences. In the scorebook the readers made their description-to-targetgram matches. The scorebook included a page of four similar-looking tangrams for each description (again, see Figure 1 for the six sets used). For each description, readers read the typed version in the notebook, then, in the scorebook, circled the tangram they thought was best described.

3.4 *Procedures*

Writing sessions took place in students' regular classrooms. In session 1, the first researcher presented all general instructions orally. In sessions 2 and 3, condition-specific instructions were written in the notebooks, thus allowing for random assignment to condition within classrooms. After oral instructions, students read condition-specific materials silently and began their writing tasks. In each session, writers were given 30 minutes to describe the three tangrams. As writers worked, the first researcher circulated and answered individual questions.

All weekly reading sessions followed the same procedures (see Table 1 for weekly sequences). Readers were provided with notebooks containing nine typed descriptions and scorebooks containing nine sets of tangrams (one targetgram and three foils per set). Readers then matched each description to the tangram they thought it best described. Readers were given 30-40 minutes to read the descriptions and decide among the tangrams.

4. RESULTS

The dependent measure was the number of correct description-to-targetgram matches made by each writer's reader. For each session, a writer could earn a score between 0 (no matches made) and 3 (all targetgrams matched correctly). Table 2 shows the mean scores by session, by condition and by grade.

Table 2. Means and standard deviations by condition, grade and session

	Session 1			Session 2			Session 3		
Condition	N	M	SD	N	M	SD	N	M	SD
Feedback									
9th-grade	18	2.17	.92	18	2.39	.85	18	2.28	.96
5th-grade	25	1.80	.76	25	2.20	.76	25	1.68	.95
Rate-Other									
9th-grade	26	2.23	.77	26	2.42	.76	26	2.42	.70
5th-grade	30	1.87	1.04	30	2.00	.95	30	2.27	.87
Read-as-the Reader									
9th-grade	32	1.75	.88	32	2.25	.84	32	2.47	.67
5th-grade	23	1.57	.59	23	2.13	1.01	23	2.26	.69

Scores were submitted to a 2 (grade) x 3 (condition) x 3 (session) analysis of variance using a multivariate approach because of the repeated measure (session). Sphericity could be assumed (Greenhouse-Geisser epsilon = .99; Huynh-Feldt epsilon = 1.00), so uncorrected values are reported. Because the writing tasks differed across sessions 1 and 2 (revising vs. composing anew), preliminary analyses of these data (Holliway & McCutchen, 2000) compared session 1 to each succeeding session independently. However, the similar pattern of results, despite the variation in task, prompted us to include all 3 sessions within a single analysis here.

The ANOVA revealed a main effect of grade, $F(1, 148) = 11.01, p = .001$. On average, ninth-grade texts yielded more matches (M = 2.25, SD = .48) than fifth-grade texts (M = 1.98, SD = .58). There was no main effect of condition, nor a grade by condition interaction ($F < 1$ in both cases). The main effect of session, $F(2, 296) = 8.76, p < .001$, was significant, with session 1 (M = 1.88, SD = .86) yielding fewer matches than session 2 (M = 2.22, SD = .87) and session 3 (M = 2.24, SD = .83). However, the session main effect was compromised by a significant interaction between session and condition, $F(4, 296) = 2.96, p = .019$. Post hoc analyses (Tukey's Honestly Significant Difference (HSD) approach) established that differences between session 1 and sessions 2 and 3 were significant only for the read-as-the-reader group (critical value = .375, $p = .05$). No other interactions reached significance ($F < 1$).

The significant interaction is depicted in Figure 2, which plots the gain scores between sessions 1 and 2 and between sessions 1 and 3 for each condition (feedback, rate-other, read-as-reader). Although the session 2 and 3 mean scores are similar for the rate-other and read-as-reader groups (see Table 2), the interaction takes into account the fact that the read-as-reader group scored somewhat lower in session 1, and this baseline difference is reflected in the gain scores.

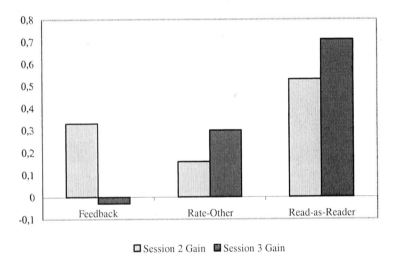

□ Session 2 Gain   ■ Session 3 Gain

Figure 2. Gain Scores across Conditions.

Students' perceptions of the value of the writing experiences were also analyzed, based on open-ended free-writes collected following completion of their tangram descriptions in session 3. We were interested in the students' perceptions of the value of their experiences as participants in the three conditions. Students portrayed their writing experiences on a variety of levels, usually characterizing the task in some way as fun or boring, insightful or uninspiring. We used the student free-write responses to generate a general coding scheme that categorized their experiences as positive or negative, useful or not useful. Examples of the coding scheme and sample student responses are presented in Table 3.

Table 3. A general coding scheme and illustrative student responses

Coding	Sample Student Responses
Positive	It was fun! But one thing I didn't get to read others and choose the shape they saw. I really wanted to, otherwise it was fun. (5th Grader in Feedback Condition)
	I thought this was fun and I think that it was teaching us how to describe better. I think it made us use our imagination. (5th Grader in Feedback Condition)
	It was a good experience, but I wish we could have matched some tangrams too. I enjoyed myself and think you did a good job! I learned a lot [sic]. (9th Grader in Rate-Other Condition)
	Though describing to shapes was kinda [sic] weird, I think that it was fun a good way of learning how to rely [sic] messages to the readers. It was fun. (9th Grader in Read-as-Reader Condition)
	I think this exercise was interesting but kinda [sic] hard. It was hard to describe a figure in your own words and your own perspective to try to get someone else to understand what you are trying to say and describe. I learned that descripfulness [sic] helps. (9th Grader in Read-as-Reader Condition)
Negative	I think this writing was boring. (5th Grader in Rate-Other Condition)
	I was about to say it is good but I am sorry to say no because it is too hard and I just want to stop doing this. I don't want to do it because it is starting to get boring. I know you're trying to make it fun but not this one try a different kind of thing that makes it fun. (5th Grader in Read-as-Reader Condition)
	This activity is not useful for my future, but it does take up boring school time. So in that sense it was good. (9th Grader in Rate-Other Condition)
	This is lame. (9th Grader in Read-as-Reader Condition)

Based on the coding scheme, we calculated the percentage of students in each condition who characterized their writing experience positively. Not all students provided a free-write, and Table 4 presents the number of students responding in each condition, as well as the percentage. We used Fisher's Exact Test to compare the percentage of positive responses from students in the feedback condition to those in the rate-other and the read-as-reader conditions. Students in the feedback condition were significantly less likely to characterize their writing experiences as positive, compared with students in the other two groups (Fisher's Exact = 6.787, p = .005).

Table 4. Student views of the value of their writing experiences

	Positive Responses	
	N Responding	% of Group
Feedback	20	46.5
Rate-Other	38	67.9
Read-as-Reader	39	70.9

5. DISCUSSION

5.1 Research Implications

Like college students (Traxler & Gernsbacher 1993), young writers in this study benefited from taking their readers' perspective. They used their reading as the reader experiences to improve the communicative adequacy of their texts when revising, and the benefits transferred when they wrote completely new descriptive essays. Although ninth graders wrote more effectively overall than fifth graders, both age groups showed similar gains when given the opportunity to take their readers' perspective.

It is difficult to attribute the benefit shown by writers in the read-as-the-reader condition to factors other than reader perspective. Writers in all three conditions received feedback about the accuracy of their readers' choices. Both the rate-other group and the read-as-the-reader group read and evaluated descriptive texts written by other students. However, only the read-as-the-reader group was asked to take their readers' perspective in the actual task of matching descriptions to tangrams, and only the read-as-the-reader group showed significant improvement in sessions 2 and 3, despite starting with lower mean scores than the other groups.

Furthermore, these young writers seemed aware of the benefit they derived from being a reader. The analysis of writers' reflections about their experiences indicated that students generally characterized their participation in the study as positive, provided they had opportunities to read other students' texts. However, students in the feedback condition were less positive than students in the rate-other and read-as-reader conditions, and many seemed to recognize the reason for their relative dissatisfaction. Due to random assignment of conditions within classrooms, students in the Feedback condition were often aware that their classmates were reading descriptions written by other students. As indicated in Table 3, students in the Feedback condition sometimes commented that they too wanted the opportunity to read other students' texts. Although the analyses of student perceptions do not mirror the reader-accuracy data exactly, students' perceptions indicate that students were aware that opportunities to act as reader could be valuable to them as writers.

Thus far we have documented improvements in readers' ability to match descriptions to targetgrams (the dependent measure in this study) resulting from reading as the reader. However, we have yet to identify changes in writing strategies due to enhanced reader perspective. Initial text analyses of the descriptive essays generated in this study reveal few structural differences that can be associated with condition. Many writers began their descriptive essays with an analogy followed by descriptive phrases that characterized the organization of the tangram. For example, one student wrote: "It looks like a goose. It has a long zigzagging neck. It has a small head and a pointed beak. Its body is kinda [sic] long and it has two feet on top of each other." Future research might include protocol analysis to shed further light on the discourse strategies that students employ as they attempt to meet their readers' informational needs.

5.2 Classroom Implications

Admittedly, ours was not a study of how to best teach writing in classroom settings. Rather, we began with a theoretical model of revision (Hayes et al., 1987; Traxler & Gernsbacher, 1992, 1993) and examined assumptions of the model via experimental manipulations. Any classroom implications, therefore, are implications only in the broadest sense.

This research adds to a body of literature (e.g., Beal, 1996; Cameron et al., 1996; Daniles, 1990; Frank, 1992; Oliver, 1995) exploring instructional conditions that help young writers envision how their readers interpret their texts. Although we explored a rather constrained form of descriptive writing, the study offers empirical support for the widespread classroom practice of peer editing and peer response. Peer editing is assumed to improve the specific texts under consideration, but there is also an assumption of transfer to the writing and revising processes of all students involved - those who provide feedback as well as those who receive it. In evaluating the texts of their peers, students are in effect asked to take the reader's perspective. The results of the present study suggest, however, that peer response may be most effective when peers actually use the text in some way. Using a text in a concrete context may force students to confront the text's strengths and weaknesses in ways they are unable to do within a more abstract context. For example, if students are provided with clear guidelines for responding to written work (via scoring rubrics, etc.), they may more easily transfer those experiences to their own writing.

An adaptation of the writing/reading exercise used in this study might be a useful addition to a teacher's repertoire of classroom activities. In discussing her "writer's tool box," Harper (1997), a practicing teacher, described five revision tools that have worked with her middle school students. One such tool is her "snapshot." Students compose written snapshots similar to detailed photographic snapshots. Such snapshots compel students to attend closely to physical detail. Asking students to match written descriptive snapshots to actual photographs may provide students with concrete feedback about the power of their words to evoke images for their readers.

5.3 *Conclusion*

Bruner (1996) suggested that any theory of learning must include *perspectivability*. In Bruner's cultural psychological approach to education, "the perspectival tenet" states "to understand well what something 'means' requires some awareness of the alternative meanings that can be attached to the matter under scrutiny" (p. 13). Similarly, Olson (1994) suggested that understanding that other people have different experiential perspectives is tantamount to becoming literate. Distinguishing the "said" (that which is explicit) from the "intended" (that which is implicit) requires a perspective on the reciprocity between reader, writer, and written text that is challenging even for experienced writers and readers. Reading-as-the-reader is one revision strategy that may assist young writers in taking a small step toward the literacy of perspectivability.

AUTHOR NOTE

Work reported here was partially supported by NIH grant HD33812-06.

REVISION OF FORM AND MEANING IN LEARNING TO WRITE COMPREHENSIBLE TEXT

AMOS VAN GELDEREN & RON OOSTDAM

University of Amsterdam, The Netherlands

Abstract. In this chapter we give a theoretical account of the roles of form and meaning in the revision process of inexperienced writers. The account is based upon theories about the writing process and cognitive constraints in working memory. From a review of empirical studies of children's revising skills, it appears that their attention is almost exclusively focused on form related issues whereas revision on the level of meaning seldom occurs. We present a model in which the roles of form and meaning in revision on local and global text levels are systematically described. Next we explore the implications for instruction in which two dimensions of learning are distinguished: "explicitness of instruction" and "focus of instruction." We go into the feasibility of facilitating linguistic fluency in order to improve meaning-oriented revision processes. Finally some questions for further research into the effectiveness of instructional conditions are raised.

Keywords: Revision, writing, linguistic fluency, focus on form, focus on meaning, cognitive processes, implicit instruction, explicit instruction

1. INTRODUCTION

Text revision is probably one of the most complex skills for writing. It depends on both linguistic and extra-linguistic skills. *Linguistic* skills are dependent on lexical, syntactic, phonologic, morphologic and orthographic knowledge of a certain language. They appear to be essential, because manipulating linguistic units within and between sentences is the most obvious – and most observable – aspect of revision activities. By *extra-linguistic skills* we refer to conceptual knowledge, metacognition, discourse knowledge and topic knowledge relevant to the writing task. This distinction between linguistic and extra-linguistic skills is cognitive, not disciplinary. Discourse decisions and pragmatic issues have both aspects. For example an extra-linguistic aspect is realizing that a situation has certain pragmatic characteristics (e.g., being polite); a linguistic aspect is knowing which words are appropriate to use in that situation (e.g., using the word "sir"). Some influential models of revision (Cf. Bereiter & Scardamalia, 1987; Flower, Hayes, Carey, Schriver, & Stratman, 1986) stress extra-linguistic aspects, focusing on cognitive processes like comparison, diagnosis and operation. Linguistic skills that are needed to carry out these processes successfully are not specified in these models. We focus on revision from a *communicative perspective*: producing text that is comprehensible to the readership. The importance of extra-linguistic skills in this context is evident. Nevertheless also linguistic skills are at stake here. We may assume that all the above-mentioned aspects are at work in producing comprehensible text.

We define revision in the same way as is commonly done in the literature. In the words of Fitzgerald (1987): "Revision means making any changes at any point in the writing process. It involves identifying discrepancies between intended and instantiated text, deciding what could or should be changed in the text and how to make desired changes (...)" (p. 484). In this chapter we will address the revision processes of inexperienced writers and how these processes can be facilitated in an educational context. Although we acknowledge the importance of extra-linguistic skills for revision, we will focus upon the way *linguistic fluency* determines the revision process on both the level of meaning and form. Thereby we assume that working memory limitations play an important role in revision skill. Improving linguistic fluency will result in less working memory load by translation problems and therefore there will be more attention to meaning related problems (Cf. Grabe, 2001; Kellogg, 1996; McCutchen, 1996; McCutchen, Covill, Hoyne, & Mildes, 1994; Snellings, Van Gelderen, & De Glopper, 2002).

After a definition of linguistic fluency we will present a review of studies into children's revision skills. Two different levels of revision are distinguished: the level of meaning communicated and the level of linguistic form in which the meaning is expressed. We pay special attention to the role of linguistic fluency in spoken and written language. Next we give a systematic account of the role of form and meaning in the writing and revising process. The resulting model is based upon existing models of the writing process and identifies several revision processes of form and meaning. This identification is a necessary step in proposing facilitations directed at the improvement of revision skills depending on linguistic fluency. Finally we explore ways of improving linguistic fluency that are generated in contemporary discussions about mother tongue (L1) and second language (L2) learning. Central issues in this discussion are the role of explicit and implicit learning of linguistic rules and the implications for focus on form and meaning in language education. Aiming at linguistic fluency does not necessarily mean that children should be instructed in explicit rules for building and rephrasing sentences. It can also be hypothesized that linguistic skills are better served when children's attention is focused on communicative meaning so that linguistic fluency is acquired in a more implicit way (Cf. Krashen, 1981).

We conclude by discussing some questions for research into the effectiveness of instructional approaches for improving linguistic fluency directed at facilitating revision of form and meaning.

2. DEFINING LINGUISTIC FLUENCY

Linguistic fluency is usually defined as the ability to produce language in a fast rate (Chenoweth & Hayes, 2001; Schmidt, 1992). Fluency is distinguished from *language proficiency*, because in the latter also semantic and syntactic knowledge and the ability to produce coherent and appropriate text are included. Although correct usage of language is not our criterion for fluency some quality criteria do apply. According to us the ability to produce various word combinations and sentence structures is also an aspect of fluency. We assume that these aspects – although they might be less important in oral communication (Cf. Van Gelderen, 1994) – are important in writing and especially in revision. For successful revision it is essential that the writer can choose from various lexical entries and syntactic structures in order to actually improve drafts. In speaking fluency can be inferred directly from the language output of the production processes, but in the writing process fluency may not be directly inferred from output behavior. Fluent writers do not have to write fast, although they efficiently access and retrieve a great number of words and syntactic structures (Cf. Chenoweth & Hayes, 2001). In other words fluency indicates the *accessibility* and *retrievability* of linguistic knowledge.

There are several theories about how such accessibility might develop. According to Anderson (1983) the knowledge within the long-term memory develops from a declarative stage to a procedural stage. Declarative knowledge is explicit rule-based knowledge. It delineates in an explicit way how to achieve a certain outcome. Procedural knowledge is seen as the result of repetitive use of the declarative knowledge in the same domain. Whereas declarative knowledge depends on conscious cognitive processing, procedural knowledge can proceed automatically, without conscious monitoring. Fluency develops, according to this view by the "proceduralization" of declarative knowledge. According to Anderson (1983) these two kinds of knowledge are interfaced, whereas Squire (1992) and Willingham, Nissen and Bullemer (1989) argue for a non-interface position between declarative and procedural knowledge. This means that declarative knowledge does not influence procedural knowledge and vice versa. There are also theories that explain the acquisition of linguistic fluency from a connectionist point of view (Cf. Ellis, 1996; Hulstijn, 1997). According to this view the basic principle of language learning is the "Law of Contiguity" (James, 1890). According to this "law" associations between stimuli are the most important mechanisms of learning. This kind of explanation of fluency predicts that pure rehearsal of exposure to linguistic stimuli is very important for learning. The more times linguistic units are presented in combination the more likely the combination will be learned. The more often this repetitive exposure, the stronger the connection between the units for access and retrieval will be. This process eventually results in the availability of "chunks" of linguistic units, ready for use in a given syntactic structure. Linguistic knowledge is therefore represented in the form of a network of interconnected, parallel-computing nodes.

3. FORM AND MEANING IN CHILDREN'S REVISIONS

In previous studies into elementary students' revision skills, it has been found that these students (and older students) almost exclusively revise in order to correct errors of linguistic *form*: spelling, punctuation, syntax or idiom (Cf. Fitzgerald, 1987; Flower et al., 1986; National Assessment of Educational Progress, 1977; Nold, 1981). Rethinking and rephrasing the *meaning* of what is being communicated seems to be very rare in these students' revision process. Somehow this observation is surprising, given that children's awareness of the *meaning* of text presumably is developmentally primary to their awareness of *forms* (Cf. Galambos & Goldin-Meadow, 1990). Moreover models of the writing process generally assume that meaning related processes, like idea generation, organization and selection, have priority over linguistic processes, like lexical selection and syntactic structuring (Cf. Bereiter & Scardamalia, 1987; Hayes, 1996; Hayes & Flower, 1980; Kellogg, 1996).

There are several explanations for the neglect of revision on the level of meaning communicated. One is Bereiter and Scardamalia's (1987) description of "knowledge telling" as the basic process of composition of inexperienced writers. In short, the process consists of the separate generation of an idea for each following sentence of a text, thereby producing rather isolated sentences with poor coherence that contain little, communicatively relevant information (see also McCutchen & Perfetti, 1982). Knowledge telling is a result of the absence of reactions of a live interaction partner. In the conversational situation in which text production originates, the partner provides the necessary signals for elaborating on, improving or correcting text already produced. In the typical writing situation at school there is no substitute for this kind of cuing so communicative problems may pass completely undetected.

Some other explanations for the neglect of revision on the level of meaning can be added to the "knowledge telling" explanation. Van Gelderen (1997) quotes Garner's (1990) analysis of the reasons children have for not using strategies that are potentially available to them. He mentions several explanations. Important factors for successful meaning-related revision are the ability to comprehend text adequately, awareness of meaning-level problems and checking reformulations. All of these explanations focus on extra-linguistic aspects of revision. Children are not sufficiently attentive to *meaning related problems* in the text they are producing. But *linguistic* problems that children have in manipulating words in sentences can also play an important role, especially when a communicative problem has been detected and the child is trying to solve it by changing words and structures. A central problem in revision from a communicative point of view is the integration of linguistic and extra-linguistic resources in reformulation. Writers have to keep in mind the knowledge they have of their subject, what they want to communicate, who they want to communicate to and what they know about that person(s). At the same time they have to manipulate words, sentences and their syntactic, semantic and pragmatic implications in order to express their ideas correctly and appropriately. It is rather likely that such complex integration leads to cognitive overload, especially in the case of inexperienced writers (Cf. Scardamalia, 1981). Flower and Hayes (1980) speak in this context of "juggling constraints."

4.   FLUENCY IN SPOKEN AND WRITTEN LANGUAGE

Kellogg (1996) developed and tested a model in which working memory capacity restricts what writers can and cannot do. The load placed on working memory by lexical and syntactic decisions in (re)formulation can thus prevent non-fluent writers to focus on meaning communicated (Cf. Chenoweth & Hayes, 2001; McCutchen, 1996; McCutchen et al., 1994). The linguistic constraints in writing are in many ways new to inexperienced writers. Though they can be fluent in *spoken* discourse – and many of them are – expressing their thoughts in written form deprives them of many instruments that they normally use to convey meaning in interaction: gestures, personal and physical contact, intonation, pauses, redundant formulation, lax syntax and self-repairs (Cf. Chafe, 1986; Levelt, 1989; Van Gelderen, 1994). The contrast with written communication is large indeed. Personalized aspects of communication are absent in most writing situations; prosodic instruments are not available; lexical and syntactic constraints are much tighter than in spoken discourse and self-repairs must be made invisible to the readership. As a result of the extra-linguistic context of most writing situations the writer has to deal with the conciseness of written language. Requirements like preciseness, clarity, and depersonalization severely constrain the linguistic form that written texts take. This form must be a simplification and densification of the richness of oral communication. To avoid misunderstandings the writer must be much more cautious than the speaker. Lacking the non-verbal and prosodic ways of communication and lacking possibilities for redundancy and overt repair, utterances on paper may become ambiguous in unexpected ways. Each single lexical decision might have diverse consequences for the way the text will be interpreted by the reader. Therefore each word is a potential candidate for conscious attention and revision. Fluent writers are supposed to relieve the burden of this task by using automated (or proceduralized) processes for formulation and evaluation of relatively large chunks of language (Anderson, 1995; Chenoweth & Hayes, 2001). Children, being non-fluent writers, thus may restrict attention to the forms of the language in order to prevent working memory to be exhausted.

We assume that all of the above difficulties – both linguistic and extra-linguistic – play a role in children's avoidance of revision of meaning. There are however individual differences between students. Van Gelderen (1997) carried out a study with 30 L1-students (grades 5-6) to explore qualitative and quantitative aspects of their revisions from the point of view of the CDO-model of Bereiter and Scardamalia (1987). In this study facilitating conditions were applied for revision on the level of meaning: revision was directed to someone else's text, encouragement was given on-line by the experimenter, and standard phrases for evaluation and operation were provided, focusing on evaluation of text meaning instead of linguistic correctness. Half of the students detected, diagnosed and even removed many meaning problems in the expository text. Some children did notice and others did not notice these problems. Moreover some children did succeed in adequately diagnosing the problems and operating on the sentences, while others did not. Although many students succeeded in removing meaning problems, these revisions rarely lead to a better text. Instead new problems often emerged, a result that has also been reported by Perl

(1975) and Bereiter and Scardamalia (1987). It appeared that linguistic problems often prevented successful reformulation.

Some more or less successful attempts have been made to facilitate children's revision skills by offering support on the *extra-linguistic* side. Bereiter and Scardamalia (1987) report studies in what they call "procedural facilitations" of the processes of comparison, diagnosis and operation. They supplied evaluative, diagnostic and directive phrases to focus learners' attention on meaning related problems. Chanquoy (2001) found positive effects of postponing revision to a moment where a first draft has been completed. Hacker, Plumb, Butterfield, Quathamer, and Heineken (1994) found a positive effect of questioning on the detection of meaning related problems.

At this point we want to focus on a theoretical underpinning of facilitation on the *linguistic* side of revision. In the next section we will therefore present a model in which the linguistic and the extra-linguistic aspects of the revision process are described in more detail.

5.   MODELING REVISION OF FORM AND MEANING

In this section we describe the role of form and meaning in the production and revision of written language. This description helps to identify specific problems that exist for students with poor linguistic fluency. We are especially interested in the role such problems play in the way form and meaning are interwoven on local and global text levels. A descriptive model is presented, based upon other models for language production (Cf. Bereiter & Scardamalia, 1987; Hayes, 1996; Hayes & Flower, 1980; Kellogg, 1996; Levelt, 1989). The model describes text production processes on the *local* level and the *global* level of a text. Within the model subprocesses and their mutual relation(s) are identified by which several revision processes can be distinguished and described (see next section). The model (see Figure 1) describes the roles of long-term memory (in which linguistic and extra-linguistic knowledge are situated) and working memory (in which the processes of text production and revision are planned, executed and controlled). Figure 1 also visualizes the place of task analysis in relation to the production and revision processes.

5.1   *Analysis of the Task Environment*

We presume that the *task environment* lies at the beginning of each writing process and defines the reasons for starting the process of written text production. The environment can be an *external agent*, like a writing assignment given by the teacher or an *internal agent*, like when the writer feels the need to communicate a certain message. In both cases a task analysis will result in a *global task representation* that defines writing goals, topic, readership, and global text characteristics (genre, length, structure). Task analysis draws mainly upon extra-linguistic knowledge. The more experienced a writer, the more sophisticated the global task representation will be. The actual process of task analysis takes place in working memory and requires its complete capacity. In order to relieve working memory the output of the task analysis is stored in long-term memory. Although the task analysis is visualized in Figure 1, the process is not elaborated upon here. Other publications give more detail on this (Cf. Bialystok, 1991; Canale & Swain, 1980; Oostdam & Rijlaarsdam, 1995; Sijtstra, 1991).

5.2 Long-term Memory

Within the model we distinguish two main knowledge stores: *extra-linguistic* and *linguistic*. The *linguistic knowledge* refers to knowledge of a specific language (L1 or L2): syntax, lexicon, morphology, punctuation and orthography. This type of knowledge is essential for the translating process that takes place in working memory. The *extra-linguistic knowledge* refers to knowledge in many different fields. In this context we pay attention to two important extra-linguistic knowledge fields for the production and revision of written text: *conceptual* knowledge and *discourse* knowledge. By *conceptual knowledge* we refer to knowledge about relations between ideas and content knowledge relevant for the topic of the writing task. For example, if one has to write about the way a machine works, conceptual knowledge about this machine is necessary. In some writing situations the conceptual knowledge in long-term memory will be sufficient. In other situations it may be necessary to acquire new conceptual knowledge by consulting external resources. *Discourse knowledge* appeals to knowledge of the communicative situation. Examples are knowledge about characteristics of the readers, socio-cultural definitions of politeness and formal/informal situations, organizational principles for different types of texts, like story-grammars and genres. Both types of extra-linguistic knowledge – conceptual and discourse – are important in analyzing the writing task (forming a global task representation) and in the writing and revision process itself.

Long-term memory also allows storage of output from working memory. In Figure 1 two relevant types of output are visualized: *global task representation* and *global text representation*. The global task representation is output from the process of task analysis, mentioned previously. Based upon this task representation the planner generates the global text representation containing a conceptual outline of the text to be produced. For example, if the task representation defines the writing task as a short fairy tale for young children, then the global text representation might contain concrete ideas about who are in the story, how it begins, what exciting events are to be described and how it ends.

5.3 Working Memory

In the model working memory includes three major mechanisms for text production and revision: the *planner*, the *translator* and the *reviewer*. Through the interaction of these three mechanisms *proposed text* is produced.

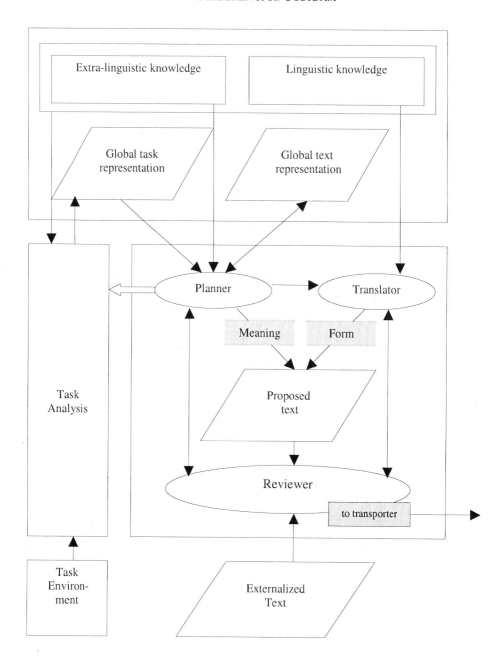

Figure 1. A model for situating form and meaning in written text production.
Normal arrows indicate the direction of information; the deviant arrow signals a switch to
task analysis processes; parallelograms indicate changing representations; ellipses symbolize
cognitive mechanisms.

In concordance with other models of the writing process we presume that the planning process can be subdivided into *generating*, *selecting* and *organizing* retrieved information from long-term memory. The global task representation together with the extra-linguistic knowledge will guide the processes of idea generating, idea selecting and idea organizing that are carried out by the *planner*. These sub-processes interact: the generation of new information determines the selection and organization of information and vice versa.

5.3.1   Global Text Production

The planner can retrieve information from the global task representation in order to propose a conceptual outline for the text to be written. This global *text* representation assimilates the task constraints from the global *task* representation. The planner also has access to the store of extra-linguistic knowledge. This process of information retrieval will most probably occur in terms of conceptual networks of associated ideas. Because the planners' functions are generating, selecting and organizing information on a conceptual and discourse level, the planner is exclusively directed to the meaning level of the text.

Although the planner is not capable of changing the global task representation, this does not mean that the global task representation cannot change during the writing process. The planner can decide that the task environment has to be reanalyzed at any moment during the writing process. Such a decision means an interruption of text production processes, because the limited capacity of working memory does not allow parallel processing of task analysis and text production. A deviant arrow in Figure 1 depicts this mode switch.

After constructing a *global* text representation the planner has two options: 1) direct storage of the conceptual outline in long-term memory, 2) making (a part of) the representation object of critical reflection in working memory. In the latter case the planner puts the global text representation in the proposed text box, by specifying intended meanings. Simultaneously it sends the translator the meanings to be translated in linguistic form. The translator consults linguistic knowledge from long-term memory and retrieves the forms fitting the meaning and sends these forms to the proposed text box. In this box forms and meanings are connected in a preliminary way. The reviewer *checks* whether the resulting text is in accordance with the intended meaning communicated by the planner. When the reviewer detects that the forms do not adequately convey the intended meaning it will produce a diagnosis and signals this to the translator. This process can go on until the reviewer decides that meaning and form are acceptably combined. Then the reviewer sends a signal to the *transporter* (see Figure 2).

The transporter acts under the authority of the reviewer. In Figure 1 an arrow from the reviewer indicates that the proposed text is sent to the transporter. The parallelograms in Figure 2 are identical to the ones in Figure 1. There are two possibilities now. First the proposed text can be placed in the global text representation (like an outline). Second the proposed text can be externalized. The task of the transporter is twofold: 1) retrieve and save textual representations in which *meaning <u>and</u> form* are (preliminarily) connected, and 2) transcribe textual representations into external-ized text.

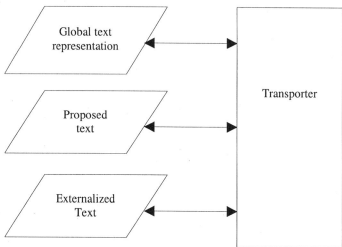

Figure 2. Transport of text representations in which form and meaning are connected.

5.3.2   Local Text Production

On the level of *local* text production (producing sentences) the model predicts essen-tially the same processes as described above. Again, the planner produces meaning units, guided by the global text representation, to be transformed by the *translator* in a specific linguistic form. This results in a *proposed text* in which meaning and form are connected. Again the reviewer *checks* whether the resulting text is in accordance with both the intended meaning communicated by the planner and criteria of linguis-tic correctness. In case a problem is detected, the reviewer will produce a diagnosis and signals this to the translator. The translator then has to choose words and struc-tures that are better suited to express the idea and avoid linguistic errors. To this end the translator consults linguistic knowledge in long-term memory. After the re-viewer has approved a new formulation in the proposed text box, the proposed text can be externalized by means of the transporter.

5.3.3   Functions of the Reviewer

The main functions of the *reviewer* are to check the meaning of the text on a concep-tual level and the connection between meaning and form. This implies that the re-viewer must have access to stored knowledge in long-term memory in order to re-trieve relevant criteria to judge the quality of the text on both meaning and form. In our model the reviewer has access to the linguistic and extra-linguistic knowledge in long-term memory via the planner and the translator.

In some models (Cf. Flower & Hayes, 1980) the revision module not only detects mistakes and diagnoses them but is also capable of improving text. In fact, the reviewer is an "all-rounder" and incorporates all the processes situated in the other components of the model. We prefer a clearer distinction between the processes of the planner, the translator and the reviewer. The task of producing the conceptual meaning of the text is delegated to the planner. The task of translating the conceptual meaning in a linguistic form is delegated to the translator. The task to detect and diagnose problems on the combination of meaning and form is delegated to the reviewer. In case the reviewer decides a problem exists and diagnoses the problem, he signals the planner or the translator to solve the problem. The reviewer itself is not capable to act as a problem solver. In Figure 3 the detection and diagnosis of problems by the reviewer is visualized.

The reviewing process starts with checking phrases in the proposed text. First the translation of the intended meaning of the planner is checked (question A in Figure 3). The reviewer may detect a discrepancy between intended meaning and the meaning as communicated in the proposed text or linguistic errors (No-option). In that case the reviewer decides upon a diagnosis of the problem and sends it to the translator. The translator generates a renewed linguistic proposal to express the intended meaning, which is checked again by the reviewer. This process may continue until a satisfying translation is established. Essentially this stage of written text production is not different from spoken text production (Cf. Levelt, 1989). In this stage the reviewing process of the proposed text is restricted to the translation. The writing process of "knowledge tellers" is often restricted to this isolated review of proposed text, without checks in the context of the text already written.

If the reviewer decides that the proposed text is satisfactory, there are two options. First the reviewer may check the acceptability of the meaning intended by the planner within the externalized text (question B in Figure 3). Second the reviewer may check the correctness of the linguistic form of the proposed text in the externalized text (question C). So at this point the reviewer may choose to attend to a multitude of extra-linguistic and linguistic criteria for assessing the accuracy of the resulting text. But, as we know, working memory capacity is limited and cognitive overload becomes a risk. Therefore inexperienced writers are likely to restrict their attention to only a few criteria. The competition between questions B and C in Figure 3 might explain why inexperienced writers restrict their attention during this stage of the reviewing process almost exclusively to criteria of linguistic form.

If the reviewer detects no problems, it can continue the reviewing process for next phrases (the Yes-options in Figure 3). In case problems are detected in the meaning communicated (the left hand No-option), such as problems of coherence or consistency, the reviewer constructs a diagnosis and sends it to the *planner*. Subsequently, the planner generates a renewed proposal for proposed text based on extra-linguistic knowledge, the global text representation and the global task representation. In case problems are detected on the linguistic side (the right hand No-option), such as the use of pronouns or noun-verb agreement, the reviewer constructs a diagnosis and sends it to the *translator* in order to propose a renewed translation.

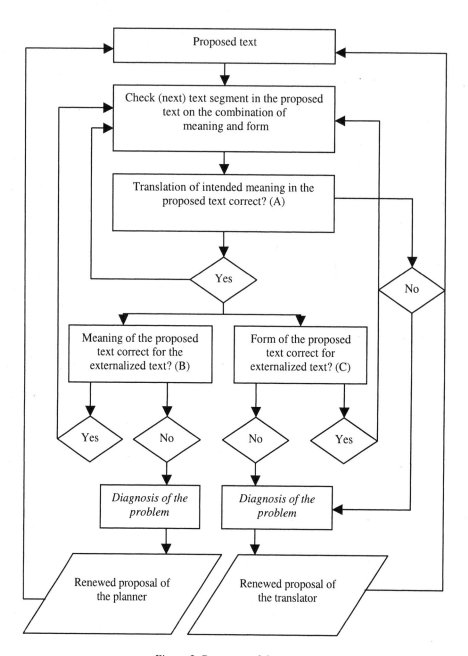

Figure 3. Processes of the reviewer.

Our model allows detection of problems concerning the meaning intended by the planner only when the proposed text is considered in the context of the externalized text. This does not mean that the text has to be actually *transcribed*. This process of checking the meaning of proposed text can take place before, during or after transport. We assume that experienced writers are able to make this check internally, before the proposed text has been externalized. The advantage is obviously that this prevents continuous rewriting.

6.   CLASSIFICATION OF REVISION ACTIVITIES DIRECTED TO MEANING AND FORM

Four levels of revision relevant to the form/meaning dichotomy can now be distinguished. We assume that these levels are of increasing cognitive complexity. The demands of linguistic fluency for successful operation on each successive level also rise. The reason for this is that the context of revision develops from very narrow local context (proposed text) to broader textual context (externalized text).

The first level is *revision of proposed text*. During this process detection and diagnosis are directed to the translation of intended meaning apart from externalized text (question A in Figure 3). The main question is whether the intended meaning is satisfactorily expressed by the linguistic form (syntactic, semantic and pragmatic) as given by the translator. Assuming that the planner has not made an error (which the reviewer cannot detect in this stage) translating problems may occur on different levels. There may be an operating problem (the translator does not function adequately) or an accessibility problem (insufficient chunking of linguistic units and insufficient linguistic knowledge, resulting in linguistic dysfluency). The reviewer is not capable of monitoring the planner's ideas, because he cannot compare the intended meaning of the planner with externalized text at this stage. Thus level-1 revisions are always directed solely at the form of utterances.

The second level deals with *revision of form of local externalized text*. In this case detection and diagnosis are given with respect to the correctness of the linguistic form of the proposed text in relation to the externalized text so far (question C in Figure 3). The main question is whether the linguistic form of the proposed text fits into the written text (syntactic, orthographic, standard usage or punctuation). This process can also take place when the proposed text (or a part of it) is being (or has been) externalized. This type of revision can be characterized as error correction. The reviewer checks the syntactic context for the proposed text and may detect errors and diagnose them. The translator subsequently has to fix such errors on the basis of the diagnosis of the reviewer. This revision process can be confronted with the same kinds of problems that were mentioned above. In this case however the appeal on linguistic fluency is larger, because there are more linguistic variables to be manipulated when proposed text is to be placed in externalized text. Moreover the process of checking for linguistic correctness has to compete with the next level in which attention is directed at the meaning of the resulting text.

The third level deals with *revision of meaning of local externalized text*. In this case detection and diagnosis are given with respect to the connection of the meaning of the proposed text to the meaning of preceding sentences in the externalized text (question B in Figure 3). In this process the reviewer checks whether the intended meaning of the planner holds when the proposed text is placed in the externalized text. The main question is whether the meaning of the proposed text meets criteria for *local* coherence and consistence. If problems exist, the planner receives a diagnosis from the reviewer and puts in motion a revision process. This process may be obstructed by problems on different levels. There may be a problem on operating level (the planner does not function adequately) or on the level of access and retrieval (insufficient conceptual knowledge and poor cognitive fluency).

The fourth level deals with *revision of meaning of global externalized text*. In this case detection and diagnosis are directed to the connection of the meaning of the proposed text (or draft) to the meaning of the externalized text as a whole (question B in Figure 3, from a global perspective). The main question is whether the meaning of the text meets the global text representation and global task representation as well as criteria for global coherence and consistence (parts of the extra-linguistic knowledge). The reviewer uses these global criteria to assess the adequacy of individual sentences and of global text structure. The revision process starts when the reviewer detects a problem and the planner receives a diagnosis. The operation can be directed at formulating a new proposed text or at rearranging bigger parts. The difficulty of this level thus lies in the complex interplay between local and global considerations for text revision. Different sorts of problems may obstruct the process. Again there can be an operating problem (the planner does not function adequately), an access and retrieval problem (insufficient conceptual and discourse knowledge and poor cognitive fluency), or global text representation problem (unclear notion of readership, insufficient information about the communicative context, etc.).

The four levels of revision are determined by the different roles that the writer assigns to form and meaning in the revision process. Between the levels 2 and 3 there is a crucial transition from merely form-focused revision processes to mainly meaning-focused revision. The meaning-focused levels, however always *imply* revisions of form. Therefore they are more complex, because the writer needs to detect conceptual or discourse-based problems first and subsequently has to diagnose and solve the problems by a more adequate proposal (from the planner) followed by new linguistic translations. Therefore we assume that on the levels 3 and 4 linguistic fluency is a more stringent condition for successful revision than it is on the levels 1 and 2. Although meaning is a very important criterion for revision on level 1, most of the attention is focused on processes of translation and reformulation. On the levels 3 and 4, however, the meaning and form aspects compete for working memory access (the so-called "juggling constraints").

7.   INSTRUCTIONAL APPROACHES FOR IMPROVING LINGUISTIC FLUENCY

The previous paragraphs identify revision processes directed to meaning and form that occur during writing. The description of these levels of revision indicates possibilities for facilitations to improve the revision process of inexperienced writers. In this respect the model can help in answering questions about the interaction between cognitive and instructional processes when revision is an object of school learning.

As our interest is in improvement of linguistic fluency, we want to explore ways in which this can be done according to theories of the role of linguistic knowledge in L1 and L2 learning. Discussions about the role of linguistic awareness in language learning are with us for a long time. Both in school practice and in scientific discourse about the conditions for a good language curriculum "grammar" has been one of the most debated topics. More than half of the previous century the teaching of grammar was generally regarded as a hallmark of good practice for language education, no matter who the learners were (children, adolescents, adults) or what the learning was about (L1, L2 or a foreign language). From the seventies on, a more critical attitude towards so-called traditional grammar grew amongst educationalists, both from a pedagogic and a linguistic point of view. In mother tongue education there were debates questioning the relation between subject matter of grammar education and the communicative skills that students' actually had to learn. Also the fundamental question was raised whether explicit knowledge about sentence structure is necessary for understanding and producing grammatical utterances. One of the first demonstrations that implicit learning is important in the syntactic acquisition process are the experiments with artificial grammars by Reber (1967). From the point of view of second language acquisition Krashen (1982) put forward the idea that all that is necessary for successful L2-acquisition is meaningful communication in the L2 (see also Robinson, 1997). Any focus on formal aspects of the language was considered non-productive by Krashen, because this kind of explicit knowledge has no relation with actual usage and does not transfer to communicative skill. Therefore a *focus on meaning* was stressed by Krashen (1981) and his followers as the main factor for successful (second) language acquisition. This was a dominating theme in L2-theory and practice during the eighties and part of the nineties of the previous century. Lately a counter movement set in, proposing that a *focus on form* is a key factor for successful L2-learning (Cf. Doughty & Williams, 1998; Long, 1991; Norris & Ortega, 2000). According to this view learners will keep on making the same mistakes over and over again if formal aspects of L2 are systematically neglected. Focus on form (not formS, like Long insists to discriminate it from the traditionalist view on grammar) means that the attention in the classroom mainly stays on the level of communicative meaning, but that at the same time learners are confronted with some form related issues that are supposed to be at their level.

The previous discussion makes clear that awareness of linguistic form can be an important condition for acquisition of certain structures and thus for aspects of linguistic fluency. On the other hand it is still debated how important this awareness is in the context of communicative language learning in general (Cf. Ellis, 1994). It might be that many linguistic structures are learned without conscious *noticing* (Schmidt, 1993) while learners are solely focused on meaning. This is "pure" implicit learning. But it can also be the case that *noticing* specific linguistic structures is essential for learning, so that students must be (explicitly) confronted with these forms. This is explicit learning directed to form, but focus on meaning still dominates. Furthermore there is discussion about the role of explicit knowledge of linguistic rules or regularities (e.g., explaining word order in sentences). There are studies indicating that the effect of explicit knowledge of rules on linguistic fluency may depend upon the *complexity* of the rules in question (Cf. Keyzer, 1995; Reber, 1989; Robinson, 1996). This explicit learning of rules goes one step beyond simple noticing by explaining or generalizing how certain structures are designed.

The theoretical debate about the role of awareness of linguistic forms and knowledge of linguistic rules has made it clear that there are no simple answers to questions like the following: Is it better to learn language and its usage by mere exposure to as much meaningful input as possible, or should explicit noticing and/or knowledge of rules accompany this input? Two dimensions of instruction are at stake here that can have an independent effect on learning outcomes. The first dimension we call "focus of instruction" (form or meaning). The second we call "explicitness of instruction" (implicit or explicit). In Table 1 these two dimensions are depicted.

Table 1. Two dimensions for facilitating linguistic fluency

	Explicitness of instruction	
	Implicit learning of linguistic structures with attention to *linguistic forms*	*Explicit* learning of linguistic structures with attention to *linguistic forms*
Focus of instruction		
	Implicit learning of linguistic structures with attention to *meaning*	*Explicit* learning of linguistic structures with attention to *meaning*

In the above the theme of debate was learning of linguistic structures in general (often in oral communication). In discussions about writing education the same questions have been raised into the role of teaching explicit rules for language use (Cf. Hillocks, 1984; Van Gelderen, Couzijn, & Hendrix, 2000). Therefore, in the case of revision it is obviously relevant too. For successful revision it is necessary that linguistic errors are detected, diagnosed and corrected with some certainty. Explicit knowledge of rules can help the inexperienced writer in carrying out these processes. On the other hand some revision processes might be carried out more efficiently, drawing on implicit knowledge of sentence structure, especially when explicit rules are hard to apply.

8.   USING REVISION EXERCISES FOR LEARNING TO WRITE COMPREHENSIBLE TEXT

In our model a view has been given of revision as an integrated part of the writing process. Actually the writing process as we view it consists for the greatest part of revision processes. We assume that form and meaning are separate aspects of the revision process and as such play a distinctive role in the learning of revision skills. Meaning is superimposed over form in the sense that conceptual and discourse decisions have priority over their linguistic translations. However, studies of children's revision skills have shown that their attention during revision is unilaterally directed to correctness of linguistic form. In terms of the model that we presented this can be explained by assuming that poor linguistic fluency prevents working memory capacity to be spent on meaning related problems. In order to prevent overload of working memory children therefore restrict their attention to local form-related issues. Apart from that, poverty of extra-linguistic resources plays a role in the absence of meaning-related revisions in children's texts.

Here we discuss implications for facilitating children's attention to meaning related problems in revision by improving their linguistic fluency. We differentiated three sub-processes of revision: detect, diagnose and operate. Detect refers to the process of comparison between actual and (internally represented) intended text on the level of form and meaning. Diagnose refers to the process in which the specific problem is identified. Operate refers to the process of repairing. Facilitating revision skills by improving linguistic fluency thus means that each of these sub-processes should be involved. Children should therefore be given the opportunity to exercise their linguistic knowledge both in *reception* and *production* tasks. By reception tasks we refer to the use of linguistic knowledge for decoding (detect and diagnose), while by production tasks we refer to the application of linguistic knowledge for recoding (operate). Reception tasks require a different use of linguistic knowledge in comparison to production tasks. For reception tasks it suffices to apply rather intuitively represented linguistic knowledge, whereas production tasks require a more conscious control of linguistic structures. Probably production tasks are also more difficult on average than reception tasks.

It seems plausible that training of linguistic fluency for revision is more effective in the context of real writing tasks than in isolated exercises. Given the fact that children rarely get to the point in which they actually revise on the level of meaning it is advisable that they learn to apply linguistic knowledge for communicative purposes. This would guarantee a more easy transfer to real writing contexts. On the other hand tasks should *urge* students to practice their revision skills. One of the major impediments for improving revision on the level of communicative content is that students rather avoid it instead of practicing it.

We have differentiated four levels of revision, presuming that improving linguistic fluency is needed on each of these levels. Revision on the level of proposed text (level 1) draws on linguistic fluency, because the translator must retrieve chunks of suitable language from the store of linguistic knowledge. Revision of form on local externalized text (level 2) also presupposes the use of linguistic fluency because the ability to detect and correct linguistic problems fully depends upon the accessibility of relevant linguistic knowledge (Cf. Hacker et al., 1994). Considering the revision of meaning of the local and global externalized text (levels 3 and 4) fluent word and structure recognition are prerequisites for detection, diagnosis and operation on the level of meaning.

If we want to improve linguistic fluency we can try to simulate the receptive and productive processes of revision at each of the four levels. As the aim is improving fluency – which means that the linguistic knowledge must become easily accessible – *repetitive* practice of the same words and structures is a very important factor in this kind of training (Cf. Segalowitz, Poulsen, & Komoda, 1991).

Revision exercise → Linguistic fluency → Better text revision → Comprehensible text

Figure 4. Hierarchy of instructional objectives for learning to write comprehensible text.

Figure 4 pictures the hierarchical organization of instructional objectives that we propose. It can be seen that we start with revision exercises in order to improve linguistic fluency, that in its turn results in better revisions, because the translation of intended meaning by the planner improves. Because of this students become more capable of writing comprehensible texts. We will give some examples of how the discrimination of the four levels of revision can be used to define useful revision exercises.

For example, to simulate cognitive processes involved in level-1 revisions we can design a production exercise in which given faulty translations must be reformulated on the basis of given concepts represented in pictures. By simulating such an isolated process in which no externalized text is present to fit in, learner attention is directed to the mere formulation of a concept. A disadvantage of this kind of exercises is that there is no wider meaningful context for text production. These exercises however might be useful for beginning first and second language learners. For more advanced learners, however, isolated simulations of level-1 revisions do not seem very useful.

To simulate level-2 revisions it is possible to design exercises in which students' attention is focused on linguistic form, for example on detecting and correcting certain syntactic errors, in a meaningful context. The fact that error-correction is placed in a meaningful context implies that learner attention is focused on form, while distraction by meaning processing can occur. This makes the process of form revision more realistic in comparison to more traditional (isolated) exercises in error-correction.

For simulation of level-3 revision exercises can be designed in which learners' attention is focused on meaning, for example by checking whether propositions in a given sentence are consistent with previous propositions in the text. This implies that the linguistic knowledge that has to be applied will not receive conscious attention by the learners. Because the same structures are repetitively presented - although in different contexts - this can be regarded as *implicit* learning of linguistic structure.

For simulation of level-4 revision we can present students with sentences (or bigger parts of the text) that violate global characteristics of the text, like coherence, structure or logical/temporal relations. Level-4 revisions will lead to a new cycle of proposed and externalized text production. So level-4 revisions may also add to the training of linguistic fluency. But this level of revision is also the domain of strategic training aimed at improving conceptual and organizational skills for writing.

9. CONCLUSION

In this conclusion we want to raise some questions concerning the effectiveness of instructional approaches as outlined above. What kind of training of linguistic fluency actually facilitates writing and revision skills? This question has not been addressed experimentally yet. We will briefly sketch possibilities for experimental research into optimal conditions derived from our previously mentioned dimensions of instruction: "explicitness of instruction" and "focus of instruction." The cells in Table 1 indicate four conditions for instruction. The four conditions can be characterized as: *implicit* learning with attention to linguistic *forms, explicit* learning with attention to linguistic *forms, implicit* learning with attention to *meaning,* and *explicit* learning with attention to *meaning.*

We suggest that the effectiveness of these conditions be tested by using the revision exercises mentioned above. If we use simulations on level-1 form and meaning can be separated for example by the following instructions. Given a picture of a certain event (a boy kicking a ball) with a linguistic translation that incorrectly represents it ("the boy is picking the ball") the students have to detect, diagnose and correct the problem, while being focused on meaning. A focus on form can be realized by the same picture, but with a syntactic error like "the boy is the ball kicking." As already mentioned such level-1 simulations seem suited for beginning learners of a language, but not for more advanced learners. Level-2 simulations lend themselves only to a focus on form approach, because in this case correction of linguistic errors (syntax, usage and spelling) in externalized text is the main objective. Conversely level-3 simulations are only suitable in a focus on meaning condition, because learners have to detect, diagnose and correct problems in the way the intended meaning of the planner is being expressed in the externalized text. Simulations on level-4 are also primarily suitable for a focus on meaning approach, because on this level global text characteristics like the structure and the intended readership determine local and global text revisions. Because of this we feel that level-4 simulations are less suitable for the training of linguistic fluency. As explained in the previous paragraph it is essential that this training includes the *repeated* use of certain linguistic structures, which is hard to realize when transformations are needed from a global perspective on the text.

For the distinction between implicit and explicit instruction all mentioned simulations are equally suited. In the implicit conditions it is essential that the same linguistic structures are presented in different texts as often as possible, but without explication of these structures. In the explicit conditions these linguistic structures are also repeated over different texts and exercises, but here underlying rules or regularities are explicitly taught. In the Appendix an example is given of a reception exercise for all four conditions that we distinguish. This exercise consists of simulations of level-2 (focus on forms) and level-3 (focus on meaning) and also contains the linguistic rules to be used in the explicit conditions. The effect of the conditions can be measured by (production) revision tasks at all levels. The object is to find out whether each condition has more or less effect on linguistic fluency in order to produce better revisions of form and meaning in the resulting text.

Some other variables are of interest for our proposed line of study. First there is the question to the interaction of the instruction conditions with linguistic domains (syntax, lexis, morphology, pragmatics). Second we have to consider the possibility that several linguistic parameters play a role in the effectiveness of the instruction, such as rule governedness, difficulty of explicit rules and frequency of usage. Finally it is important to pay attention to the influence of individual differences between students, like their level of language proficiency, their language background (L1 or L2) or their level of writing experience. Experimental studies should not only touch on the effectiveness of the four distinguished learning conditions for revision, but also unravel the interaction between learning conditions and the above mentioned linguistic variables.

AUTHOR NOTE

We want to express our gratitude to Sarah Ransdell, for her thoroughgoing and useful comments on a draft of this chapter.

APPENDIX. EXAMPLE EXERCISE IN FOUR CONDITIONS

Knowledge of rules given in the explicit conditions
Rule: Sentences consist of sentence parts. [Omar/ walks/on the street] Each part of a sentence always has a <u>kernel.</u> You cannot leave it out. In the next sentence the parts consist of kernels only. You cannot delete any word. [The boy/has/the ball] You can however extend the parts. [The *handsome* boy *with the black hair* has the *red* ball *that Ilse is looking for*] The italicized pieces do not belong to the kernels. You can leave them out. But they give more information about the kernel. They give a *commentary* on it. So, the commentary says more about the kernel but can be deleted. Commentary can be placed before or behind the kernel. [before: *handsome* boy; after: ball *that Ilse is looking for*]

Reception exercise
[Two texts about snowboarding; sentences of text 1a contain only kernels; sentences in text 1b contain kernels and commentary. After completion, students check their own answers in separate booklet.]

Text 1a
Did you know that snowboarding is a sport? It is the sport of Bianca de Wit. This girl intends to become a champion. Sliding on a board from a slope, is what she likes. Et cetera

Text 1b
Did you know that snowboarding is a very exciting sport? It is the favourite sport of Bianca de Wit, a thirteen-year-old girl with blond tresses and hefty calves from Rotterdam. This girl, now already the top-best of her age, intends to become a real

champion. Sliding on a narrow board as fast as she can from a steep slope, is what she likes best on her winter holiday. Et cetera.

Condition 1 Focus on form/implicit	Condition 2 Focus on form/explicit	Condition 3 Focus on meaning/ im- plicit	Condition 4 Focus on meaning/ explicit
Check the pieces that have been added in text 1b. [It is observed that some pieces of a sentence can be deleted, while the sentence remains correct.]	Check the pieces that are <u>commentary</u> in text 1b. Commentary can be placed before or after the kernel.	Why are the underlined pieces in text 1b interesting? Check one of the following answers: a) extra information about snowboarding, b) it helps to understand the text, c) it is fun to read.	Why are the <u>commentaries</u> in text 1b interesting? Check one of the following answers: a) extra information about snowboarding, b) it helps to understand the text, c) it is fun to read.

INSIGHTS FROM INSTRUCTIONAL RESEARCH ON REVISION WITH STRUGGLING WRITERS

CHARLES A. MACARTHUR*, STEVE GRAHAM**, & KAREN R. HARRIS**

*University of Delaware, USA, ** University of Maryland, USA*

Abstract. In this chapter, we review research on the revision processes of struggling writers, primarily students with learning disabilities (LD). Throughout the chapter, we focus on how instructional research that is based on cognitive and social-cognitive models of writing can contribute to understanding these processes as well as to improving instruction. Descriptive studies, based on interviews and writing tasks, and experimental studies designed to isolate components of the revising process have shown that struggling writers have a limited conception of revising, have less knowledge about evaluation criteria, are less likely to detect and diagnose problems, and have difficulty making effective revisions even after finding problems. Instructional studies have demonstrated the effectiveness of approaches that provide explicit instruction in cognitive and metacognitive strategies in combination with word processing and interaction with peers and teachers.

Keywords: Writing, revision, cognitive processes, instruction, word processing, strategies

1. INTRODUCTION

Revision as practiced by expert writers is a complex process requiring awareness of audience, a mental representation of goals and plans for the text, ability to read critically, knowledge of common evaluative criteria and writing problems at the text level as well as the local level, a repertoire of revising strategies, and the general language and writing skills to improve problematic aspects of the text (Fitzgerald, 1987; Flower, Hayes, Carey, Schriver, & Stratman, 1986). Many professional writers describe revising as a critical aspect of the writing process that helps them to develop their ideas and communicate effectively. For example, the writer Susan Sontag (2000) entitled an article on her writing processes, "Directions: Write, Read, Rewrite. Repeat Steps 2 and 3 as Needed." In contrast, revision by children and less competent writers is generally a more straightforward process focused on local problems with mechanics and language rather than meaning and overall organization. Children engage in little revision and make few changes that affect the meaning of the text. In general, older and more competent writers make more revisions involving meaning and theme-level changes (Fitzgerald, 1987; McCutchen, 1995).

Students with learning problems struggle with revising, as with all aspects of composing. In comparison to better writers, they have less awareness of audience and less knowledge about evaluative criteria for good writing; they tend to emphasize mechanical criteria at the expense of substantive criteria; and they often fail to improve their writing or make it worse when they do revise (Graham, Harris, Mac-Arthur, & Schwartz, 1991; McCutchen, 1995). Instructional research with struggling writers poses interesting challenges and can offer insights into the cognitive and social processes required for effective revision. In this chapter, we review research on the revision processes of struggling writers, primarily students with learning disabilities (LD). Throughout the chapter, we focus on how instructional research that is based on cognitive and social-cognitive models of writing can contribute to understanding these processes as well as to improving instruction.

Most of the research reviewed in this chapter was conducted in the USA with students with LD. Learning disabilities are a heterogeneous group of disorders presumed to be due to central nervous system development that interfere with listening, speaking, reading, writing, mathematics, or reasoning (National Joint Commission on Learning Disabilities, 1998). LD is often operationalized to include individuals with average intelligence and significant difficulties with academic learning that are not due to other problems such as poor instruction, emotional problems, and cultural differences. Procedures for identification of LD continue to be controversial. Although the research reviewed in this chapter was conducted primarily with students with LD, we believe that it is appropriate to make cautious generalizations to immature writers and other students who struggle with writing.

2. REVISING PROCESSES OF STUDENTS WITH LEARNING PROBLEMS

Research on revision processes and revision instruction with students with LD has been based on cognitive (Bereiter & Scardamalia, 1987; Flower & Hayes, 1981; Flower et al., 1986; Hayes, 1996; McCutchen, 1995; Scardamalia & Bereiter, 1983) and socio-cognitive (Flower, 1994) models of writing and revising. All of these models view reviewing/revising as a goal-driven problem-solving process that can be called upon at any time during the writing process to evaluate and change plans, sentences formed in the mind, or actual written text. In the influential model of revising developed by Flower and colleagues (1986), the major process components are evaluation, which includes detection and diagnosis of problems, and strategy selection. Evaluation is a constructive process, based on active reading comprehension, in which the writer creates a mental representation of the text as written (see also Hayes, 1996, on the importance of reading comprehension to evaluation). Beyond reading for comprehension, the writer evaluates the text by imposing criteria based on general goals for writing (e.g., clarity, grammar) and goals specific to the task (e.g., persuading a particular audience). In addition to general detection of problems, evaluation may also include more specific diagnosis of problems. According to Flower et al., the amount of diagnosis in a particular revising episode depends not only on the expertise of the writer but also on the nature and extent of the problem. Often low-level problems call forth almost automatic diagnoses together with specific solutions (e.g., a problem with subject-verb agreement). On the other hand, higher-level problems of content or organization may result in a general diagnosis based on heuristics. The amount of diagnosis is related to strategy selection. The main strategy decision, other than deciding to ignore the problem, is whether simply to re-write the section or to diagnose and fix the problem. In some cases, it is simpler to re-write and re-evaluate than to attempt a diagnosis. Thus, Flower et al. contrast a simple detect/rewrite strategy with a more complex diagnose/revise strategy. In addition to evaluation and strategy selection, the model also includes task definition (e.g., deciding to proofread versus focus on meaning) and actually modifying the text.

Writers may have difficulty revising due to limited knowledge or skills at any stage in the process. They may define revision in a limited way, such as cleaning up surface errors. They may have difficulty detecting problems in the text because poor reading comprehension skills limit an accurate representation of the actual text. Detection of problems can also be limited by lack of knowledge of evaluation criteria for writing or a weak representation of the goals and plans for their intended text. Diagnosis requires more precise knowledge of evaluation criteria and common writing problems. Because the diagnose/revise strategy requires knowledge of evaluation criteria and specific means or tactics for fixing problems, less expert writers may rely excessively on a simple detect/rewrite strategy. In addition, the process of actually making changes may be limited by weak general language and writing skills. Finally, overall metacognitive control of the complex revising process may be limited. Without efficient metacognitive strategies, the complexities of managing detection, diagnosis, and actual revision while keeping in mind the overall goals for the text may strain limited working memory capacity.

2.1 Descriptive Studies

Research on the revising processes of students with learning problems has included both descriptive studies, based on interviews and writing tasks, and experiments designed to isolate components of the process. Interview methods, sometimes combined with writing and revising tasks, have provided general descriptions of students' knowledge about revising. Wong and her colleagues (Wong, Wong, & Blenkinsop, 1989) interviewed adolescents with LD and normally-achieving students. Students with LD made substantially more comments related to mechanical concerns such as spelling and sentence structure and fewer comments focused on higher order cognitive processes such as idea generation, organization, planning, revising, and audience awareness. Another interview study (Graham, Schwartz, & MacArthur, 1993) with students in grades 4-5 and 7-8 found that students with LD, in comparison with average students, had a less mature conception of writing that focused more on mechanical than on substantive concerns. Across questions about the nature of good writing, activities of good writers, reasons for other students' writing difficulties, and their own revising activities, students with LD placed less emphasis on substantive issues of content and organization and more on mechanical concerns such as spelling, handwriting, and length. The results of these two studies can be explained in a variety of ways: Students with LD may have less knowledge of substantive criteria for good writing; mechanical issues may be more salient because of greater problems in that area; and their instruction may have focused on the mechanics of writing.

A study by Englert and her colleagues (Englert, Raphael, Anderson, Gregg, & Anthony, 1989) included an interview that focused specifically on students' knowledge about expository texts and its relationship to their reading and writing performance. In the interview, fourth- and fifth-grade students (high-achieving, low-achieving, and LD) were asked to give advice to another student about planning and revising information for a compare/contrast essay. On the topic of revising, students were asked to examine the beginning of an essay comparing two fast food restaurants, to evaluate the essay, to make suggestions for continuing it, and to revise and complete the essay. While the high-achieving students recognized that the essay only mentioned one restaurant and made appropriate revisions that included similarities and differences, the students with LD and many of the low-achieving students failed to notice that the essay did not meet structural requirements and revised the essay by adding more content on one restaurant or mentioning only similarities. In this case, lack of knowledge about evaluation criteria for a compare/contrast essay prevented detection of the major problem and made effective revision difficult.

MacArthur, Graham, and Schwartz (1991) investigated LD students' knowledge of revision and revising performance using interviews and writing assessments. Students' predominate conception of revision, as revealed in the interviews, was correction of errors. However, when presented with a specific text containing numerous problems, they were able to make some substantive suggestions for revision – mostly addition of information. Few students detected problems with organization or insignificant details. Actual revisions of stories and persuasive essays written by the students consisted mainly of surface changes. More importantly, fewer than half of all revisions were rated as improvements. Furthermore, no overall change in length, quality, or mechanical errors was found between drafts. The only type of revision that correlated with change in quality was changes at the sentence level. Sentence additions consistently improved quality, whereas sentence deletions consistently impaired quality. Two implications for instruction were drawn. First, teaching students to add information should be effective and relatively easier than teaching more complex criteria and strategies such as organization. Second, the use of word processors should reduce negative sentence deletions because most of them appeared to be due to accidents or lack of motivation during recopying.

Interview studies must be interpreted with caution. Responses to interview questions may reflect students' knowledge of writing, their primary concerns about writing, their ability to express their knowledge, and their beliefs about what adults would like them to say. However, the results of the interviews were consistent with the students' revising performance on artificial and natural writing tasks. The results are also consistent with other research showing that younger and less competent writers make fewer meaning-changing revisions and are less likely to improve their compositions by revising (Fitzgerald, 1987). In this sense, students with LD may simply represent the low end of the continuum. In addition, the descriptive studies of students with LD provide evidence about the reasons for limited revising skills. Such students have a less mature conception of writing that emphasizes mechanical criteria for quality. They have limited knowledge of substantive evaluation criteria, such as text organization, as indicated by interview responses and the fact that most of their substantive revisions were limited to addition of information. Even at the level of surface changes, these students were generally unable to improve their texts and often made them worse, perhaps, due to generally weak reading and writing skills.

2.2 *Experimental Studies*

Experimental studies can be designed to test particular hypotheses about the cognitive processes involved in writing (Bereiter & Scardamalia, 1987, Chapter 2). A few such studies have focused on the revising processes of students with LD. Graham, MacArthur, and Schwartz (1995) designed a study to test two theoretical explanations for limited revising performance. First, students may focus on surface revisions because they have a limited conception of revising as proofreading and lack knowledge of more substantive evaluation criteria. Second, students may focus on minor problems because they lack the executive control to regulate the complexities of the revising process while considering the entire composition. This study investigated the effects of providing students with a specific substantive goal to make their paper more interesting by adding information, in comparison to a general goal to improve their paper. The specific goal directed students to an important substantive concern and gave them the specific criterion of adding three items of information. In addition, to determine whether performance was limited by problems regulating the overall process, some students received procedural facilitation (Bereiter & Scardamalia, 1987) in the form of prompts to generate five ideas, select the most important, and decide where to insert them. Students who were assigned the specific substantive goal made more revisions that affected meaning, particularly additions, than the control group. More importantly, the specific goal resulted in greater improvement in overall quality. Use of the procedural facilitator in combination with the specific goal did not further affect students' revising or the quality of their text. The results support the theory that students focus on surface revisions because they lack knowledge of substantive goals for revising or fail to use that knowledge when revising. The failure to find an effect for procedural facilitation did not necessarily demonstrate that executive control is not a problem. Another explanation is that the specific goal provided sufficient executive support by directing students to a single focus for revising.

Graham and his colleagues (De La Paz, Swanson, & Graham, 1998; Graham, 1997) conducted two studies focused on the role of executive control in revising with students with LD. Graham (1997) provided students (in grades five and six) with procedural facilitation designed to reduce the burden of executive control by prompting students to move through the steps of a revising process and by limiting the number of evaluative and tactical decisions made. The procedural facilitation was a modified form of a routine developed by Scardamalia and Bereiter (1983) that included three basic elements: compare, diagnose, and operate (CDO). Students revised one sentence at a time. For each sentence, they selected one of seven possible evaluations (e.g., "This doesn't sound right." or "This is good."; Compare), explained orally how the evaluation applied (Diagnose), selected one of five tactics for revision (e.g., "Change wording.") and actually made the revision (Revise). Thus, the CDO process provided executive support and suggested evaluation criteria to apply. A control group revised with a general prompt to improve their paper. The procedural support did not affect the overall number of revisions nor the quality of the compositions. However, it did affect the quality of revisions. Students in the experimental group made more non-surface revisions that were rated better as well as more revisions rated worse. Students reported that the process made revising easier. Overall, the experiment provided qualified support for the hypothesis that executive control was a significant problem for this group of students. However, students continued to have difficulties with the individual components of the revising process, including detecting and diagnosing problems and actually making revisions.

The experiment was replicated with some modifications with eighth-grade students with LD with more substantial effects (De La Paz et al., 1998). In this study, students wrote persuasive essays instead of stories, and the procedure was modified to direct students to consider overall problems with the text (e.g., "Part of the essay is not in the right order.") before evaluating each sentence separately. The procedural support resulted in significant increases in the number of non-surface revisions, both meaning-changing and meaning-preserving. In particular, students in the experimental group made seven times as many sentence-level revisions. As in the previous study, increases were noted in revisions that improved the essays and revisions that made them worse. However, in this study, the procedural support affected essay quality positively; two-thirds of experimental students improved their essays by revising compared to one-sixth of the control students. Students did have difficulty with components of the process, but overall the executive support helped students revise more effectively. The greater effects in this study compared to the earlier study (Graham, 1997) may have been due to the age of the students or to the modified process that including evaluating the entire essay before focusing on individual sentences.

Taken together the descriptive and experimental studies indicate that students with learning problems have difficulty with many aspects of the revising process. First, they have a limited conception of revising as proofreading or fixing minor errors. Second, they have less knowledge than better writers about characteristics of good writing that can be used as evaluative criteria in revising. Consequently, they are less likely to detect problems and to diagnose them accurately. Third, they have difficulty with the executive control processes involved in managing the complexities of the revising process. Finally, their limited general writing skills make it difficult for them to make effective revisions even when they do identify a problem.

The CDO routine has some promise as an instructional intervention. In fact, Bereiter and Scardamalia (1987) reported some success in using a modified version of the procedure for instruction with normally-achieving students. However, it is probably more appropriate to design instructional procedures that make use of the principles involved in these studies by teaching students evaluation criteria and revising tactics along with strategies for managing the entire process. In addition, given the evidence on students' tendency to make additional errors during recopying and the general problem of motivating students to revise, it would be worthwhile to investigate the impact of word processing on revision. In the next section, we review research on the effectiveness of strategy instruction and the impact of word processing on revising by students with learning problems.

3.   INTERVENTIONS TO IMPROVE REVISING

3.1 *Word Processing*

Word processors are flexible writing tools that may assist poor writers with many aspects of composing, particularly revision. The ability to correct errors and produce an attractive printed publication may be motivating to writers who often face difficulties with handwriting and spelling. The editing power makes it possible to revise extensively without tedious recopying. As discussed above (MacArthur, Graham, & Schwartz, 1991), students with LD and other struggling writers often introduce new errors during recopying. Furthermore, the ease of reading printed text in contrast to handwritten text may facilitate revision.

A meta-analysis (Bangert-Drowns, 1993) found that the use of word processing in instructional programs for normally-achieving students produced positive, though modest effects on writing quality. Recent studies have reported that students who are experienced with word processing produce higher quality papers on tests when permitted to use the computers than when required to write by hand (Russell, 1999). A few studies (MacArthur, Graham, Schwartz, & Shafer, 1995; Morocco, Dalton, & Tivñan, 1990) indicate that word processing together with writing instruction can enhance the writing of students with LD. However, none of these studies specifically analyzed the impact of word processing on revising.

Two studies have specifically analyzed the effects of word processing on revising for struggling writers. Both studies were conducted with students who had had instruction and substantial experience using word processors. Vacc (1987) studied eighth-grade students with mild retardation using a single-subject, ABAB design in which students alternated between handwriting and word processing. With word processing, students composed more slowly and wrote fewer words, though no consistent differences were found in overall quality of writing. Revision was measured only during initial drafting and no second draft was produced. Students made more revisions during drafting using the word processor. Most revisions were attempts to correct spelling and punctuation.

MacArthur and Graham (1987) compared composing by fifth- and sixth-grade students with LD via handwriting and word processing. Although students composed more slowly with word processing, the final drafts of papers written with a word processor did not differ from those written by hand on any of the measures used in the study including overall quality, length, story structure, vocabulary, syntactic complexity, or errors in spelling, capitalization, and punctuation. With regard to revision, no differences were found in the number of revisions, level of text affected (e.g., word, phrase, sentence), operation (e.g., addition, deletion), or proportion of revisions that affected meaning. In both conditions, a large majority of revisions were minor changes in spelling, capitalization, or word choice that had no impact on meaning. Moreover, these changes were ineffective because there were no differences between first and second draft in proportion of mechanical errors or in quality. However, there was a difference in when revisions were made. With word processing, students made more revisions during writing of the first draft, whereas most revisions with handwriting were made between the first and second drafts. This difference is understandable. Word processing facilitates minor error corrections during typing, whereas handwriting results in minor changes during recopying.

A reasonable interpretation of the findings of these studies is that mere access to word processing will not substantially affect the writing processes or products of struggling writers, but that word processing may facilitate instruction about writing processes and enhance motivation in ways that improve their writing. In the next section, we report on studies that used word processing in conjunction with instruction on cognitive strategies for revising.

3.2 Cognitive Strategies Instruction

The cognitive research mentioned in the introduction to this article demonstrated that proficient writers possess a repertoire of strategies for planning and revising, a wide range of knowledge about writing, and self-regulation strategies that enable them to use their knowledge and strategies flexibly to meet goals. The basic premise of cognitive strategy instruction is that students can be taught to use more mature and effective strategies. General agreement exists that strategy instruction should address the following components: (1) mastery of task-specific strategies; (2) understanding of the use, significance, and limitations of those strategies; (3) metacognitive strategies for self-regulation (e.g., selecting strategies, monitoring performance); (4) substantive knowledge and skills; and (5) motivation (Pressley & Wharton-McDonald, 1997; Schunk, 1989). Several models of strategy instruction have been developed including reciprocal teaching (Palincsar & Brown, 1984), the Kansas learning strategies model (Deshler & Schumaker, 1986), explicit explanation (Duffy, Roehler, & Rackliffe, 1986), self-regulated strategy development (Harris & Graham, 1995), and transactional strategy instruction (Pressley et al., 1992). Common to all of these models are explicit explanation and modeling of strategies, interactive support and scaffolding as students learn the strategies, and gradual fading of support as students develop competence.

The effectiveness of strategy instruction in improving the academic performance of students with learning problems has been well demonstrated (Pressley et al., 1997). In particular, the writing performance of students with LD has been improved by teaching strategies for planning and revising (Englert, Raphael, Anderson, Anthony, & Stevens, 1991; Graham et al., 1991; Harris & Graham, 1995).

Graham and MacArthur (1988) used the self-regulated strategy development (SRSD) model to teach a strategy for revising persuasive essays to elementary school students with LD. The SRSD model places special emphasis on the development of self-regulation strategies such as goal setting, the use of self-instructions to support effort and motivation, self-monitoring and evaluation, and self-reinforcement (Harris & Graham, 1995). The revising strategy focused primarily on substantive revisions specific to persuasive writing, such as stating the thesis clearly, giving and supporting additional reasons, and increasing the coherence of text. The strategy contained specific evaluation criteria as well as a routine for managing the overall revising process. Students were instructed to read their essay, find the thesis statement and check its clarity, add two reasons, and check each sentence for clarity, connection to the thesis, possible elaboration, and errors. Self-regulation included self-instructions about problem definition, self-evaluation, and self-reinforcement. Essays were composed on a word processor. The strategy was investigated using a multiple probe across subjects design with three students. The strategy resulted in increases in substantive revisions (meaning-changing) as well as total revisions. More important, improvements were found for all students on two quality measures – improvement from first to second draft and quality of the final draft. Furthermore, effects were maintained over time and generalized to writing via handwriting. Finally, students' self-efficacy as writers increased.

The use of peer response groups to support revising is based on an understanding of writing as a social process as well as a cognitive process. Writing is an interaction between writer and reader (Nystrand, 1986a, 1986b). Expert writers consider audience throughout the writing process as they set goals, generate content, consider word choices, and evaluate the potential impact of their text (Flower, 1994). Peer response groups may help in the development of revising skill by providing an immediate and familiar audience to respond directly to students' writing. However, the literature on peer response groups has reported mixed impact on students' revision and writing (DiPardo & Freedman, 1988). The combination of strategy instruction and peer response might be more effective than either one alone.

MacArthur and his colleagues conducted two studies of a reciprocal peer revision strategy (MacArthur, Schwartz, & Graham, 1991; Stoddard & MacArthur, 1993) designed to guide students in both the cognitive and social aspects of response and revision. Peer response was thought to enhance strategy instruction by providing a real reader, by offering reciprocal experience as both author and editor, and by encouraging students to pose questions and explain their thinking. Cognitive support included evaluation criteria as well as an overall strategy for identifying problems, discussing questions, and making revisions. Prior research had shown that students with LD often lack knowledge of evaluation criteria (MacArthur, Graham, & Schwartz, 1991). Hillocks's meta-analysis of writing instruction (1986) showed that teaching evaluation criteria together with practice in revising based on those criteria was an effective approach. The peer revising strategy guided students in the following steps: students listened to each other read their papers, commented on positive aspects of the papers, asked questions and made suggestions based on specific evaluation criteria, and discussed how to improve the papers. After revising for substance, pairs of students helped each other fix errors in spelling, capitalization, and punctuation. As part of instruction, students practiced applying specific evaluation criteria (e.g., Clarity: Is any part of the paper hard to understand?) and revising their papers. Revision of minor problems in spelling and grammar was deferred to a second stage of editing. Word processing was used in both studies.

The first study of the reciprocal peer revising strategy (Stoddard & MacArthur, 1993) used a multiple-probe design across pairs of students with six middle-school students with LD. On the pretests, students made few substantive revisions and did not improve the quality of their papers by revising. Following instruction, all students made more substantive revisions, the proportion of revisions rated as improvements increased substantially, and second drafts were rated as qualitatively better than first drafts. Furthermore, the overall quality of final drafts increased from pretest to posttest. The gains generalized to writing and revising without a partner and to writing via handwriting, and were maintained on one and two-month follow-up assessments.

The second study (MacArthur, Schwartz, & Graham, 1991) extended the findings to instruction by classroom teachers in their classes for students with LD. The classrooms had been engaged in a larger writing project including word processing, writing workshop, and strategy instruction, and students had been using the word processor and engaging in peer response groups for five months. Students in the strategy classes, in comparison to control classes that used word processing and writing workshop including peer response groups, made more substantive revisions and produced papers of higher quality following peer response. These results generalized only partly to revising without peer support. Without support, students in the strategy classes made more revisions but did not produce higher quality papers. On a metacognitive interview, strategy students demonstrated greater awareness of evaluative criteria for writing. This study demonstrated that adding explicit instruction and guidance in cognitive strategies enhanced the effectiveness of peer response groups.

A study by Wong and her colleagues (Wong et al., 1994) investigated whether peer dialogues added to the effectiveness of revising instruction provided by the teacher (research assistants in this case). Adolescents with LD or with limited English proficiency learned to revise through "interactive dialogues." Teachers engaged students in individual dialogues about their rough drafts. Teachers focused initially on any parts of the text that were not clear and then on whether the theme or topic of the essay was clear and stated at the beginning and end. Teachers explicitly identified problems, explained the problems, offered suggestions for improvement, and continued the dialogue until the problems were resolved. Thus, although no specific strategy was taught, teachers did provide explicit guidance based on two evaluation criteria. After such dialogues about four essays, students were randomly assigned to a peer-dialogue condition or to continued teacher dialogues. In the peer-dialogue condition, students worked in pairs following the routine earlier used with the teacher; the teacher observed and guided the interaction. Both groups demonstrated improvement from pretest to posttest in clarity and thematic salience of their essays, and both groups performed better than a no-treatment control group. However, no differences were found between teacher-dialogue and peer-dialogue conditions.

In addition to these studies of specific revising strategies, we should mention two large-scale studies of comprehensive writing instruction that included strategy instruction in both planning and revising. Both instructional programs provided coordinated instruction in multiple strategies over the course of a full year. Both also stressed the importance of establishing a social environment in which students wrote for meaningful purposes and discussed their writing with teachers and peers.

The Cognitive Strategies in Writing Instruction (CSIW) program (Englert et al., 1991) included instruction in expository text structures and strategies for planning and revising text based on text structure knowledge. Planning strategies focused on brainstorming ideas followed by using one of several text structures (e.g., compare/contrast) to organize and elaborate the ideas. Revising strategies focused on asking evaluation questions appropriate to the particular text structure in peer and teacher conferences, as well as general evaluation questions. In a year-long evaluation of the program, fourth and fifth-grade students with and without LD made significant gains in expository writing on text structures included in the instructional program and also on a transfer measure in which students wrote on a topic of their own choosing.

The Computers and Writing Project (CWIP, MacArthur et al., 1995) integrated word processing and strategy instruction. The curriculum included strategies for planning and revising, both of which were designed to be flexible enough to apply to a wide range of writing tasks. Students applied the two strategies to a variety of writing genre, including stories, persuasive essays, and reports. The planning strategy, which was based on prior research (Graham et al., 1991), involved the use of common text structures to generate and organize content. For revising, the reciprocal peer revising strategy described above was used. The evaluation questions within the revising strategy were varied as needed to adapt to different genre and levels of student skill. The curriculum was evaluated over two years in grades four through eight in classes for students with LD. Students in the program made significant gains in comparison to a control group on both narrative and informative writing.

These comprehensive writing programs demonstrate the importance of integrating instruction in planning and revising. One of the major purposes of instruction in revision, besides actually improving students' revising, is to help them develop skills and knowledge about good writing that will improve their initial drafts. This outcome is facilitated when strategies for planning and strategies for revising incorporate similar components of good writing. For example, in both the CSIW and CWIP program, planning strategies were based on text structure components, and revising strategies included questions about these components. In addition, the comprehensive programs demonstrate the importance of providing meaningful writing tasks and social interaction. Strategies are goal-directed approaches that will only make sense to students in a context in which their writing has meaningful communicative goals.

4.   CONCLUDING COMMENTS

The combination of research on cognitive processes and instructional research reviewed in this chapter has paid off in improved instructional methods and greater understanding of the cognitive difficulties of struggling writers. The research demonstrates that instruction based on cognitive and socio-cognitive models of the writing process can help struggling writers to revise more effectively and improve the overall quality of their writing. In return, the instructional research confirms and extends our understanding of the cognitive processes involved. For example, the interview studies revealed that students had a limited conception of revising as fixing errors and had little awareness of substantive criteria (Englert et al., 1989; Graham et al., 1993; MacArthur, Graham, & Schwartz, 1991; Wong et al., 1989). A brief experimental intervention established that providing students with a clear substantive criterion for revising (i.e., to make it more interesting by adding information) resulted in more substantive and higher quality revisions (Graham et al., 1995) More extensive interventions included instruction in using a variety of evaluative criteria and documented that students' knowledge of criteria as well as their revising improved (Graham & MacArthur, 1988; MacArthur, Schwartz, & Graham, 1991; Stoddard & MacArthur, 1993). Similarly, the theory that students had difficulty with the executive control processes involved in managing the complexities of the revision process was supported in experimental interventions that improved revising performance by providing executive support. Extended interventions provided executive support in the form of strategies with organized steps as well as other self-regulation features. Thus, the instructional studies confirm the importance of knowledge of evaluation criteria and executive control in the revising process.

Further research is needed to extend our understanding of revising processes and how they interact with other cognitive processes as well as to develop additional effective instructional interventions. One area in need of research, specifically with struggling writers, is the relationship between revising processes and students' difficulties with basic processes of transcription and sentence generation. Research comparing composing via dictation and handwriting has shown that transcription processes interfere with overall composing processes for struggling writers (Graham, 1990; MacArthur & Graham, 1987). When permitted to dictate, students with LD produce compositions that are higher in quality. Similarly, difficulties with transcription processes may interfere with revising by causing students to focus excessively on error correction or by making it difficult for students to read their own compositions. Several of the studies reviewed above (De La Paz et al., 1998; MacArthur, Schwartz, & Graham, 1991) attempted to reduce this problem by directing students to ignore mechanical errors or to correct them in a second stage of revising. More specific studies are needed. Struggling writers may also have difficulties with language that impede fluent sentence generation. These difficulties may explain why so few revisions were rated as improvements (Graham, 1997; MacArthur, Graham, & Schwartz, 1991). One way to approach this problem would be to use instructional approaches targeted on sentence generation, such as sentence combining, and investigate the impact on revising.

Another area in which further research could advance our understanding is the role of social interaction and peer response in revising. Peer and teacher dialogue were important components in both of the comprehensive writing programs that were reviewed (Englert et al., 1991; MacArthur et al., 1995). On the other hand, another study found no benefit of adding peer response to teacher response (Wong et al., 1994). Revising strategies both with peer response (Stoddard & MacArthur, 1993) and without (Graham & MacArthur, 1988) have been found to be effective, and one study showed that the combination of strategy instruction and peer response was more effective than peer response alone (MacArthur, Schwartz, & Graham, 1991). There are good theoretical reasons to think that peer response is important (Flower, 1994), and studies with normally-achieving students have described what happens in peer response groups (Dipardo & Freedman, 1988). Research is needed to investigate the effects of peer response as an instructional component. Furthermore, research is needed that describes the discourse in peer interaction in sufficient detail to understand its connection to students' thinking and to connect it to changes in students' actual revising.

INTEGRATED WRITING INSTRUCTION AND THE DEVELOPMENT OF REVISION SKILLS

LINDA ALLAL

University of Geneva, Switzerland

Abstract. Research on writing instruction in the elementary grades is reviewed, based on findings from classroom investigations of multifaceted programs and from experimental studies of factors affecting the acquisition of revision skills. The principles underlying an integrated sociocognitive (IS) approach to writing instruction are presented, as are the results of a year-long field study in 20 classes comparing this approach to a componential skills (CS) approach. The results of this study show significant but modest effects of the IS approach on students' ability to revise narrative text in second and sixth grades. Analysis of developmental trends between the two grades shows several important changes in students' revision skills, namely an increase in revisions affecting text organization and semantics, as well as increased concern for grammatical rather than lexical aspects of spelling. Very substantial interindividual variation is found, however, in each grade. The findings are discussed in relationship to other studies of writing instruction and revision.

Keywords: Writing instruction, sociocognitive approach, text revision, spelling, elementary school

1. WRITING INSTRUCTION IN ELEMENTARY SCHOOL

Language instruction has long been dominated by a componential skills approach which entails the separation of the curriculum into component areas (reading, writing, vocabulary, spelling, grammar, etc.) and the organization of activities focused on each area (Gehrke, Knapp, & Sirotnik, 1992; Langer, 1984). In the area of writing, elementary school students often spend more time doing exercises intended to improve their ability to write than in actually producing extended text. Although students are expected to proofread and correct formal errors in their writing, instructional activities rarely allow learning about the process of revision. Under these circumstances, it is not surprising that young students tend to produce short texts, make few revisions and that those made concern primarily surface features (spelling, punctuation) having little effect on the meaning and the general structure of the text (Fitzgerald, 1987). Although the time allotted to text production appears to have increased in recent years, the teaching of isolated skills by means of exercises is still widespread in elementary classrooms, particularly classrooms in low-income, ethnic minority communities (Davies, Clarke, & Rhodes, 1994) and those receiving students with learning disabilities (Palinscar & Klenk, 1992).

Alternative approaches to writing instruction have introduced major changes of perspective. The "writing process" approach (Calkins, 1986; Graves, 1983) has generated widespread acceptance of the basic principle that learning to write is a constructive, interactive and contextualized process. This implies that learners are actively engaged in all aspects of writing (planning, composing, revising multiple drafts of their texts), that the interactions among members of a writing community are a source of support and a means of transforming on-going work, that writing projects take place in authentic contexts of communication involving audiences inside and outside the classroom. The work on situated cognition has provided theoretical grounding for the design of "literacy apprenticeships" in the classroom which mirror authentic literacy practices outside of school. As described by Resnick (1990):

> Children work to produce a product that will be used by others [...]: they work collaboratively, but under conditions in which individuals are held responsible for their work; they use tools and apparatus appropriate to the problem; they read and critique each other's writing; they are called upon to elaborate and defend their own work until it reaches a community standard. (p. 183)

Research on writing instruction includes both classroom-based investigations carried out over extended periods of time with complex, multifaceted programs and studies focused on specific factors that are likely to influence the instructional process. We will briefly examine the approaches developed by two groups of researchers who have made major, sustained contributions to research linking classroom investigations with focused inquiry on writing instruction. Although both have worked primarily with special education teachers and students, the orientation of their work is broadly relevant to all elementary grades. Findings from this research and from other sources have identified factors of instructional significance which influence the acquisition of revision skills.

Graham, Harris and their colleagues (Graham & Harris, 1997; Harris & Graham, 1992, 1996; Harris, Schmidt, & Graham, 1998) have proposed an integrated instructional approach combining the basic principles of writing process with the procedures they have developed for Self-regulated strategy development (SRSD). The six steps of SRSD constitute a "metascript" which proceeds as follows: (1) develop student background knowledge, (2) conference on strategy goals and significance, (3) modeling of the strategy by the teacher, (4) strategy memorization by the student, (5) collaborative practice with scaffolding provided by the teacher, (6) independent student performance (fading out of scaffolds). The self-regulation strategies developed with this approach include goal setting, self-instructions, self-monitoring and self-reinforcement with respect to the different aspects of the writing process (planning, composing, revising). In addition, writing activities are combined with explicit, systematic instruction in basic skills, such as spelling and handwriting. As Graham and Harris (1997) have pointed out, explicit instruction can be carried out with innovative techniques and does not have to be synonymous with mindless drill and rule following. The association of word processing with strategy instruction aims at providing a supportive environment for improving student writing and revising skills (Graham & MacArthur, 1988; MacArthur, Graham, Schwartz, & Shafer, 1995). The extensive classroom research carried out by Graham, Harris, MacArthur and their colleagues has been methodically linked to controlled experimentation designed to test the effects of different components of the SRSD model on different aspects of writing. The findings, particularly those concerning revision, are presented in the MacArthur, Graham and Harris chapter of this book.

The conception of writing instruction developed by Englert and her colleagues is situated in a Vygotskian social constructivist framework. An initial model known as Cognitive strategy instruction in writing (CSWI) includes several components: reading and analyzing texts before writing, teacher modeling of writing strategies, collaborative dialogue between students and teachers, internalization of the dialogue by the student, use of procedural facilitation in the form of "think sheets," and student participation in the construction of socially shared meanings within a literacy community (Englert, 1992). More recent models, such as Literary environments for accelerated progress (LEAP), accentuate the role of genres as a reference for writing, the integration of reading and writing with other subject matter areas and the place of peer collaboration in the constitution of a community of practice (Englert et al., 1995; Englert, Berry, & Dunsmore, 2001). In these models, revision is seen as a socially mediated activity developed in situations of joint text production, in teacher-student dialogues about texts and in reciprocal peer response to written work. Classroom-based research has shown the positive impact of the LEAP model on the quality of children's writing and on the processes peer interaction about writing, but has not provided specific indications about effects on revision skills.

In order to understand how learning to revise can contribute to learning to write, research based on complex instructional models needs to be combined with experimental studies focused on specific factors affecting student revision. Existing studies have shown five factors to be particularly relevant for enhancing students' understanding of revision and their ability to improve writing through revision.

1) Direct instruction, based on charts outlining revision operations, teacher modeling, and extensive practice on sample texts, was found to increase children's knowledge about revision as well as the amount of revision they carried out (Fitzgerald & Markham, 1987). The impact of direct instruction on revision was more pronounced when the writing task was situated in a meaningful communication context (Cameron, Hunt, & Linton, 1996).

2) Greater knowledge about the writing topic tended to increase revision for meaning (Butterfield, Hacker, & Plumb, 1994; McCutchen, Francis, & Kerr, 1997). Knowledge about text genre (e.g., the structure of expository text) also influenced the types of revisions made by students (Englert, Raphael, Anderson, Gregg, & Anthony, 1989).

3) Setting goals for revision, for example the goal of adding information (Graham, MacArthur, & Schwartz, 1995), led to increased revision for meaning and improvement of text quality.

4) Procedural facilitation, in particular the CDO (compare, diagnose, operate) procedure proposed by Bereiter and Scardamalia (1987), was shown to be an effec-

tive means of guiding the types of revisions made by students and the improvement of text quality (De La Paz, Swanson, & Graham, 1998).

5) Instruction in a reciprocal peer revision strategy helped students to learn evaluation criteria, increase substantive revisions and improve text quality (MacArthur, Schwarz, & Graham, 1991). Joint peer revision of a common text was shown to have a positive effect on subsequent individual revision activity and on metacognitive reflection about writing (see the Rouiller chapter in this book).

The integrated sociocognitive approach to writing instruction developed in our own research has incorporated features from the instructional models and the experimental studies reviewed here.

2. AN INTEGRATED SOCIOCOGNITIVE APPROACH TO WRITING INSTRUCTION

In the official, elementary school curriculum of French-speaking Switzerland (COROME, 1997), writing instruction is based on principles quite close to those of the process writing perspective except in one main respect: Students' writing is not usually based on free choice of topic and type of text. The curriculum is structured around writing sequences focused on different text genres (Schneuwly & Dolz, 1997). In general, an entire class works on a sequence involving a specified genre, topic and audience. Individualization occurs primarily in the way in which each student treats the topic and interprets the constraints of the genre. Exchanges among students and with the teacher concern how and why texts of a same genre on a same topic addressed to the same audience nevertheless differ in significant and interesting ways. In this approach, considerable importance is given to students learning about the macrostructural features and the textual organizers that characterize a given genre. For example, when writing narrative texts, students learn about story grammar and about organizers that mark the temporal structure of the narration (*a long time ago, one day, suddenly, finally,* etc.).

The writing sequences developed in our research adopt this genre-based framework, but introduce two other instructional design features. The first is the systematic integration of basic skill activities within writing sequences. Our approach is similar in this respect to the integrated instruction advocated by Graham and Harris (1997; Harris, Schmidt, & Graham, 1998), but it places more emphasis on functional links between basic skills and text genres. For example, in a sixth-grade sequence involving the composition of a historical narrative, the basic skill objectives concern verb morphology and the coordinated use of verb tenses appropriate to this genre. The second instructional design feature developed in our sequences concerns the forms of sociocognitive regulation which support students' composing and revising activities. In a social constructivist perspective similar to that of Englert (1992), several forms of scaffolding are introduced in each text production situation: teacher-student dialogues, peer collaboration and interactive tool construction and use. Our approach does not, on the other hand, give the same importance to explicit strategy instruction as that found in the SRSD and CSWI models.

The writing sequences based on our integrated sociocognitive approach have a spiral structure, as shown in Figure 1. This structure is derived from the concept of the spiral curriculum proposed by Bruner (1960) and from recent research on situated cognition and learning (Allal, 2001). A detailed presentation of the sequences is proposed in Allal et al. (2001).

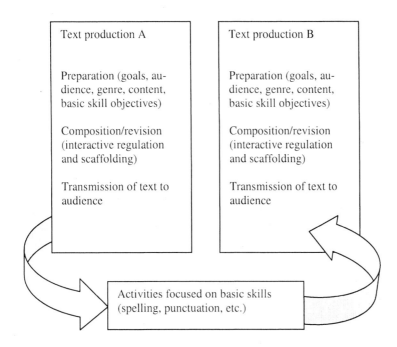

Figure 1. Structure of the integrated sociocognitive instructional sequence.

Each sequence includes two situations of text production. They concern the same genre and are both situated in authentic contexts of communication, but the topics differ. Situation A allows students to discover the characteristics of the genre and to work on associated basic skills while composing and revising their texts. Production of text A is followed by activities which focus on aspects of basic skills (lexical and grammatical aspects of spelling, punctuation conventions) which were a source of difficulty when writing text A and/or which need further consolidation. Situation B allows students to reactivate the knowledge and skills acquired in the previous activities and to reuse this knowledge and these skills in the production of a second text. The spiral thus proceeds from a complex learning situation, to simpler, more specific tasks, and then to another complex situation.

This spiral conception can be illustrated by the following sequence developed for second grade. In situation A, the students compose and revise recipes for a witch's brew; all the texts are to be assembled in a collective "Magic recipe book" for the class library. The basic skill objectives concern use of the letter *s*, both for the transcription of sounds (*s* vs. *ss*) and as a marker of the plural in noun-article agreement (e.g., *les hérissons* [the hedgehogs]). The situation B involves production of a set of instructions for a disguise using various objects and articles of clothing; once written and revised, the texts are exchanged among students who try to draw the disguises described by their classmates.

Each situation of text production includes two phases. The preparation phase starts with the definition of the writing project (its aim, the topic, the genre, the intended audience). The students then read and analyze texts of the same genre as the one to be produced. Both macrostructural and microstructural features are noted on charts for future reference during writing. Through a collective discussion or exchanges in small groups, ideas about the possible content of the text are evoked and listed. This preliminary work on content is designed to assure that each student can draw on a collective pool of ideas while writing. The basic skill objectives of the sequence are then specified and the teacher helps students construct or complete a "guide" to be used while carrying out the writing task. The guide summarizes spelling and punctuation rules which are illustrated with examples drawn from curricular materials and from the students' own writing.

The second phase of the sequence involves composition and revision of a text by each student. Different forms of scaffolding are introduced to assure "interactive regulation" of student activity (Allal, 1988). On-line revision during writing is encouraged by teacher intervention and guidance. Standard reference materials and the student's personalized guide are used during composing and for deferred revision of completed drafts. Several forms of scripted peer interaction (O'Donnell, 1999) are proposed to foster more in-depth transformations than those initially carried out by each student. For example, in one sixth-grade sequence, student dyads exchange the newspaper reports they have each written and use different colored markers to indicate places where changes appear to be needed. The reports are then returned to their respective authors for revision. In a subsequent exchange, the dyad discusses why certain changes were made and others not carried out. Transmission of the texts to the intended audience, inside or outside the classroom, provides further feedback about the quality of the revised texts. At the end of the sequence, the teacher asks the students to express orally and/or in writing their metacognitive reflections about what they learned during the sequence and what aspects of writing they need to still work on.

The basic skill activities which intervene between the text production situations are of two types, as defined by Jaffré (1986) in work on the didactics of writing and spelling. Deferred activities are based on difficulties encountered during the first writing situation and on errors observed in the students' texts. For example, sentences could be selected from students' texts and used to construct an activity focused on an aspect of grammatical spelling such as article-noun-adjective agreement. Detached activities, on the other hand, do not maintain a functional link with the text production situation; they consist most often in exercises selected in available curricular materials. Both activities are adapted according to student needs and may entail peer tutoring or cooperative learning structures.

The remainder of this chapter will present and discuss the results of a year-long field study conducted in second and sixth grades. The purpose of this study was to determine how teachers implemented the writing sequences based our integrated sociocognitive (IS) approach and what the effects were on students' revision skills and on their acquisition of both lexical and grammatical aspects of spelling. The results of the IS classes were compared to those of classes using used the curricular materials provided by the school system. These materials reflect a componential skills (CS) approach in which text production is carried out in a communicative, genre-based perspective but basic skills are learned by decontextualized exercises and dictations having no connection with situations of text production. Our presentation will also examine developmental trends in revision between second and sixth grades and the nature and extent of individual differences in each grade.

3. METHOD

Our study was based on a quasi-experimental design comparing the integrated sociocognitive (IS) and componential skills (CS) approaches to writing instruction in second and sixth grades. Since one aim of the study was to determine whether students following the IS sequences would acquire spelling skills comparable to those of the CS students who used the official curricular materials, pretest and posttest measures of spelling were collected at the beginning and the end of the school year. In order to determine the impact of instruction on students' revision skills, as well as the evolution of these skills between second and sixth grade, we designed an activity of narrative text production that could be carried out at the end of the school year in IS and CS classes of both grades. In addition, meetings with IS and CS teachers and classroom visits during the year provided information on how instructional activities were being implemented in the classroom. A complete presentation of the findings of our research is provided in Allal et al. (2001). The present chapter focuses on the final activity of narrative text production and revision.

3.1 Sample

The sample was composed of students from 12 second-grade classes in the public school system of the cantons of Geneva (8 classes) and Vaud (4 classes) and from 8 sixth-grade classes in Geneva. Half of the classes in each grade followed the IS sequences developed by our research team, while the other half used the usual curricular materials reflecting a CS approach. The data presented here concern 226 second-grade students and 135 sixth-grade students who carried out the narrative text production activity at the end of the school year.

At the beginning of the school year, the average age of the children was 7 years, 6 months in second grade and 11 years, 8 months in sixth grade. The sample distribution of students' families according to their socioeconomic status showed an under-representation of students from low socioeconomic backgrounds in second grade and an over-representation of this category in sixth grade. Since socioeconomic status and language achievement in school tend to be moderately correlated, it is probable that our data do not include an adequate sampling of the two extremes of elementary students' competencies in writing, as found among the lowest-achieving second graders and the highest-achieving sixth graders. The percentage of children whose mother tongue was French was higher in second grade (73%), and slightly higher in sixth grade (68%), than the overall percentage in the Geneva canton (62%). This type of data was not available for the Vaud sample.

3.2 *Text Production Activity*

In each class, the students produced a narrative text on the basis of pictures showing the adventures of a postman whose keys are stolen by a chicken while he's having a nap after a picnic. The sixth-grade students received a series of 10 pictures. In second grade, a selection of 5 pictures showing key episodes was provided. The writing activity was designed with an authentic communication goal so as to encourage students to produce texts as interesting and well written as possible. The aim was to produce booklets in which different text passages would be inserted next to the corresponding pictures; the booklets produced by the second-grade children were to be given to their parents, and those produced by the sixth-graders to younger students (7-8 years) attending the same school. In second grade, the activity took place in three sessions: a preparation session involving analysis of narrative text structure and discussion of ideas suggested by the pictures, a drafting session, and a session devoted to revision of the drafts. In sixth-grade, preparation and drafting took place in a single session, revision in a second session.

3.3 *Data Coding and Analysis*

Two types of data concerning the narrative text production were analyzed. First a series of indicators was calculated to describe general characteristics of the students' texts. These indicators were defined as follows:
- number of words in the draft of the student's text,
- number of incorrect words (i.e., words containing one or more spelling errors),
- percentage of incorrect words: (indicator 2/indicator 1) x 100,
- number of transformations made by the student when revising the draft,
- density of the transformations: (indicator 4/indicator 1) x 100.

Secondly, a multidimensional system of coding was defined to characterize the transformations carried out on each draft (see Allal, 2000, for a presentation of the application of this system in several studies of student writing). We use the term transformation to refer to an observable change marked on a draft in a situation of deferred revision. This term allows us to differentiate the products of revision (text transformations) from the overall process of revision. In each revised draft, the units of transformation are identified and each unit is coded on several dimensions. The size of a unit can vary from one letter or symbol (accent, punctuation mark) to several sentences inserted or displaced as a bloc in the draft.

In the analysis presented here, three dimensions of transformation were coded:
1) type of transformation: addition, deletion, substitution, rearrangement;
2) object of the transformation: semantics (changes of meaning and vocabulary), text organization (primarily operations of segmentation, connection, cohesion, changes of verb tense, use of narrative organizers), spelling (grammatical aspects, including punctuation, and lexical aspects);

3) relationship of the transformation to language conventions: conventional transformation that is correctly carried out, or that is incorrect, optional transformation not required by language conventions and which thus reflect author's voice.

Our coding scheme differs from other systems commonly used in studies of revision in several respects. Most systems distinguish two categories regarding the object of transformation: surface changes which do not affect meaning (spelling, punctuation) and changes which transform meaning. Our system introduces a third category, text organization, which is particularly important in a genre-based approach to writing. The transformations in this category contribute to the structuring of a text in a cohesive and coherent manner which facilitates reader comprehension.

In order to illustrate our coding system, here are two examples of coded transformations.

Example 1. In the expression *le facteur alla vers le chat* [the postman went toward the cat], *le facteur* is replaced by *il* [he].

This transformation is coded as a *substitution* affecting *text organization* (pronominalization which can reinforce cohesion), and as having an *optional* character (the use of pronominalization is not strictly required by language conventions).

Example 2. In the expression *les clés font du bruit* [the keys make noise], the letter *s* is added to *bruit*:

This is coded as an *addition* which changes a grammatical aspect of *spelling*, and which is *incorrect* with respect to language conventions (if an *s* is added to *bruit*, the article *du* must changed to *des*).

Coding was based on a detailed guide which assured a high degree of intercoder reliability (88% to 97%, depending on the dimension and the grade).

4. RESULTS

For each set of data, we first examine the effects of IS vs. CS instruction and then look at the evolution of student skills between second and sixth grades. After these analyses, we provide an illustration of the types of individual differences shown by students at the end of sixth grade.

4.1 *Characteristics of Student Texts*

Table 1 presents the means on each indicator for the students following the CS and the IS instructional approaches in second and in sixth grade.

*Table 1. Characteristics of the students' texts, mean indicators by grade
and instructional approach*

Indicator	Second grade		Sixth grade	
	CS (n = 113)	IS (n = 113)	CS (n = 65)	IS (n = 70)
Nb. of words	100.5	91.4	381.0	340.2
Nb. of incorrect words	30.5	27.9	35.2	31.5
% of incorrect words	30.7	31.4	9.7	10.1
Nb. of transformations	5.3	5.7	14.5	15.0
Density of transformations (in %)	5.4	6.6	3.9	4.9

Analysis of variance showed only one significant difference between the CS and IS conditions: a higher density of transformations in the second-grade IS classes ($F(1, 224) = 3.978, p = .047$).

In a second series of ANOVAs, the effect of instructional approach was tested for three sub-groups of students: the upper, middle and lower thirds on the distribution of students' scores on the spelling test administered at the beginning of the school year. In these analyses, a significant difference was found in sixth grade for the students in the upper third with respect to the number of incorrect words in the initial draft of the narration: IS students' drafts contained an average of 15.7 incorrect words, while CS students drafts contained an average of 24.6 ($F(1, 42) = 5.891, p = .020$).

These results show that the IS approach had a significant but modest effect in two areas. In second grade, the IS students tended to write shorter drafts but made relatively more revisions (as shown by a higher density of transformation). In sixth grade, among the students who had a high level of skill in spelling at the beginning of the year, those participating in IS instruction produced texts with fewer errors than those following CS instruction. This appears to suggest that IS instruction allows students with a high initial level of basic skill mastery to increase the automatization of these skills and/or their capacity to make on-line revisions while writing.

While the effects of the two types of instruction are not highly differentiated, the data in Table 1 show important differences between second and sixth grades. Although the data are cross-sectional, rather than longitudinal, they provide some useful indications regarding the evolution of students' composing and revising skills between second and sixth grades. Our discussion will refer to averages on each indicator (across instructional approaches) and to additional data regarding the distribution of the indicators.

At the end of second grade, the students' drafts have an average length of 96 words, of which approximately 30% are incorrect. The students generally make 5 or 6 transformations, which means that a very large number of words remains uncorrected in most drafts at the end of the revision session. On each indicator, a very wide range of individual differences is observed. Text length varies from 36 to 183 words (for 98% of the students, with several extreme cases of drafts of 245 to 380 words). The percentage of incorrect words varies from 5% to 65%, and the number of transformations from 0 to 22.

At the end of elementary school, the texts of the sixth-grade students show substantial differences from those of second-graders. The average length increases (from 96 to 360 words); the percentage of incorrect words decreases (from around 30% to 10%); the average number of transformations increases (from 5.5 to 14.8). These changes reflect the children's increased competency in producing correct drafts and in revising them. The number of errors left uncorrected is nevertheless quite large (an average close to 25 words per text). One can note, in addition, that the density of transformations is in fact lower in sixth than in second grade (4.6 vs. 6.0). Moreover, interindividual variation remains very high at the end of elementary school: Draft length varies from 161 to 683 words (except for one case of a 842-word draft), the percentage of incorrect words varies from less than 1% to 32%, the number of transformations from 0 (for 5 students) to 67. This means that some sixth graders produce shorter texts and/or texts with proportionately more errors than is the case for some second graders.

4.2 Text Transformations

For each of the three dimensions of transformation, χ^2 tests were carried out to determine if the distributions of the IS and CS instructional conditions differed. With respect to the operations used to carry out transformations, the effect of instructional approach was non significant in both grades. Moreover, a very similar pattern was found in both grades. The vast majority of the transformations (around 85%) were either additions or substitutions (the former being somewhat more frequent in sixth-grade); deletions accounted for around 10% of the transformations and rearrangements for less than 5%.

Table 2 presents the distribution of the transformations according to their object (semantics, text organization, spelling) and for two subcategories of spelling (grammatical, including punctuation, and lexical). In second grade, there are no significant difference between the distributions of the IS and CS instructional approaches. In sixth grade, the χ^2 test shows a significant difference between the approaches for the three main categories ($\chi^2 (2, N = 1990) = 20.204$, $p < .001$), but not for the spelling subcategories. The distributions show that the students participating in the IS instruction made relatively more transformations of spelling and text organization, and relatively fewer revisions of semantics, as compared to the CS students. This finding is coherent with the emphasis placed in the IS approach on organizational factors linked to genre and on the production of correctly written texts to be transmitted to an audience of younger students. It raises, however, several questions which are discussed in the final section of the chapter.

Table 2. Objects of transformation, distribution in % by instructional approach

Object	Second grade		Sixth grade	
	CS	IS	CS	IS
Semantics	5.8	7.8	18.8	11.7
Text organization	22.3	25.6	32.7	34.0
Spelling	71.8	66.6	48.6	54.3
Grammatical	35.0	40.3	58.1	57.3
Lexical	65.0	59.7	41.9	42.7

Although the general pattern of the distributions in Table 2 is similar in both grades, several important differences can be seen between second and sixth grades. In second grade, around 70% of the transformations are focussed on spelling. By the end of elementary school, spelling transformations account for approximately half of the students' revisions, and the transformations affecting text organization and semantics increase correspondingly. A second important change occurs in the subcategories of spelling transformations. In second grade, around 60% of these transformations concern the lexical aspects of spelling (including word segmentation), whereas in sixth grade nearly 60% of the transformations involve grammatical aspects of spelling (verb inflections for different tenses, markers of subject-verb agreement and of article-noun-adjective agreement, punctuation marks). The data in Table 2 suggest that increasing competency in text production and revision between second and sixth grades involves two processes. Increasing mastery of spelling allows students to focus to a larger extent on revisions of text organization and meaning, and within the area of spelling, increased automatization of lexical knowledge facilitates control of the complexities of the grammatical aspects of spelling.

Table 3 presents data on a third dimension of transformation: the relationship of the transformation to language conventions. While no significant differences were found between instructional approaches in either grade, several important differences can be seen between the grades. The transformations carried out by second graders are focused almost exclusively on conventional aspects of writing (67% of the transformations are carried out correctly and 23% incorrectly). Only 10% of their transformations can be classified as optional, that is, as reflecting author's license to make changes not required by language conventions. In sixth grade, conventional considerations continue to account for large majority of the transformations, but incorrect changes decrease (from 23% to 11%) and optional transformations increase (from around 10% to nearly 24%). These findings are consistent with those in Table 2 showing the increase of transformations of text organization and semantics in sixth-grade. They suggest that as children's knowledge of spelling and ability to proofread become more automatized, they acquire the capacity to exercise author's license and revise aspects of text organization and meaning that are not dictated by language convention.

Table 3. *Optional vs. conventional transformations,
distribution in % by instructional approach*

Relation to convention	Second grade		Sixth grade	
	CS	IS	CS	IS
Optional	9.2	10.0	26.0	21.9
Conventional	90.8	90.0	74.0	78.1
Correct	67.3	66.8	63.2	67.1
Incorrect	23.5	23.2	10.8	11.0

5. INDIVIDUAL DIFFERENCES AT THE END OF ELEMENTARY SCHOOL

Although general changes intervene in children's capacity to produce and revise texts between second and sixth grades, the individual differences that remain at the end of elementary school are striking. They can be illustrated by the situation of two students from a same IS class: Yann (who had the lowest score on the spelling test administered at the beginning of the year) and Marion (who had the highest score).

Yann's draft of 235 words included 74 incorrect words (31.5%), whereas Marion's draft of 683 words contained 5 errors (0.7%). Marion carried out 9 transformations: 1 of spelling, 5 concerning text organization and 3 semantics. Yann carried out 29 transformations: 21 concerning spelling, 6 text organization and 2 semantics. These findings support the idea that mastery of basic skills lets the student focus revision efforts on higher-order aspects of text production (89% of Marion's transformations concern text organization and semantics, compared to 28% of Yann's transformations). Nevertheless, it is worth noting that in absolute terms the number of higher-order transformations is equivalent for the two children (8 transformations each). Yann appears capable of transforming text organization and semantics but has to invest most of his revision effort on spelling. Examination of Yann's draft shows that he has acquired substantial skill in several aspects of narrative text production: use of organizers (e.g., *a long time ago, as usual, suddenly*) and coordination of past definite and past indefinite tenses. In contrast, his spelling skill remains very limited for a sixth grader, both in the lexical area (particularly as regards double consonants, e.g., *letre* instead of *lettre*) and in the grammatical area (errors of verb inflections and confusion of infinitive and past participle). Unfortunately, given the usual norms of promotion from elementary to secondary school, Yann's problems of spelling (more than 50 words remain incorrect after revision) are likely to prevent recognition of the knowledge he does have concerning narrative text structure.

6.   DEVELOPMENTAL TRENDS AND THE DESIGN OF INSTRUCTION

In this final section, we first summarize the major differences between second and sixth-grade students' revision skills, independently of instructional approach. We also consider the effects that the writing situation may have on the characteristics of student production and revision. We then examine the effects of the integrated sociocognitive approach to instruction, as compared to those of the componential skills approach. Finally, the implications of our research results for designing more effective instruction in writing and revision are discussed.

The major differences between second and sixth grades can be summarized as follows. Sixth-grade students, on the average, as compared to second-graders:
1)   produced longer drafts which contained relatively fewer spelling errors;
2)   made more transformations of text organization and semantics and correspondingly fewer transformations of spelling;
3)   when revising spelling, made relatively more transformations of grammatical aspects and correspondingly fewer modifications of lexical aspects;
4)   produced more optional transformations and carried out conventional transformations with greater accuracy.

The first finding reflects two factors which cannot be dissociated in our data: the children's increasing knowledge and automatization of writing skills plus their capacity to integrate on-line revision within the process of composition. This change, in conjunction with the second finding concerning the objects of deferred revision, is globally coherent with studies showing that progressive mastery of spelling, as a component of translating, allows children to produce texts more fluently (Graham, Berninger, Abbott, Abbott, & Whitaker, 1997), and to invest more cognitive resources in on-line planning and revision of higher-order text features (McCutchen, Covill, Hayne, & Mildes, 1994). The third finding, concerning sub-categories of spelling, can be interpreted in a similar manner: As students consolidate their lexical knowledge, they are able to devote more consideration to the complex grammatical aspects of French spelling. The fourth finding supports the idea that increasing ease in conventional revision of spelling and punctuation goes along with greater use of author's license to make higher-order changes of text organization and meaning.

The differences between second and sixth-grade students show highly similar patterns whether instruction is based on the IS or the CS approach. This suggests that developmental language processes play a significant role in the acquisition revision skills and that instruction needs to take these processes into account. Although evidence of developmental trends is quite clear-cut on the average, it should nevertheless be emphasized that there are substantial individual differences among students in each grade.

Another factor which appears to be similar in both grades, and both instructional conditions, is the influence of the type of writing activity on students' drafts and revisions. Students in all classes showed a great deal of interest in the narrative writing activity which involved an authentic communication goal (production of illustrated booklets to be read by other children). This appears to have had a stimulating effect on text production. The second-grade students produced drafts with an average length of around 100 words, which is considerably more than the average of 24 words reported by Cameron et al. (1996) on the basis on large-scale samples of classroom writing in second grade. The sixth-grade students also produced longer drafts (averaging around 360 words) than those obtained in other studies of sixth graders (averages of around 200 words in research by Bereiter and Scardamalia, 1987, and by Fitzgerald and Markham, 1987). A substantial student investment in writing extended text means that the occasions for carrying out revisions are also expanded. This is potentially an advantage for student learning about the multiple facets of revision but it could also lead to lower rates of revision if students are faced with too many errors to correct. Comparing our sixth-grade data to the fifth-grade data collected under similar circumstances (deferred revision of narrative text) by Chanquoy (2001), we see that our sixth graders produced longer drafts (around 360 vs. 110 words, on the average) containing a smaller percentage of incorrect words (10% vs. 20%); on the other hand, our students carried out relatively fewer revisions (around 5 transformations per 100 words vs. 23 per 100 words in Chanquoy's study). This finding raises the following question. Although authentic communication situations have advantages with respect to student motivation and the production of extended text, should more constrained writing tasks also be used to foster systematic practice in revision skills focussed on different categories of text content and form? This would imply that targeted text revision activities be inserted in the spiral instructional sequence along with the activities focused on basic skills (see Figure 1).

We will now examine the effects of the two forms of writing instruction carried out in our research. Our analyses showed that the integrated sociocognitive approach had three significant effects on students' revisions, as compared to the componential skills approach. Second-grade students in IS classes made relatively more transformations of their drafts. Among sixth graders who had a high initial level of spelling skill, IS students produced drafts with fewer errors, which implies enhanced translating fluency and/or better integration of on-line revision during drafting. With respect to deferred revisions of an existing draft, sixth-graders in IS classes tended to carry out relatively more transformations of spelling and of text organization, and relatively fewer transformations of semantics.

The first two findings can be considered as positive, albeit modest, effects of the integrated sociocognitive approach. The third finding is open to differing interpretations. Most studies of revision consider increases in transformations affecting meaning, as compared to surface transformations, as a sign of progress in the mastery of the revision process. From this perspective, the IS approach could be judged as producing a negative effect on revision. We think, however, that the dichotomy between surface and meaning revisions fails to take into account the complexities encountered by elementary school students when making transformations of text organization and of spelling, particularly when writing in French. Although corrections of spelling errors are generally classified as surface revisions, they constitute transformations of considerable complexity in French because of their grammatical aspects. This is particularly true for unvoiced markers of noun group agreement and of subject-verb agreement, which are a major source of difficulty for elementary school students (Largy, 2001), and can even lead to mistakes by adult experts under conditions of cognitive overload (Fayol & Largy, 1992). In situations of text production and revision, the grammatical aspects of spelling concern relations not only between words but also between sentences; for example, it may be necessary to add a feminine and/or plural marker on a past participle to assure agreement with a noun in a previous sentence (*La clé est tombée subitement....Cachée sous le buisson, elle*...[The key suddenly fell... Hidden under a bush, it...]; since *clé* is feminine, an *e* needs to be added to the past participle *caché*). Mastery of the grammatical aspects of French spelling is quite difficult and continues to be a challenge for the majority of students throughout the elementary school years (Bétrix Köhler, 1995).

Our data show that although spelling corrections constituted about 50% of the transformations made by sixth-grade students, a substantial number of spelling errors remained in most texts (on the average approximately 25 errors in texts of 350 words). Improvement in the area of spelling is therefore a goal that cannot be neglected if elementary school writers want to assure reader comprehension of their texts. In a genre-based approach to text production, improvements in text structure are equally important for reader comprehension and, in some cases, are closely linked to grammatical aspects of spelling. We would argue, moreover, that for elementary school students, increased concern for text organization and spelling is a sign of transition along the continuum described by Bereiter and Scardamalia (1987), from a strategy of "knowledge telling," centered on transcribing ideas as they come to mind, toward a strategy of "knowledge transforming," aimed at producing a text that is comprehensible for others.

Although the IS approach to writing instruction had several significant effects, its overall impact was less pronounced than had been expected. This outcome is due in part to the high degree of interindividual variability encountered in both grades. High variability among second-grade writers is not really surprising since, in any new area of learning, it is common to observe a very wide range of variation in learners' behaviors, rates of progress and complexities of outcome. Other research has also found important individual differences among young writers, not only before an instructional intervention but also after the intervention (Berninger, Abbott, Whitaker, Sylvester, & Nolen, 1995). The persistence of a high degree of diversity until the end of sixth grade is more of a problem. It means that a substantial number of the students do not manage to consolidate effective writing and revision strategies before entering secondary school and are therefore likely to encounter literacy-related difficulties in their subsequent studies. This of course raises the question of how to enhance the effectiveness of writing instruction for *all* elementary school students. Although the IS sequences we developed offered meaningful contexts for writing, various forms of sociocognitive scaffolding and occasions for integrated skill construction, they did not include direct strategy instruction of the type emphasized in the SRSD and CSWI models (see section 1). It is possible that, for a sizeable proportion of the elementary school population, direct strategy instruction is needed to insure that learners take full advantage of the other components of an integrated sociocognitive approach. In summary, while conserving the discursive and motivational advantages associated with text production in contexts of authentic communication, it appears to be important to design instruction that includes explicit guidance in the operations of text revision, as well as tasks focused on the different objects of these operations.

AUTHOR NOTE

The research reported in this chapter was supported by a grant (no. 4033-035811) from the Swiss National Research Foundation.

EFFECTS OF COLLABORATIVE REVISION ON CHILDREN'S ABILITY TO WRITE UNDER-STANDABLE NARRATIVE TEXTS

PIETRO BOSCOLO & KATIA ASCORTI

University of Padova, Italy

Abstract. The chapter focuses on elementary and middle school children's revision of written narrative texts in an interactive situation. The study had two closely-related objectives. The first was to analyze the effects of collaborative revision on children's ability to anticipate their readers' need for comprehension, as well as to check comprehensibility when revising texts written by others. The second objective was to analyze the role of children's verbal interaction and discussion while revising. Children's ideas were investigated in a concrete writing-reading situation: that is, a child wrote a text, a classmate gave feedback on its comprehensibility, both discussed the suggested corrections. The hypothesis was that through collaborative revision children might improve their writing skills. A total of 122 students from an elementary and a middle school in Padova (Italy) participated in the study. For each grade level (4, 6, and 8), there was an experimental and a control group. The results showed improvement for the experimental group children both in writing and revising after the collaborative revision sessions. The participants' attitudes towards revision emerging from peer interaction are presented and discussed.

Keywords: Collaborative revision, narrative writing, audience awareness

1. INTRODUCTION

Since the early 1980s, when the cognitive approach "discovered" writing as a promising research field, written production has been investigated as an essentially individual ability or process. Studies on collaborative writing, mostly distributed between the 80s and early 90s, were stimulated in particular by the development of personal computer technology, which suggested interesting possibilities for analyzing new ways of learning and designing more effective learning environments (Crook, 1994; Heap, 1989b; Kumpulainen, 1996; Pontecorvo & Paoletti, 1991).

The theoretical framework of most of these studies was related to Piagetian and, to a greater extent, Vygotskian theories. On the one hand, according to Piagetian theory, the social interaction required by collaboration fosters cognitive development in that it produces cognitive conflict, and therefore the need for children to reconcile and integrate different points of view (e.g., Daiute, 1986; Daiute & Dalton, 1988; Dale, 1993). On the other, research on collaborative learning has generally supported Vygotsky's idea that learning is a social process in which the child's development is stimulated by interaction with more competent peers and adults. Through interaction, mediated by language, a child internalizes the "tools" – knowledge, rules and meanings – elaborated by his/her culture (Daiute & Dalton, 1993; Heap, 1989a; McLane, 1990). From this perspective, a collaborative writing task, particularly one involving peers with different levels of competence, can increase children's mastery and awareness of the functions of writing.

In the 1990s, there was a renewed interest in collaborative writing thanks to the development of studies on the effects of writing on learning (Tynjälä, Mason, & Lonka, 2001), on the one hand, and the expansion of social constructivist approaches to literacy learning on the other. Some studies have demonstrated that collaborative writing helps children develop learning and reasoning skills, particularly in the scientific domain (e.g., Dale, 1994; Dunn, 1996; Keys, 1994, 1995; Tynjälä, 2001). In quite a different theoretical framework, the social constructivist approach has led to a new conceptualization of writing which has diminished the individualistic view of the cognitive approach and emphasized the social aspects of literate practices. The social constructivist approach is quite complex; contributions from various research fields converge, and an exhaustive treatment is beyond the objectives of the present chapter. The aspect of this approach which we underline here, strongly influenced by Vygotskian theory, is that literacy learning is not, or not only, the acquisition of "general" reading and writing abilities, but of socially and culturally marked practices, including behaviors, beliefs, meanings and modes of interaction. Writing, specifically, is a cultural practice in that it is aimed at reaching objectives (e.g., communicating, informing, recording information) through specific genres and contexts consolidated in a culture. Writing is a social practice not only because it involves the writer's relationships with the reader or audience, but also because the writer shares with other past and present writers the conceptual and linguistic tools of a genre and thus participates in a discourse community. From this perspective, collaboration is only one aspect, although a most representative one, of writing as a social practice (Spivey, 1997).

Collaborative writing is a somewhat generic label in that writing includes various processes (Hayes & Flower, 1980), and collaboration may regard some or all of them. For instance, some studies have focused on planning and idea generation (e.g., Flower, Wallace, Norris, & Burnett, 1994; Morani & Pontecorvo, 1995), whereas others have underlined the effects of collaboration on production and revision (Zammuner, 1995). Relatively few studies have focused on collaborative revision, although revision has been more or less explicitly considered in almost all studies on collaborative writing. Zammuner (1995) compared fourth-graders' computer production and revision of narrative texts across three experimental conditions: individual production/individual revision (participants wrote and revised their own texts); individual production/dyad revision (each participant wrote a text individually, and revised it together with another); dyad production/dyad revision (two children wrote a narrative cooperatively and then revised it). Regarding revision, children were asked to re-read their story, detect mistakes to be corrected and "make the story better." Results showed that when children revised their texts, they improved them from the viewpoints of errors, story structure and idea quantity. The greatest improvement was found in the writing condition where students wrote the narrative individually and revised it together with another child. When revising the individual production in collaboration, they focused on its linguistic aspects (e.g., more syntactic complexity), and introduced more information about characters' internal reactions. Zammuner concluded that the presence of an interlocutor seemed to be more useful when revising than writing a text, and that the revising process was most effective when carried out with a peer who did not contribute to the production, and therefore had a more detached attitude to the written text.

Zammuner's (1995) study has been referred to extensively for its dissimilarity from other studies on revision. Unlike most studies on collaborative writing, it neatly distinguished the role of revision from planning and drafting. However, as in other studies, participants were given a general instruction to revise (to make the text better and/or identify errors), that is an instruction very similar to the one teachers usually give when asking students to revise texts. The research focus was on the effects of revision on text quality, but the interactive aspects of collaborative revision were not considered.

The study we will present in this chapter had two objectives which differentiate it from most studies on this topic. The first objective was to investigate the effects of collaborative revision, not in terms of general improvement (text length, syntax, ideas, etc.), but with respect to a specific variable, namely, children's awareness of audience when writing a narrative text. The second objective was to analyze the ways students of different grade levels approach revision of a peer's text, that is, how they interact when identifying gaps or inconsistencies and suggesting improvements to be made. Therefore, in this study collaborative revision is not considered only for its effects on writing, but also as a form of verbal interaction during which students' attitudes towards revising can emerge.

2. STUDYING COLLABORATIVE REVISION

One of the crucial problems for research on written composition is the development of the writer's audience awareness, that is how writers consider their readers' need to understand. Over the last two decades a substantial body of empirical studies has been generated on this topic (see reviews in Hillocks, 1986; Langer & Flihan, 2000; Nelson & Calfee, 1998; Tierney & Shanahan, 1991). These studies can be grouped into two categories. The first regards how writers of different levels develop an awareness of audience (e.g., Boscolo & Cisotto, 1999; Crowhurst & Piché, 1979; Kroll, 1986; Roen & Willey, 1988; Rubin & Piché, 1979; Wollman-Bonilla, 2001), as analyzed through specific text features, such as syntactic complexity, stylistic and rhetorical features and changes in meaning. The second group includes studies aimed at improving audience awareness through instructional intervention. Some of these studies (e.g., Newkirk, 1982; Tierney, Leys, & Rogers, 1984) have demonstrated that collaborative learning experiences, such as sharing one's writing with other students in class, positively influences students' audience awareness. Other, more numerous studies, have considered the role of feedback in writers' awareness. Several scholars have argued that a writer's sensitivity to audience can be increased if information is provided on the reader's viewpoint regarding written text clarity. For instance, Schriver (1992) designed a method called "reader-protocol teaching", which consists of giving writers feedback about how readers reacted to their texts. This feedback should enable writers to build a mental model of readers and their comprehension problems. The results of Schriver's study showed that college students trained with the reader-protocol method were more able to diagnose readers' problems than the control group. Lumbelli and her associates (Lumbelli, Paoletti, Camagni, & Frausin, 1996; Lumbelli, Paoletti, & Frausin, 1999) criticized Schriver's (1992) method because readers' feedback about the written texts consisted in pointing out difficulties they encountered in reading (e.g., "this text needs an example", or "this section makes the idea too hard to understand"), not the processes underlying those difficulties (e.g., how a reader tries to build a representation of what is being read, what elements the reader finds abstract or vague, or how the reader evaluates the plausibility of inferences). Lumbelli and her associates (1996, 1999) adopted a different method, presenting their participants (sixth graders) with a reader protocol that explained which elaboration and inferential processes led to the solution of comprehension problems. The children were asked to read and correct texts containing unclear and missing information. During correction, the children listened to an adult's recorded comments, which included questions and inferences related to the unclear and missing parts. Thus, the protocol simulated the processes an expert reader carries out automatically (e.g., gap-filling or resolving incoherence) when detecting a comprehension problem. Unlike Schriver (1992), Lumbelli and her associates also hypothesized, but failed to demonstrate, that making comprehension problems explicit by thinking aloud techniques had a positive influence on children's ability to write clearer texts.

The present study focuses on elementary and middle school children's revision of written narrative texts in an interactive situation. Children's ideas were investigated in a concrete writing-reading situation: that is, a child wrote a text, a classmate gave feedback on its comprehensibility, and they decided together on the appropriate corrections. From a methodological perspective, collaborative revision allows a researcher to analyze reading-writing relationships more thoroughly, in that a participant assumes the double role of writer and reader. The hypothesis was that through verbal interaction and peer feedback, children's ideas of what makes a text understandable would emerge. We formulated the following research questions:

- Does the experience of collaborative revision have any effect on elementary and middle school children's ability, when writing, to anticipate readers' need for comprehension? And, if so, are these differential effects related to grade? The verbal interaction through which a reader/reviser underlines lack of clarity, asks the writer for clarification, and/or suggests how to improve it, was expected to have a positive effect on children's ability both to detect lack of clarity in texts written by others and to avoid gaps and/or inconsistencies when writing.

- How do students check narrative texts for comprehensibility? Do they differentiate their responses and comments according to the specific types of information gaps? How do the writers react? Are there any differences as related to school grade?

In the previous section, we argued that the present study differed from most studies on revision by its focus on the awareness of audience and on verbal interaction. It also differs from studies on audience awareness in two main aspects. First, whereas most previous studies have focused on the written production of procedural or explanatory texts (but see Kroll, 1985), the present study concerns narrative writing, which is a common activity in elementary and middle school. There is an important difference in audience awareness between narrative and explanatory, or procedural writing. Narrative comprehension requires continuous inference generation because the writer (or teller) does not give all the information needed for comprehension, but only what he/she considers relevant and/or necessary for the reader's understanding. In order to build a coherent text representation the reader often has to infer what is only implicit in the text being read (e.g., why a character did a certain action, or how another character reacted to it). Thus, the writer implicitly refers to the reader's prior schematic knowledge (knowledge of human feelings, experiences and interactions usually described in a narrative) and discourse knowledge (structure and features of a story or narrative) (Alexander, Hare, & Schallert, 1991). The reader's inferential activity is much more limited in explanatory and procedural texts because he/she needs precise information that the writer has the "responsibility" to supply. Comprehending a written explanation means organizing text information (e.g., a rule, procedure, or concept) clearly and coherently. Therefore, information gaps are to be carefully avoided. Narrative reading is also aimed at coherent text representation, but the reader's attitude is less "demanding." Not only does the reader have to fill in information gaps by using prior knowledge; sometimes the writer uses strategies such as delaying or not giving information to create suspense, doubt or curiosity – in a word, "expectation" – on the part of the reader.

The second aspect regards audience specification. Unlike most studies in this research field, we did not specify the type of reader to whom the participants' texts would be addressed. There was an important reason for not doing so. The audience is usually not specified in narrative writing assignments in school. Thus, we conformed to a procedure followed at any grade level by language teachers who are traditionally children's only audience. In summary, the aim of revision was specific (focusing on gaps and inconsistencies, not errors), whereas the audience was unspecified.

3. METHOD

3.1 Participants

The students of two grade 4, two grade 6, and two grade 8 classes of an elementary and a middle school in Padova (Italy) participated in the study. There were a total of 122 students (M = 50, F = 72). For each grade level a coin was tossed to determine the experimental and control classes. The groups were composed as follows:

	Experimental Group	Control Group
Grade 4	20 (M = 6, F = 14)	20 (M = 5, F = 15)
Grade 6	20 (M = 10, F = 10)	19 (M = 10, F = 9)
Grade 8	24 (M = 13, F = 11)	19 (M = 6, F = 13)

3.2 Procedure and Materials

The study, conducted between January and April 2000, was divided into three phases.

3.2.1   Phase 1

Both the written production and revision tasks were performed in the classroom.

Written production. All participants were asked to write a narrative text ("An un-expected event which happened during a trip or short journey you had with your family, class or a small group of friends").

Individual revision. All participants were asked to read a text (a personal report written by an anonymous eighth grader) and identify all the information gaps and unclear points that might make it difficult for a reader to understand. They were also required to explain why these points were not clear, and to suggest an appropriate correction. The text had been manipulated by the authors and included eight hard-to-understand points, which emerged from a pilot study. These points represented three types of unclear expression common in children's narrative writing: deixis; information gaps, due to referential ambiguity and lack of a causal relationship between text segments; inconsistencies caused by contradictory information.

In the instructions the participants were told they had to focus on text clarity, not content or correctness. To avoid, or at least limit the young revisers' "hypercorrection" (i.e., exaggerated severity in correcting, as seen in the pilot study), the participants were reminded that a good text is one which doesn't "tell" everything, but only what is necessary for the reader to understand.

3.2.2   Phase 2

Two conditions are contrasted: collaborative revision and teacher correction.

Collaborative revision. The experimental groups wrote two narrative texts, four weeks apart. The first was about a personal event ("The time my parents were very angry with me"), the second was an invented story ("I have made friends with a foreign boy/girl"). The students were invited to be clear when writing. The collaborative revision was carried out by students in pairs who first worked on one and then the other written text. Thus, each participant in the experimental group acted as an author twice (true and invented narrative) and twice as a reviser. The reviser was told to read the peer's text to individuate gaps or expressions which made comprehension difficult, ask the author for clarification, discuss text clarity with the author and negotiate an appropriate correction. The collaborative revision was performed outside the classroom, in a quiet room, two children at a time, and was audio-recorded. Each session lasted about 20 minutes.

Teacher correction. The same narrative production tasks were assigned to the control classes, and were corrected by the language skills teachers.

3.2.3   Phase 3

Both the experimental and control group children were assigned a new written production task ("A party with my friends") and a revision task (a new manipulated written text with the same number and types of comprehension difficulties).

3.3 *Data Analysis*

The participants' written narratives and revisions performed at the beginning and end of the intervention were used as pre- and post-intervention measures. A few participants missed the writing task either at the beginning or the end of the intervention, thus there were fewer participants in the writing task (n = 114, M = 42, F = 72) than in the revision task

3.3.1   Written Narratives

Each text was divided into T-units (Hunt, 1983), and for each text the ratio of information gaps to length (number of T-units) was computed. Information gaps were identified and rated on a 4-point scale according to their "seriousness":

- A gap was rated 1 when it could be filled in by a simple inference. For instance:

    ...on the way to Genoa, my mother heard a noise and we stopped.

Since the writer had previously said that she and her family went to Genoa by car, the lack of information about the origin of the noise is easily resolved.

- Deixis and reference to events known to the writer but not the reader were rated 2:

    ...when I went on a trip with my class, not here, but Lunate...

The writer has not considered that it is not clear what "here" refers to.

- Comprehension difficulty was rated 3 when it could be overcome by relatively complex inferential processes, from which only a plausible solution is obtained:

    ...we found that fool of a brother of mine in a very big hall with the attendant.

To make the sentence meaningful, a reader must infer that the boy, who was lost, had been found, taken into a very large room, and handed over to an attendant.

- Finally, inconsistencies and hard to understand passages, unresolvable by inference, were rated 4:

> My cousin had invited me to his school's End-of-Year party and because I went to Chile
> (where I was born) every two years for a holiday, I decided to accept.

This is the only reference to Chile, and its relationship to the school party is utterly obscure.

Two judges, trained by the first author to detect information gaps in written texts, read the narratives, and identified and rated gaps, ambiguities and inconsistencies. They stopped reading when they found a point (word, clause, or sentence) which was not easily understandable, that is, left a sense of uncertainty in the reader. They agreed on 90% of the identified sources of comprehension difficulty and resolved the other cases by discussion. For each text, the sum of ratings was computed, and divided by the number of T-units.

3.3.2   Individual Revision

Each participant was assigned four scores. Two scores, from 0 to 8, regarded the gaps, as matched with expected corrections in the manipulated texts before and after the collaborative revision sessions. Two other scores (before and after) regarded the participants' "severity" of corrections, that is the additional gaps a participant might identify on the basis of his/her revising attitude. These "severity" scores had no maximum.

3.3.3   Collaborative Revision

Collaborative revision was articulated into the following steps, which were common to the dyads of all three school levels. First, the reader started to read the peer's text, and stopped when an unclear point was found. Then the reader either asked the writer for clarification, and, after his/her response, proposed how to change the written text. Or, in the case of less serious gaps or inconsistencies, the reader underlined the lack of clarity and proposed how to improve the text. In both cases the interaction usually ended with the writer's acceptance of the changes proposed by the reviser, and the correction of the text.

In the revision sequence variability basically regarded the ways readers pointed out lack of clarity in the written narrative. From an analysis of audiorecorded peer interactions two main types of the reader comments emerged: requests and suggestions. Requests were aimed at obtaining clarifications and explanations from the writers. They were asked when the reader did not understand a paragraph, sentence or short expression. Suggestions were aimed at improving a segment of the text which the reader viewed as incomplete or unclear, albeit understandable. Although a request for clarification is by no means incompatible with a suggestion for improving the text, and usually precedes it, requests and suggestions seemed to belong to two different revision stances.

The following list gives the definitions of the main request and suggestion categories, as well as illustrations of each:

Requests

- *Text clarification.* The reader's question regards the meaning of a word, expression or sentence he/she can't understand. Example: the reader identifies a gap which can easily be filled by an inference, or an expression which appears imprecise, such as a metaphor or irony. The reader's attitude is sometimes hypercorrective and the writer's objection is that the requested specification is not needed.
Example:

Text:	My mother called a glazier without telling my father.
R:	Why without telling him?
W(riter):	Because he would be very angry about how much it cost. Do I have to add it?
R:	It would be better.

Another example:

Text:	My brother and I bashed into a mirror. The mirror was signed and was handed down for generations in my family.
R:	What does it mean the mirror was signed?
W:	It was signed with a dedication by my grandfather if I remember right; perhaps I should add it.

- *Event clarification.* The reader's question regards the event narrated, not the written text. The request is motivated by apparent inconsistency or scarce plausibility.
Example:

Text:	That afternoon me and my cousin were playing ball on the grass. It was her turn to throw but I threw so hard that she couldn't catch it and it broke a window.
R(eader):	But who threw it, you or her?

Another example:

Text:	At last my mother found me and I, on seeing her, calmed down and ran to her.
R:	Did your mother find you because you stepped onto the stage or because she was able to see you?

- *Gap filling.* The reader underlines a deixis or gap by asking a generic question (Who? What?)
Example:

Text:	Once a group of friends and I went to the banks of a river in a nearby village for a picnic.
R:	Near to what? I don't understand: Do you mean close to the village where we live?
W:	In a village close to ours.

Suggestions

- *Correction.* The reader underlines inadequate expressions and/or repetitions, and suggests how to change or remove them.

Example:

Text:	That day I made my parents really flipped.
R.:	Here it's clear what you mean by "flipped, but perhaps in a composition it's better to use the right words.
W:	You mean: 'That day I made my parents really angry.' Is that better?

- *Addition*. The reader suggests adding an explanation or specification to make the text clearer.
  Example:

Text:	However, when I returned home my parents were there waiting for me, ready to tell me off. They punished me for a week.
R:	You could also say what sort of punishment they gave you!

- *Inference*. The reader suggests specifying the cause of a character's behavior.
  Example:

Text:	Because of that quarrel, I did not play with Vanessa for two days.
R:	Here you could write that you were angry to Vanessa because it was her fault that you were punished.

4. RESULTS

4.1 *Written Narratives*

The information gap scores obtained by participants in the phase 3 writing task after the sessions of collaborative revision ("A party with my friends") were submitted to an analysis of covariance (ANCOVA) with grade level and experimental condition as between-subject factors and the information gap score obtained in the phase 1 writing task ("An unexpected event which happened during a trip or short journey…") as the covariate (see Table 1).

Table 1. Means, standard deviations, and adjusted means for gap scores, by experimental condition and grade

Grade	Collaborative revision		Teacher correction	
	Means (SD)	Adjusted Means	Means (SD)	Adjusted Means
Grade 4	7.47 (6.55)	6.90	14.65 (9.55)	14.43
Grade 6	3.26 (4.45)	3.14	11.88 (12.23)	11.99
Grade 8	3.57 (6.65)	4.28	12.61 (10.46)	12.66

A significant correlation of the covariate with the dependent measure was found $(F(1, 107) = 9.82, p < .01, \eta2 = .08)$. The main effect of experimental condition was significant ($F(1, 107) = 28.23$, p < .01, $\eta^2 = .21$) but the effect of grade was not. The collaborative revision group produced texts with fewer information gaps.

4.2 Individual Revision

Two ANCOVAs were carried out, one regarding the number of information gaps identified by participants in the manipulated texts (Table 2), and the other on the "hypercorrection" scores, that is the gaps identified in addition to the manipulated ones (Table 3).

Table 2. Means, standard deviations, and adjusted means for identification of gaps, by experimental condition and grade

Grade	Collaborative revision		Teacher correction	
	Means (SD)	Adjusted Means	Means (SD)	Adjusted Means
Grade 4	3.45 (1.47)	3.38	1.40 (0.82)	1.45
Grade 6	2.63 (1.21)	2.79	3.16 (1.38)	3.18
Grade 8	4.54 (1.47)	4.41	2.32 (2.11)	2.32

The first ANCOVA showed no significant effect of the covariate; significant main effects were found for grade level, $F(2, 114) = 4.46$, $p < .05$, $\eta^2 = .07$ and experimental condition, $F(1, 114) = 20.58$, $p < .01$, $\eta^2 = .15$. The collaborative revision participants identified more information gaps. The effect of grade level, although significant, failed to show the expected trend, since sixth-graders' performance was worse than that of fourth-graders.

Table 3. Means, standard deviations, and adjusted means for hypercorrection scores, by experimental condition and grade

Grade	Collaborative revision		Teacher correction	
	Means (SD)	Adjusted Means	Means (SD)	Adjusted Means
Grade 4	1.75 (.97)	1.71	1.25 (1.07)	1.30
Grade 6	.58 (.69)	.61	1.16 (0.69)	1.17
Grade 8	1.04 (.75)	.99	.63 (0.76)	.64

Regarding the hypercorrection scores (Table 3), no significant effect was found for the covariate and for the experimental condition. The analysis showed a significant main effect of grade level, $F(1, 114) = 8.37$, $p < .01$, $\eta^2 = .13$ and a significant grade x condition interaction, $F(2, 114) = 3.75$, $p < .05$, $\eta^2 = .06$. Older students were less severe than younger ones when revising, but the developmental trend was not linear.

4.3 *Collaborative Revision*

Table 4 provides data on requests and suggestions during collaborative revision.

Table 4. Percentage of requests and suggestions, by grade and type of story (percentages are calculated on the frequencies in each column)

	Grade	True Story 4th	6th	8th	Invented Story 4th	6th	8th
Request	Text Clarification	40	25	18	27	27	55
	Event Clarification	20	14	_	46	11	_
	Gap filling	_	11	_	13	16	14
Suggestion	Correction	20	9	41	7	33	4
	Addition	13	2	32	7	13	23
	Inference	7	19	9	_	_	4
Total Number of Reader Comments		15	43	22	15	.29	22

For each type of story and grade level, the number of requests and percentages are indicates, as are the percentages computed on the total number of comments from all readers. At each grade level, a sizeable number of participants made no comments on their peers' written narratives. Older students proposed more suggestions than requests for revising the true story, and more requests for the invented story, whereas the younger ones used requests extensively for both types of stories.

5. DISCUSSION

This study had two objectives. The first regarded the effects of collaborative revision on children's awareness of audience. We hypothesized that verbal interaction through which a reader/reviser underlines lack of clarity, asks the writer for clarification, and/or suggests how to improve it, would have a positive effect on children's ability to both detect lack of clarity in texts written by others and avoid gaps and/or inconsistencies when writing. The second objective was to analyse collaborative revision as an interactive situation. We focused on the reader/reviser's approach to the written narratives, that is how lack of clarity and suggestions or stimulation of text correction are indicated.

Regarding the first objective, a significant improvement in writers' awareness of the readers' need for understanding emerged; the collaborative revision participants made fewer violations of comprehensibility when writing narratives. However, no effect of grade level emerged, as either a general trend or an interaction with the experimental conditions. This unexpected result may be due to the method adopted for analyzing the violations. Although gaps and inconsistencies were rated differently, according to their degree of seriousness, a global score was given to each text. A sub-score – that is, one for deixis, one for inconsistencies, and so on – might have been more appropriate for highlighting the trends of the specific types of gaps. However, there may be a different, but not necessarily competing explanation. Participants wrote narrative texts in their usual school setting, with the teacher giving students a topic to write about. Although this procedure guarantees the ecological validity of the writing task, it puts few constraints on the writer's freedom of composition. Thus, the researcher can discover the difficulties that student writers are unable to overcome when writing, but not those that they able to avoid. A more constrained writing task, one which lists the points to be considered when narrating, would perhaps be more appropriate for setting up a comparable situation for writers of different grade levels. With respect to individual revision, a positive effect of collaborative revision was found. Students in the collaborative revision condition were able to identify a significantly larger number of information gaps in the subsequent revision task. Once again, a uniform developmental trend across grade levels was not found and the use of the global revision score may have obscured trends affecting sub-components. Regarding hypercorrection, participants' severity in revision significantly decreased with grade level, but no effect of condition emerged, whereas the significant grade x condition interaction is not easy to interpret.

From an analysis of children's interactions during collaborative revision (our second research question), two main types of reader/reviser approaches to peer texts emerged: request and suggestion. If we consider the variety of reader/reviser responses to peer texts, grouping into only two categories may seem to be an oversimplification. However, the distinction is useful for highlighting the two facets of the revising attitude adopted by students at all grade levels. That is, participants adopted two typical teacher attitudes: request aimed at making a writer aware of the lack of text clarity, and suggestion in which the request for clarification is implicit and emphasis is on how to improve the text. In imitating their teachers, however, participants used the two responses in a flexible way, as analysis of verbal interactions showed. Older students used more suggestions than requests when revising the true story, that is, they assumed a more collaborative stance, whereas younger ones seemed to view the reader's role more severely. The trend was quite different for the invented story; in this case both younger and older students made extensive use of requests. This difference between the true and invented story may be related to student perception of the "seriousness" of the two writing tasks. Inventing a story, although on a plausible topic such as making friends with a foreign peer, is perhaps not considered a "true" writing task by students in these schools. Thus, the reviser's attitude was aimed more at checking text plausibility by explanation requests than at improving its quality by suggesting changes, as was the case in a more "academic" and familiar task such as the description of a trip.

Another aspect of participants' flexible use of requests and suggestions should be emphasized. Most students showed they were able to distinguish text from event by asking questions aimed at clarifying the text but also questions aimed at checking the plausibility of the narrated event. On the one hand, at all grade levels the students, as revisers, stressed the need to help the audience understand and pointed out gaps even when the narrated experience (e.g., a trip) was common to both the writer and reviser. On the other hand, this "formal" attitude was completed by questions about the event ("what really happened?"), as a way of understanding the writer's communicative intention and helping express it more appropriately.

The analyses presented in this chapter focused on the reader/reviser stance, but we can mention some general observations of the writers' reactions to peer requests and suggestions. These interventions were rarely refused; rejection occurred only in the case of overly meticulous requests or of suggestions to expand the text in a substantial way. The writer's agreement with requests and suggestions, and negotiation with the reviser about a different text formulation regularly contributed to improving texts.

Several studies have shown that children are mostly concerned with surface level corrections when revising. This study has shown that when revision is aimed at a specific objective such as making a text understandable, children are competent in analyzing, discussing and improving texts. This result has implications for both research on revision and writing instruction.

The implication for research regards the aims of revision. In many studies conducted in the cognitive approach, revision is viewed as a multi-purpose process and participants are required to check all aspects of writing, from spelling to style. This view of revision is similar to that of many language skills teachers, who ask students to revise their texts after writing without any specific guide or objective. We think that arranging a writing situation so that revision is aimed at a specific outcome (in our case, a more comprehensible text, but the objectives might be different for different text types) rather than at generic text improvement, could contribute to a deeper analysis of the cognitive processes involved in reader/writer research through text. A comparison between two collaborative revision conditions, one in which students are asked to check text comprehensibility, the other with a generic request to revise, is the object of a study now in progress by the present authors.

The implication for writing instruction regards the dual role of collaborative revision, as a tool for improving texts and for stimulating students' discussion of their own texts. On the one hand, the positive effects of collaborative revision could be extended to other genres and other text features. On the other, verbal interaction on text comprehensibility and, in general, text quality, is a literate practice through which students can negotiate meanings, clarify their communicative intentions, compare and discuss their ideas on what characterizes a good text. This can help students not only write better, but also become aware of themselves as readers and writers.

For its humour, a sixth-grader's final comment on a peer's text is perhaps the most appropriate conclusion to this chapter:

> Well done, I didn't find anything that was incomprehensible, it is all clear. We have got better at writing compositions since we have been correcting them!... or perhaps we are more good-hearted than the teacher, who is tough.

COLLABORATIVE REVISION AND METACOGNITIVE REFLECTION IN A SITUATION OF NARRATIVE TEXT PRODUCTION

YVIANE ROUILLER

School for Teacher Education, Lausanne, Switzerland

Abstract. This chapter focuses on the role of peer interactions in a sequence of narrative text production in sixth grade. It investigates the effects of these interactions during a deferred (post-drafting) revision session and in a subsequent interview. After presenting the conceptual framework underlying this study, the text production sequence, and the methodological choices, three analyses of research results are provided and discussed. The first analysis concerns quantitative and qualitative differences with respect to the transformations carried out by dyads and individual writers. The second analysis looks at qualitative differences between the dyads most productive in revising their texts and those who are the least productive dyads. The third analysis looks at the metacognitive reflections appearing in the interview conducted with students who carried out revisions under the dyadic and under the individual conditions. In conclusion, possible modifications of the instructional situation are considered in order to enhance the impact of peer interaction on revision.

Keywords: Writing, collaborative revision, peer interaction, metacognitive reflection, elementary school, narrative text

1.   INTRODUCTION

According to Brown, Collins and Duguid (1989) " the activity in which knowledge is developed and deployed... is an integral part of what is learned" (p. 32). These authors recommend instructional approaches that integrate learning in an activity which allows students to exploit the social and physical context in order to produce useful knowledge instead of "inert" concepts. From this perspective, effective writing instruction at the elementary school level involves the creation of authentic and complex production situations which encourage students to engage in optimal self-regulation processes, especially through peer interaction. For students to activate successfully their knowledge and skills in real life situations, beyond those encountered in school, they must learn to take advantage of peer interactions, a fundamental component of such situations.

2.   CONCEPTUAL FRAMEWORK

Research on peer interaction during writing activities and on metacognitive reflection provides the framework for describing the aims of our research which compares individual and dyadic conditions of narrative text production and revision.

2.1 *Peer Interaction in Writing*

Written communication, considered as a social construction (Rafoth & Rubin, 1988), may suffer, as Bereiter and Scardamalia (1987) have pointed out, from the fact that it lacks the interpersonal interactions which stimulate oral production in conversation. The difficulties experienced by young writers when revising compositions may not be due primarily to inadequate language competencies but rather to their lack of understanding of those processes which are relevant to revision (Bereiter & Scardamalia, 1987) and to a limited comprehension monitoring ability (Beal, 1996). Teaching methods which encourage interactions between students when writing help compensate for such lacking elements by placing written production in a context of social interaction. Students working together are in a better position to put their skills into practice. They can check their representations, confront them with others and test hypotheses (Nystrand, 1986a, 1986b). They are encouraged to verbalize the inner speech which organizes writing and thus exercise more explicit control over their productions (Nunn, 1982). In terms of management of the writing situation, students who work together take the time to understand what is required (Garcia-Debanc, 1990) or to formulate their own goals rather than passively accept those prescribed by others (Newman, Griffin, & Cole, 1984).

In this context, approaches to collaborative writing and in particular conditions favoring positive effects of peer interaction on revision processes have been proposed by several authors (Dipardo & Freedman, 1988; McCarthey & McMahon, 1993; Saunders, 1989). Sociocognitive conflict, mutual control and joint regulation appear to be central when studying the interaction dynamics in revision processes (Daiute, 1989; Dale, 1994; Guerrero & Villamil, 1994). Two main categories of interactive structures are distinguished: structures in which student roles are differentiated ("spontaneous" peer assistance or peer tutoring) and structures in which student status is defined as equivalent (cooperative or collaborative situations).

When studying dyadic interactions during collaborative text composition in elementary school, Daiute (1989; Daiute & Dalton, 1988) found that students are not particularly keen to engage spontaneously in explicit planning and revision sequences. Even though peer discussions appear to be rather vague, unresolved and only implicitly related to planning and evaluation, playful collaboration often leads to productive cognitive conflicts. Daiute and Dalton (1988) have emphasized the importance of play in the zone of proximal development: "In summary, the number and the variety of the play categories which emerged from the composing sessions illustrate that children used play in complex ways to create and revise stories" (p. 13). Daiute's contributions (1989) make us aware of the fact that research hypotheses regarding text production in children are too often based on results from research done on adults (involving planning and revision as basic operations) rather than on children's specific ways of functioning.

Regarding interactions between children during text revision activities at the elementary school level, Goldberg, Roswell, and Michaels (1996) presented mixed results: peer response was unengaged, revisions sparse and superficial, scores on final drafts remained the same or decreased. Zammuner's research (1995), which focused on computer-writing under three writing conditions (individual writing/individual revision, individual writing/dyadic revision, dyadic writing/dyadic revision), showed that the greatest changes between the draft and the revised product occurred when children wrote the text individually and revised together with another child: in such cases they were able to make both more local revisions and more global ones, without explicit training.

Guerrero and Villami (1994) studied L2 revision interactions between secondary school students. Their research on the regulation dynamics established during the interaction of two students placed the concepts of regulation and control at the heart of the dynamic process. Their analysis specified the contents and kind of interactions (e.g., the kind of episode within which the utterance occurs, the degree of regulation, the type of social relationship) rather than the effects of interaction on students' texts. Several studies analyzed the effects of text co-revision on the length of finished text. Karegianes, Pascarella, and Pflaum (1980) showed that cooperation at this level led to texts which were at least as long, if not longer, and led students to pay more attention to the composition task. Kastra, Tollefson, and Gilbert (1987) found a significant positive effect of this approach on student attitudes towards writing but observed large variations between classes.

Based on previous collaborative writing research results, we have taken the following points into consideration when planning our field experiment: (1) dyadic structure can favor sustained thought and student activity (Higgins, Flower & Petraglia, 1992); (2) working on a common task usually leads to better collaboration quality (Freedman, 1987, cited by DiPardo & Freedman, 1988); (3) when students individually compose different parts of a joint text, they have more critical distance which is favorable to collaborative revision (Zammuner, 1983); (4) common planning may increase the involvement of each student in the deferred collaborative revision phase (Saunders, 1989), because it necessarily implies the coordination of both students' points of view.

2.2 Metacognitive Reflections

The concept of metacognition (Flavell, 1976), which refers to an individual's cognition about cognitive functioning, includes two dimensions: metacognitive knowledge and regulation processes.

In research on writing, metacognitive regulation processes are often present, even though they are not necessarily designated as such. For example, in the well-known model of Hayes and Flower (1980) "planning," "monitoring" and "review-ing" interact directly with the "text produced so far" in order to guide the operation of "translating." Research about self-regulation in writing has identified several metacognitive processes likely to enhance expertise in writing (Allal, 2000).

But what about the links between social interaction and metacognitive reflec-tions? In an interactive model of metacognitive regulation, Allal and Saada-Robert (1992) argued that the operations of metacognitive regulation constitute an "inter-face" which coordinates the functioning of representational networks and production processes. Brown and Palinscar (1982) pointed out that regulations (implicit and authomatized) can become conscious when difficulties or new situations are encoun-tered and their studies have shown the important role of peer interactions in the regulation process through the encouragement of explicitation and active control.

In this context, we can hypothesize that a dyadic co-production situation can raise students' awareness of their modes of functioning and, consequently, influence the modifications that they carry out during and after text production, as well as their metacognitive post-writing reflections.

2.3 *Aims of the Research*

In the present study, several aspects of peer interaction are studied through experi-mentation comparing individual and dyadic conditions of text production and revi-sion. The general hypotheses are defined as follows:

1) In a situation of narrative production, a dyadic condition (implying cooperative interactions between students writing a joint text) entails quantitatively and qualitatively different processes of revision, as compared to an individual condi-tion; the effects of dyadic interaction persist when each student individually produces a new text.
2) Analysis of the functioning of different dyads shows that the intensity, the na-ture and the balance of exchanges are linked to the quantity and quality of the revisions carried out.
3) The conditions of text production and revision (individual vs. dyadic) introduce variations in post-writing reflections of the students, especially with regard to the degree of explicitness of statements and the objects mentioned.

For more details, see Rouiller (1996, 1998).

3. METHOD

3.1 *Participants*

The research was conducted in three different sixth-grade classes of elementary pub-lic schools located in the urban zone around Geneva, in collaboration with the teach-ers. In each class, children were divided into five strata on the basis of their grades in French and within each stratum, two children were assigned to the dyadic condi-tion and the third to the individual condition. In order to favor constructive interac-tions within the dyads, the existence of positive relations between the paired children was verified with the teacher. The sample was made up of 5 dyads and 5 individual students from each class.

3.2 *Sequences of Narrative Text Production*

The writing situations were compatible with the current language curriculum in the Geneva school system. The productions were inserted in an authentic communication situation since the students wrote narrative texts that were meant to be read by younger students of their school.

All children in the three classes were asked to take an active part in two sequences of narrative text production. Each sequence was based on a different series of ten pictures corresponding to the episodes of the classical narrative superstructure. The sequence included five phases: 1) presentation of the production task, activation of the necessary knowledge and skills, and elaboration of a production guide (available throughout the rest of the sequence), 2) planning of the story, 3) writing of a draft, 4) revision of the draft, 5) transmission of the story to the intended audience. The first sequence (P1) was designed to estimate the effects of peer interactions on text production: students in the dyadic condition were asked to plan and revise texts together but wrote each half of the draft; students in the individual condition completed all five phases alone. The second sequence (P2) aimed at identifying possible transfer when all children wrote a text individually two weeks later.

3.3 *Data Collection and Analysis*

To analyze the effects of the structure of dyadic co-production between peers on the processes of revision, more than 1700 transformations were classified along four dimensions simultaneously: level of language affected by the transformation, type, object of transformation and optional vs. conventional status of the transformation. The system was developed on the basis of a previous study (Allal, Rouiller, & Saada-Robert, 1995). Transformation units were defined as observable differences between the draft and the final text. The data were coded on the basis of a detailed eight-page protocol. The effects of experimental conditions on the texts were analyzed by F tests and χ^2 tests and the results were considered significant at $p < .05$.

In order to observe the variation in the functioning of the different dyads and the links with the quantity and quality of revisions carried out, we analyzed the recordings of dyads' interactions. In this perspective, we identified two dyads whose number of transformations during the coproduction at P1 is similar to the results of each of the two individuals at the time P2 (dyads ALPHA and BETA) and three dyads whose number of transformations during the coproduction at P1 is clearly higher than the results of each individual taken separately at the time P2 (dyads GAMMA, DELTA and EPSILON). In our analysis, DE (E like equivalent) designates the dyads corresponding to the first pattern and DS (S like superior or synergetic) those corresponding to the second pattern.

We divided each interaction into sequences defined by the objects the students discussed. Subsequently, each discussion round was classified according to several dimensions: the object of the utterance, the speaker, the communicative aim, the support to which the speaker refers, the person(s) that are taken into consideration, the level of reflection expressed in the utterance.

After the two sequences of text production, the children were individually interviewed on their representations of revision. We compared the post-writing reflections of ten students working in dyads and ten matched students from the individual condition. Matching was made with respect to three criteria: the length of the text, the number of mistakes and the number of transformations carried out. Students were questioned about their conception of text revision and about the methods they employ to perform this activity. We analyzed statements made in response to three questions:

1) "What is revising a text all about for you?"
2) "What is the best way to revise a text?" (statements analyzed in two ways),
3) "How do you go about writing the best story possible in the first go, without being able to revise it later?"

4.   RESULTS

Results concerning the first hypothesis are published elsewhere (Rouiller, 1996). They are briefly summarized but the rest of this chapter focuses on the results for hypotheses 2 and 3.

4.1   *Effects on Text Revision*

The effects of the dyadic condition on modifications carried out by the students are both quantitative and qualitative. Children working in the dyadic condition carried out a larger number of revisions of their texts during the collaborative task (on the average 34 vs. 19.5 transformations). In addition, the characteristics of the transformations varied significantly between the two conditions. Regarding the object of transformations, it was principally found that the dyads carried out relatively more transformations linked to text organization (segmentation, connection, cohesion, modalization), without diminishing the number of changes linked to spelling. They also carried out optional transformations more frequently (28% vs. 23%) and made somewhat fewer incorrect transformations (6% vs. 10%)

In the P2 sequence (two weeks after the P1 sequence), significant transfer was not found with respect to the number of transformations carried out. However, there were indications of transfer with regard to the relative frequency of changes affecting text organization and spelling and the presence of optional transformations.

4.2   *Quality of Peer Interactions*

We shall consider here the data relevant to two questions:
1) What is the relationship between the verbal fluidity observed during a dyad's interaction and the quantity of text transformations?

2) What are the topics of the students' verbalization when they interact in a text revision task?

4.2.1   Verbalization and Transformations

Table 1 shows the number of transformations made to the draft, the number of transformations with respect to the number of words in the draft and the number of utterances recorded during the revision activity.

Table 1. Relationship between the number of utterances made by the students and the number of text transformations in a coproduction situation

Dyad	Number of Transformations	Ratio Transformations/ Words	Number of Utterances
DE ALPHA	17	13.8	29
BETA	20	10.6	73
DS GAMMA	47	27.8	757
DELTA	58	22.7	474
EPSILON	69	28.4	387

The data show a relationship between the number of transformations made by the students and the number of utterances during the revision. DS dyads make more transformations and their interactions include a much larger number of utterances, as compared to DE dyads. The direction of causality is not, however, clear: Do students who carry out more transformations on their text have a tendency to verbalize more about their actions? Or do dyads that verbalize more have a tendency to make more changes in their text?

By examining to the global revision strategy of the dyads, we note that the DS dyads reread more often than the DE dyads. The components of the DS dyads' strategies are more varied. When a member of a DS dyad is rereading, the partner is often called upon to take part in the resolution of encountered problems. The members of DE dyads, on the other hand, work almost exclusively in parallel to each other. Their verbalizations seem to be essentially a way of coordinating individual activities. The global revision strategy chosen by the dyad (amount of rereading, diversity of components, etc.) seems influence both the quantity of the utterances during the revision and the number of actual transformations carried out.

4.2.2   Topics of Verbalization

What do two interacting students talk about during a text revision task? Table 2 presents the proportion of utterances concerning different objects. For all the dyads, a low proportion of the utterances concerns aspects of text organization. DS dyads clearly formulate more utterances concerning spelling than do DE dyads. DE dyads on the other hand express themselves more about the semantic content of the text.

Table 2. Topics of verbalization,
% of total utterances formulated by the students of each dyad

Dyad	General	Semantics	Organization	Spelling
DE ALPHA	17.2	34.5	0.0	27.6
BETA	25.3	28.0	13.3	29.3
DS GAMMA	17.7	15.1	8.6	47.7
DELTA	19.5	12.1	5.5	46.7
EPSILON	12.9	11.6	11.3	45.6

To complete our study of the link between utterances and text transformations we investigated whether the utterances formulated by a dyad concerning a given object corresponds to the revisions carried out in the same area.

Text organization. As noted above, text organization is the object that gave rise to the least verbalization. By comparing the number of transformations and the number of interaction sequences concerning text organization, we note that there are always fewer, sometimes even many fewer, verbal sequences than the number of actual transformations. In other words, students in all the dyads transform the text organization without having talked it over together. Dolz and Schneuwly (1998) also failed to find any trace in student dialogues of text organization categories previously taught in text production situations. A possible explanation is that this language component is probably the least developed in elementary school curricular activities; students have thus acquired fewer references to discuss it than is the case for discussion of spelling mistakes, for example.

Semantics. The results do not show any difference between the DS and DE dyads. As noted above in the case of text organization, certain semantic transformations are not discussed. However, the opposite also occurs: certain exchanges about semantics do not lead to text transformations.

Spelling. There is a difference between DS and DE dyads concerning spelling. The interactions of DS dyads involve more sequences about spelling than transformations in that area. This means that certain dialogue sequences do not lead to actual transformations. The data relevant to the DE dyads show the opposite tendency. The interactions involve fewer sequences concerning spelling than the actual transformations. Again we can interpret this result in the light of the global revision strategy chosen by these students who integrate relatively few verbal exchanges in their largely individual activities.

4.2.3   Two Contrasting Dyads

A qualitative analysis taking into consideration the unique dynamics of each dyadic interaction could help explain the differences we have noted so far. We shall therefore examine two contrasting interactions: that of the dyad for which collaboration seems to have had the largest effect on the students' revision activity (dyad EPSILON) and that of the dyad showing the least effect (dyad ALPHA).

ALPHA. The work sequence of the ALPHA dyad (Charles, Susan) starts with the experimentor presenting instructions. Despite several questions aiming at ensuring the comprehension and the approval of the students, they remain silent. Then, without any previous negotiation with her partner, Susan rereads out loud the part of the text she wrote herself. She reads in a monotonous tone of voice, without any punctuation, and makes no comments. Charles does not interrupt her and continues by rereading the brief second part of the text that he had written. He then suggests they correct the spelling. Each student corrects his own part; during this stage a single verbal exchange occurs, concerning spelling. Charles proposes rereading a third time. Susan then reads the whole text out loud and her partner interrupts her to suggest some changes.

The students show little enthusiasm. They do not involve themselves very much in the task, but nevertheless correctly do what is expected of them without showing any particular reticence. Their text and their revision activity seems to reflect an attitude of "getting by with the least effort" rather than an author's behavior.

Although there were very few interactions, the participation of both students during each interaction sequence is equivalent from a quantitative point of view. However, each student tends to take a different role: Susan rereads out loud whereas Charles suggests adjustments. These different attitudes are characterized by utterances of a different level of reflection and by different proportions of interrogative and injunctive utterances. Charles is the instigator of both organized work periods. Susan accepts all of his suggestions.

Several elements seem to explain why so few verbalizations and revisions took place with the ALPHA dyad. Susan remains in the background and takes virtually no initiatives; the draft on which the dyad is working is quite limited; the students lack enthusiasm and apparent desire to communicate. The observation of the transformations performed by these two students during the second sequence of individual production (P2) could offer an explanation about Charles's qualitative dominance during the dyadic interaction. Charles demonstrates a higher level of text production than Susan. His text is much longer and contains less mistakes. He pays more attention to text organization and optional transformations, whereas Susan pays more attention to conventional aspects of language. The revision activity of

Susan at P2 does not, however, pinpoint any particular weakness. She actually makes slightly more transformations than Charles (C = 17, S = 23), which is not surprising given the large number of mistakes in her text.

EPSILON. The members of this dyad, Tony and Alan, are active from the very start of the sequence. They feel satisfied with their draft and seem proud of themselves. A sentence: "He was sad, but sad, so sad..." seems to provide a guiding link that stimulates several steps of their work (starting the activity, rereading globally a first time, rereading later focusing on punctuation). The students reread their story at least five times. The first time they do so, individually, leads to an exchange about emphasis. They then decide to correct together. While rereading a second time, they seem to put aside punctuation problems which are later taken into consideration during the third rereading. They then go through the questions of the production guide. After having checked the verb tenses, and done spot checks and corrections back and forth through the text, Alan suggests rereading it completely one more time.

The interaction between Alan and Tony is characterized by frequent utterances throughout the sequence. This autoreinforcement is especially carried out by Alan in numerous ways:

- by complimenting himself,

> Well, where could we find that... in the grammar book! God, I'm good!

- by highlighting or repeating excerpts he is proud of,

> Look, look, Tony, at what I wrote.

- by oralizing all the steps of their search,

> Alan: What verb is that? To reject?
> Tony: Perfect tense
> Alan: Wait!
> Tony: Wait!
> Alan: "He felt re rejjjjj... rejected" to reject He was feeling, he was feeling rejected, where's that? To reject, to reject, that's right... "and alone, he was sad, but..."

The two students try to draw each other towards different perspectives. When, for example, Tony suggests, for stylistic reasons, that they should not repeat the adjective "sad," Alan first reacts in a semantic perspective, then adapts himself to his partner's preoccupation:

> Tony: We should take away a "sad."
> Alan: Why? That's the story.
> Tony: "He was sad, but sad, so sad...."
> Alan: No, he was sad, but sad, so sad,...sounds stupid.

At first, Alan, who is quite competitive, seems to dominate the interaction. He even holds back his partner and tries to impose himself as the one who does the corrections. But this attitude is mostly linked to the students' favorite sentence. Tony does not, however, seem to be handicapped by his partner's behavior. He asserts and expresses himself.

Another particularity of this dyad is the way they remember joint decisions. This gives them a basis from which they can later reorient their actions. Although Alan initiates most spelling sequences, Tony participates very actively in the resolution of problems. He also tends to start rereading excerpts out loud more often than his partner. Each of the five times they reread, Alan and Tony seem to be continually comparing the sentences they are reading with a rich representation of language, which includes elaborate stylistic subtlety. It appears as if they are making successive trials until their text corresponds to some ideal representation they have of it. This does not prevent them from correcting all the small details they come across. Alan isn't satisfied with his partner's implicit agreement; he asks Tony to openly express his acceptance of suggested changes:

Tony:	Benjamin...
Alan:	He told them the story, and... told them the whole story. That's better, isn't it? No.... but you must agree, it isn't me who has to...
Tony:	Yeah, but I was thinking about it!

The functioning of the EPSILON dyad is clearly marked by the stimulating influence of the students' pleasure; they play with words and manipulate language and the parts of the text they are proud of. The students do not, however, participate to the same extent in the interactions. Alan's utterances are more numerous. They refer more explicitly to the dyad, reveal a higher level of reflection, and include more injunctive and interrogative utterances. Alan seems to initiate exchanges more easily, especially the dyad's stylistic bursts. Tony, for his part, actively participates in all the reflections under way and seems to take over the role of oral rereading. The analysis of the transformations made at P2 confirms the complimentarity of both students by showing the same tendencies as at P1. Tony completed less transformations than Alan on a slightly longer text containing less mistakes than his friend's text.

4.2.4   Metacognitive Reflections about Revision

Four analyses of students' answers to three interview questions are presented here to compare the post-writing reflections of students working in dyads (D) with those of students from the individual condition (I). Our aims were, first, to identify indications of metacognitive explicitation of revision operations and, second, to qualify the intensity and the objects of these reflections. For each analysis, a figure presents results for the ten matched students in each condition.

Question 1. The first interview question aims at highlighting the students' representations of the activity of text revision: "What is revising a text all about for you?" The two groups of students produced a similar number of brief statements. Answers were classified according to four categories:

1) G: General considerations, including reflections such as "See if the text is OK,"
2) Se: Reflections linked to semantic content such as "See if the story makes sense,"
3) T: Reflections linked to text organization such as "Check for repetitions,"

4) S: Reflections linked to spelling such as "The easy words like 'cat,' for exam-
        ple, I'm not going to look up in the dictionary."

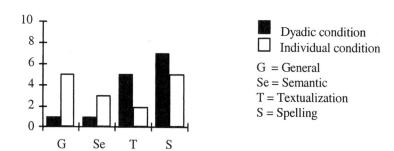

*Figure 1. Definitions of revision activity: Objects mentioned,
by experimental condition (n = 10).*

When we examine Figure 1, we observe that I students tend to make more frequent
formulations in general terms (G) and refer more to semantic content (Se), whereas
the children in the dyadic condition refer more to text organization (T) and spelling
(S), for example:

> Correct spelling mistakes, see if two sentences fit well together, if there isn't any mis-
> take due to inattention...

It is interesting to note that only one D student alluded to the reference materials
(dictionary, conjugation tables, etc.) which were constantly at the children's disposal
during the revision activity.

Question 2 a. The answers to the second question: "What is the best way to revise a text?" were classified in four categories: sequential organization of revision
activity (OS), detection of errors and other improvements (D), use of external resources (peer help, reference material, etc.) (R), general correction or modification
of the draft (C).

Figure 2 shows that 8 out of 10 students from the dyadic condition gave information concerning the sequential organization of their work. Carlo declared, for example:

> So.. looking at it word for word... and the more difficult ones especially... And all the
> little things like for example, all the little things about punctuation, ... and for exam-
> ple... the "E acute accent," [*E accent aigu*] things like that, I try to have a look at them
> again... And then the difficult words, because... apart from that, the easy words like
> "cat", for example, I'm not going to look up in the dictionary.

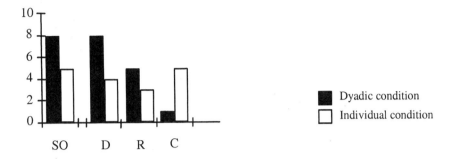

SO   sequential organization of revision
D   detection of errors and improvements
R   use of external resources
C   general ccorrection activity

Figure 2. Revision approach: Categories mentioned,
by experimental condition (n = 10).

Half of the I students also mention sequential organization, but their statements are often limited to an indication of the extent of the revision:

> I re-read from start to finish.
> I look at my sentence, and then I revise.

Most D students formulate statements which mention aspects of error detection and possible improvements:

> Well ... I take a look at all the verbs and then I see if they are more or less right, and then if ... if I'm not sure, then I have a look at the conjugation table.

In contrast, less than half of the I students make any statement whatsoever in this regard. As illustrated in the example of Carlo, the statements of D students often allude to the varying degree of difficulty of the different objects of revision, whereas this is not the case among any of the I students. D students tend to describe to a greater extent "how" they carry out their text revisions, whereas I students tend to sum things up in general terms of "correcting" or "changing."

The results show a relatively low frequency of references to the use of external resources (R) by the two groups of students. However, the statements of D students are more elaborate, including precisions about which references pertain to different objects:

> ... when reading, err, whenever there's a word I don't understand, I use the dictionary, if it's a verb... the conjugation table, and then if it's a question of sentences or something like that, I use, err ... my grammar book.

Only reference documents (dictionary, conjugation tables, grammar book) are cited as external resources used by the students; no reference is made to either classmates or to the teacher.

Question 2 b. In order to compare the complexity of the responses made by both groups of students, we focused on the number of categories present in any one response as an indicator of the degree of metacognitive explicitness. Figure 3 presents the results of this analysis. It shows that over half of the responses made by D students include at least three of the six categories we defined. Gael's (D) response, for example, illustrates three of the categories,

> To revise texts? Well, err... I always start by looking at the verbs, after that I look in... it's the words that ... that I don't know that well from ... in the dictionary, or else if there are sentences, sentence agreements or one of the, err...the... subject-verb inversions I'm not sure about, well then I ... I look them up in the grammar book, or else, err... in the conjugation table (coded SO, I, R).

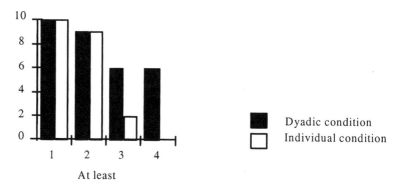

Figure 3. Revision processes: Number of categories mentioned, by experimental condition (n = 10).

The responses of I students are less elaborate, and for the most part contain statements belonging to only one or two categories. The response made by Dan (I) illustrates a response limited to only one category:

> Well, the grammar book, the dictionary ... the conjugation table. (coded R).

Question 3. The above results describe responses geared towards post-writing revision activity, whether it is carried out directly after text production or with a time lag between the session in which the rough draft is produced and a later revision session. Such responses might underestimate the extent of revision activity by neglecting transformations during the writing process itself. In order to assess the revision process carried out *on-line,* we analyzed responses to the question: "How do you go about writing the best story possible in the first go, without being able to revise it later?"

The results presented in the Figure 4 show several differences between the statements of I and D students. The biggest difference is that D students give more explicitation about production processes.

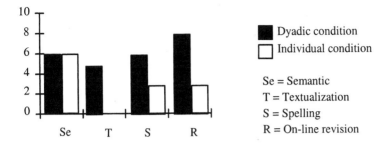

Figure 4. Drafting activity: Objects and on-line-revision,
by experimental condition (n = 10).

Half of the D students mention text organization, referring mostly to punctuation, whereas no I students do so. Six D students mention spelling, but only three I students do so. These results show the same tendencies as those found for question 1 (see Figure 1). Six students in each group made statements about the construction of the semantic content of the text. This means that references to the semantic aspects of writing are more frequent in response to this question on text production than was the case for question 1 which focused on revision.

In addition to identifying the objects mentioned by the students, Figure 4 shows the number of students who explicitly referred to the integration of revision during the drafting process. Only three I students made statements referring to on-line revision, compared to eight D students, all of whom referred to the correction of spelling while writing. The data thus suggest a greater awareness by D students of on-line revision, although we have no indicators of the transformations they actually carried out during writing.

Finally, it is interesting to note that when students were asked about what was of most help to them out of everything done in this instructional sequence, only one student of each condition spontaneously mentioned peer interaction. Both came from the same class in which peer interaction was an important part of classroom instruction. Anne (I) highlighted the supplementary burden students may face when working in groups:

> ... normally we always all work together, and then that really gets you down...

The second student, Gael, underlined her satisfaction with the work accomplished in dyads:

> Err... that's to say, it's still better in twos than all alone... yeah, 'cause in twos you get more ideas, ... when... when I was working with Cyril, (...) he asked me something, I answered, and then he agreed. When he asked me something, right, he was ... he told me something... I agreed.

In contrast with these two students, the majority of their classmates do not seem to have a strong consciousness of the role of the peer interaction in revision activity. These results are coherent with those obtained for question 2a.

5. DISCUSSION

5.1 Major Findings of our Research

Comparison of the transformations carried out under individual and dyadic conditions shows that the latter condition leads to a larger number of transformations, in
particular with respect to spelling and text organization. Qualitative analyses of dyadic functioning reveal a wide range of interactions styles. The most productive dyads (in terms of number of transformations) have very lengthy interactive exchanges
(in terms of number of utterances) and show a high level of motivation during the
revision activity; they make more use of reference materials, particularly to check
spelling errors; their verbal exchanges reflect shared control of revision choices and
the expression of metacognitive reflections. The less productive dyads tend to focus
on semantics and their verbal exchanges seem to ensure primarily the management
of their individual revision activities.

The interview data regarding the students' metacognitive reflections reveal their
conceptions of revision and the ways they approach this activity. The principal finding is that children in individual working conditions express themselves in more
general terms and formulate more statements about semantic aspects of their texts.
Children working in dyadic conditions make more references to text organization
and spelling. Moreover, they provide better descriptions of their revision activity
(mentioning various degrees of difficulty, specifying stages of error detection, of
sequential organization of their work, etc.), whereas children working individually
more often speak of "correcting" their texts. Generally speaking, these results are
coherent with Nystrand's (1986a, 1986b) observation that students working in
groups tend to consider revision as reconceptualization whereas individual writers
tend to focus on error correction.

5.2 Instructional Implications

Our research findings provide support for the use instructional approaches which
favor student interactions as a means of enhancing revision. We will discuss four
directions for future classroom research on text production and revision.
1) If a single text production sequence can lead to the effects we have observed,
     the multiplication of similar session ought to promote the cumulative acquisi-
     tion of revision strategies which are adapted to different productions contexts, in
     terms of audience, genre, etc. It would be useful to vary the composition of stu-
     dent dyads or other working groups so that students can broaden their range of
     experience and discover a variety of revision strategies, for instance, discover
     that one classmate favors a single in-depth rereading of the text to be revised,
     whereas another classmate prefers to carry out several rereadings, each specifi-
     cally focused on a certain type of transformation.
2) Our data show that the productive dyads display a high level of motivation, ne-
     gotiate their revision procedures, jointly manage the revision task and formulate
     a large number of verbalizations regarding their text transformations, but that
     these behaviors are not characteristic of all dyads. It would therefore be interest-

ing to insert one or several whole-class discussions during the text production and revision. These discussions would give students the opportunity to talk about how they proceed during revision, to compare their strategies with those of other students, to explain the advantages or disadvantages of different ways of revising. Repeated interactions of this type could gradually allow students to acquire a certain critical distance with respect to their own procedures and to develop their metacognitive reflections about the aims and means of text revision.

3) The question can be raised as to how teachers can help all students acquire the revision strategies characteristic of the productive dyads. One approach would be to integrate writing instruction in a structured cooperative learning approach. This type of approach attempts to enhance effective peer collaboration by the promotion of positive interdependence among group members, individual and group responsibility, development of cooperation skills, discussion of group processing (Howden & Kopiec, 2000; Johnson, Johnson & Holubec, 1994). A large number of studies have demonstrated the positive effects of cooperative learning structures on a variety of outcomes: academic achievement, motivation, cooperative skills, self-esteem (Johnson & Johnson, 1990; Slavin, 1983). In the cooperative learning perspective, the interactions which occur during group work and the verbalizations which refer to these interactions can gradually lead to the internalization of helping behavior and thereby promote self-regulated learning.

4) Increased student involvement in cooperative activities can allow the teacher to carry out more in-depth observations and provide more finely tuned interventions designed to regulate learning. In the case of text revision, these interventions could be situated at three levels. With respect to the overall instructional sequence, the teacher could introduce moments of explicit discussion about the aims of revision and the ways in which group members could share the responsibility for this task. At the level of group functioning, the teacher could intervene to encourage shared participation and deeper reflection. With respect to the content components of the task, the teacher could construct revision tools (e.g., checklists) in interaction with the class.

To conclude, our research shows positive effects of peer interaction on narrative text revision, but not under all circumstances. Having children work together is not sufficient to ensure productive interactions. Future research needs to show how peer interaction can be structured so as to optimize the effects on text revision.

THE STUDY OF REVISION AS A WRITING PROCESS AND AS A LEARNING-TO-WRITE PROCESS

Two Prospective Research Agendas

GERT RIJLAARSDAM*/**, MICHEL COUZIJN*, & HUUB VAN DEN BERGH**

*University of Amsterdam, The Netherlands, ** Utrecht University, The Netherlands*

Abstract. This chapter analyzes revision as a component of the writing process and as a tool for learning to write. We explore the field of revision via three excursions. The first excursion is undertaken to define revision. It is suggested that in writing research, revision should be reserved for the intentional, reflective activity during and after writing which the writer implements to improve the text. This definition excludes making transformations or other operations on pre-text. A second excursion concerns the question as to why revision has received so much attention from writing researchers. The validity of making inferences from text changes about writing processes is questioned. In the last excursion, we take the reader through the landscape of writing instruction: what difficulties do teachers and learners need to overcome to learn to write? What role can be played by revision activities? For both revision as a writing process and revision as a learning-to-write process, we propose a prospective research agenda. We conclude with some methodological considerations.

Keywords: Revision, editing, reviewing, writing process, learning to write, transformations

1. INTRODUCTION

There is a widespread notion that revision is an important part of writing and that the number and nature of revisions indicate the writer's level of expertise. Revision tends to be seen as an act of improving the quality of the outcome of writing. However, the type and frequency of the revisions that are needed depends on other factors: revision in itself is not the decisive factor of text quality. One even might claim that revision is an indication of incompetent writing, arguing that when revision is necessary, the other components of the writing process apparently were unsuccessful in some respects. Writers who are able to immediately produce an adequate draft with minimal revisions, can be considered as doing a better job than writers who need many revisions to reach the same communicative effect. The first group of writers may have planned better, had better access to lexicon and syntax, formulated more adequately, etc.

Human beings are not, however, perfect nor are their writing processes. So revision enters into the writing process, at least for some tasks and at least to some extent. Even then, revision is dependent on the quality of the other components of the writing process, on the writer, and on the writing task. *In extremis*, a weak planner may compensate with strong revision skills, and a strong planner may not need to develop a high level of skill in revision (Cf. Galbraith & Torrance, this volume). For different writers, revision is a different act with different purposes and with different outcomes (Rijlaarsdam & Van den Bergh, 1996). Generally speaking, an apparently same cognitive activity can have different functions. This is one of the reasons that Hayes et al.'s (1987) model of revision differentiated between different acts of reading (Hayes, this volume).

The writing process consists of a certain number of cognitive activities, interacting dynamically, fulfilling different roles in different phases of the process, and compensating for shortcomings in the execution of other activities (Rijlaarsdam & Van den Bergh, 1996). In principle, all combinations are possible (see Figure 3 in Hayes' chapter where various kinds of activities are connected with one another). We assume that not all combinations are equally effective and that their impact can be different at different stages of the writing process. Some patterns contribute positively to the outcome, the resulting text quality, while other patterns do not. Some patterns contribute positively only in a particular phase of the writing process, but can show a negative relation with text quality in another phase of the process.

Indeed we found in several studies cognitive activities, such as generating, goal setting, structuring, formulating, reading, and revising, are not distributed randomly over the writing process time. Secondly, we found that the functional relationship between combinations of cognitive activities can change over time. For combinations with reading activities for instance – reading followed by generating, reading followed by revision – we observed several different patterns of distribution over the process. When these combinations are related to text quality, we found that different combinations yield different effects. These cognitive activities seem to fulfill different functions in different phases or contexts of the writing process (for combinations with reading, see Breetvelt, Van den Bergh & Rijlaarsdam, 1996; for combinations with generating, Van den Bergh & Rijlaarsdam, 1999; other studies relating differences in writing process orchestration and the resulting text quality are found in Braaksma, Rijlaarsdam, Van den Bergh & Van Hout-Wolters, submitted; Levy & Ransdell, 1996; Van den Bergh, Rijlaarsdam, & Breetvelt, 1994).

Revision, as one of the three main components of writing processes with planning and formulating, interacts with these other components and the task environment, in particular the developing or developed text. The role that revision plays in

producing a communicative text depends on factors such as the level of acquaintance with the task (is it a new or a relatively routine task?), the quality of planning,
the representation of the task, the representation of "a good text", the skills of planning, translating and reviewing. In this chapter, we advocate that studying revision
activities or revision outcomes in isolation does not seem to be an adequate research
strategy.

First, we will offer a definition of revision by amending and extending certain
existing definitions. Then, we will propose and elaborate on a research agenda for
the scientific study of revision. Finally, we will go into the function of revision in
the learning-to-write process.

2.   EXCURSION 1: DEFINITION OF REVISION

In their overview of writing process models, Alamargot and Chanquoy (2001), discuss other definitions critically, and finally define a revision as:

> something (i.e., a word) is done (i.e., added, deleted, etc.) to reach a certain goal (im-
> proving style, content), at a certain text level and on a certain text (pre-text, already
> written text), at a certain moment (i.e., draft, final copy), with a certain effect (i.e., im-
> provement, neutral, decreasing effect) and with a certain cognitive cost. (p. 100)

This rich definition contains several important distinctions: revision is an intentional, goal-directed activity, operating on different objects (already-written text,
text formulated in the mind before being written), at different moments in the writing process. Alamargot and Chanquoy's definition can be read as an application of a
matrix sentence with elements of Goal (intention), Object (text level), Action (adding, deleting), Time, Result and Effect. To clarify the definition of revision, we will
discuss three components: Goal, Object and Action. This will lead to a more specific
and restricted definition. First we will start with an extension by proposing a new
element: Role.

Role. In this definition, implicitly, revision is part of a larger whole: the writing
process. This is understandable, because in any writing process at least some revision is incorporated. Revision, whether deliberately implemented or not, is thus a
means to compensate for the level of quality of other processes (planning, formulating), and for shortcomings due to cognitive load. However, there are also instances
in which revision of the text itself is the goal of the activity. In many professional
situations, the text is already given, written by someone else or by various others,
and the task of the reviser is to adapt the text to the demands of the communicative
situation. We propose to include the role of the reviser in the definition in such a
way that various revision tasks are included. Roles thus include: author, co-author,
and reviser.

In education, revision is often implemented as a learning activity. Revising texts
or fragments that are not written by the students themselves is a common learning
activity with various goals: to acquire revision skill itself by practicing it, to apply
newly learned rules, heuristics and knowledge about spelling, syntax (e.g., sentence
combining), text structure, pragmatics and rhetoric, to apply particular revision operations (deleting, adding information), or to evaluate texts by applying criteria for

"good texts". This last type of revision is covered in the new definition which includes the role "reviser".

Object. Next we will consider the type of text *(pre-text, already written* text) being revised. Hayes (this volume) points out an inconsistency in the text he and Linda Flower wrote about the reviewing component of their 1980 model (Hayes & Flower, 1980). But when we read the 1980 chapter and later models, we interpret what Hayes sees as an inconsistency as a major distinction: Reviewing is the internal, mental process, and revising ("editing") is an external activity. The decisive distinction is the input of the process, which can be either a thought or idea, or written text in some format. We agree with this proposal, being aware that one of the three factors that define a process is the type of input material (Guilford, 1971), for instance, semantic or symbolic. It is unnecessary to include all evaluative activities during writing in the definition of revision, given the fact that Hayes proposes other labels to describe other kinds of evaluative activities: (1) Evaluating (and ordering) ideas corresponds to the sub-process *structuring* (Hayes & Flower, 1980; Hayes, 1996) that is part of the planning or reflection component. (2) Evaluating pre-text, that is, text already verbalized internally but not actually written, can be considered part of the translating component of the writing process model. Structuring – evaluating ideas –, evaluating pre-text, and evaluating text belong to the process category that Scardamalia and Bereiter (1986) label as reprocessing: The writer deals with an object she already created. Because of the different functions and different material that serve as input, we propose to reserve the term revision for evaluative activities with *written text as input*: Revision (called reviewing in Hayes & Flower, 1980, and text interpretation in Hayes, 1996) is the writing process component that connects already written text with the continuation of the writing process.

Goal. Is revision a goal-driven, intentional process? In Alamargot and Chanquoy's definition, the activity is goal-oriented: "something (i.e., a word) is done (i.e., added, deleted, etc.) to reach a certain goal (improving style, content)...." This intentional aspect is why Hayes and Flower (1980) made a distinction between reviewing and editing. Editing is an automatically released activity that may interrupt any writing sub-process without disturbing the continuation of the overall activity. In the writing-aloud protocols we studied (Rijlaarsdam, 1987), we observed many instances of corrections during translating and transcribing acts. The writer produces some text, and within this production, corrects a letter, and adds a comma, without really interrupting the main process: she continues by producing the next text fragment. Or she finishes a sentence, reads the sentence back, as a springboard for generating another sentence, and while she reads, she adds a word, corrects a letter, deletes a comma, and continues the generation of another sentence. In both examples, there is some parallel processing: "translating" or "generation" is "on", and at the same time, automatic correction is "on." This kind of correction does not result in different writing plans, only in text changes (see the next section on Action).

We propose to reserve the term revision for the *goal-directed processes* of reviewing already written text, thereby excluding automatically executed editing processes. What belongs to revising and to editing is largely dependent on the writer's expertise. We are aware that this distinction, and the assumption that the distinction depends on the writer's expertise and revision template (revision task schema, Hayes, this volume), complicates the definition of revision and editing.

Action. A last element to reconsider is the start of the definition, the action itself: "something (i.e., a word) is done (i.e., added, deleted, etc.) ...." The result of the revision process is not restricted to the written text (see Hayes, this volume). When writers revise, they compare at least two representations: the representation of the intended and the representation of the actual text (Scardamalia & Bereiter, 1983; Hayes, 1996). This comparison can result in various changes in the actual text *and/or* in changes in the intended text. It may largely depend on the drafting strategy and on the stage of the writing process whether revision is used as a *forward search strategy* (to construct the writer's disposition towards the topic, as Galbraith calls it) or as a *backward updating strategy* (to accommodate the text to the rhetorical goals). This perspective is in line with the multifunctional perspective on cognitive writing activities we expressed before: revision can serve various functions, depending on the general writing strategy of a particular writer and the phase of the writing process at large. We found, for instance, that for young students (15 years old) "evaluating text," as part of revision, was positively related to text quality in the first phase of writing processes, while "changing text" was negatively related to quality in the same phase. This might indicate that better writers of this age evaluate the relatively small amount of already written text in the beginning of the writing process for the purpose of exploring meaning instead of checking quality of text (Breetvelt, Van den Bergh & Rijlaarsdam, 1994).

It is even possible that an act of revision can result in nothing more than re-confirming the writer's text and plan: revision can result in confidence that this (part of the) text will affect the reader as the writer intended. Even though nothing has been added to or deleted from the text, the process of revision has taken place. We propose to reserve the term revision for the entire act of *re*-vision: reading (part) of the text with the goal to improve the text, which may result in text corrections or transformations (Allal, this volume), and/or modifications of plans.

Definition. Having considered these four elements of the matrix sentence underlying the definition, we re-define the revision as:

> The (co)author or reviser reviews (part of) the already-written text, to reach a certain goal (communication goal, learning goal), at a certain text level, at a certain moment (i.e., draft, final copy), with a certain effect (i.e., improvement, neutral, weakening effect), at a certain level (text, plan, learning), and with a certain cognitive cost.

From now on, we will distinguish between revision as a *re*-view process and the changes made in the text: Using Allal's terminology, when we refer to changes made in the text, we will call them transformations instead of revisions.

3.   EXCURSION 2: WHY STUDY REVISION?

The widespread interest in studying revision could stem from the fact that revision is the easiest process to observe because of the physical actions and the visible traces in textual output. Transformations made in and between drafts are relatively easy to identify, and even easier since the introduction of key-logging systems (see for various applications, Olive & Levy, 2002). But what do transformations tell us other than that transformations were made? From transformations alone it is difficult to infer something about the other components of the revision process, let alone the writing process at large. In a study, we invited thirty 15-year-old students to write, under writing aloud conditions, two persuasive essays, based on some documentation about the topics. In one session varying between 60 to 90 minutes, they wrote a draft and a final version. We noted that about 6.6% of all cognitive activities involved transformations, 5.6% evaluations of already-written text, and 17.2% rereading already-written text. So the observed transformations formed just the tip of the iceberg (Van den Bergh & Rijlaarsdam, 2001). This would not be a problem if transformations clearly indicated which other processes triggered these transformations. But that was not the case: all kinds of cognitive activities were found preceding the transformations. Evaluating already written text preceded 30% of the transformation. So in less than a third of the 6.6% of operations entailing transformations, we found what one can call a "revision string": evaluation followed by transformation. But it is misleading to infer more general conclusions about the process of evaluation via transformations. When we counted the instances of evaluation of already-written text, and related these to the activities that follow these instances, it became clear that many instances of evaluation were not followed by transformations. For instance, 98% of instances of evaluation at the paragraph level were not followed by transformations. Similar results were obtained for evaluating at the sentence level (73% were not followed by transformations). The conclusion follows that transformations visible in text do not allow us to make inferences about the revision process as a whole.

Why writing researchers study transformations or revision is all the more pressing when we take into account that the relationship between transformations in the text and text quality has not yet been clearly established. In intervention studies, researchers succeeded in some cases in increasing the number of transformations made to the text, but text quality was not improved (Scardamalia & Bereiter, 1983). MacArthur, Graham and Harris (this volume) report descriptive and intervention studies showing that (1) fewer than 50% of the revisions were improvements, but no differences between draft and final version on text length or text quality were found; the only revisions that correlated positively with text quality were the addition of sentences; and (2) adding information improved text quality (Graham, MacArthur, & Schwartz, 1995). From writing process studies, we know that making transformations proved to be negatively related to text quality in the first and second of three phases of writing processes of 15-year-old students and had no effects in the last phase of writing (a writing aloud study by Breetvelt et al., 1994). In a similar study, where cognitive activities involved in revision were analyzed with a more detailed grid, some significant correlations with text quality were found. But still, the number of non-significant relations outnumbered the significant relations. However, the good news was that the six cognitive behaviors we distinguished accounted together for 42% of the variance in text quality.[1] The bad news is that three of the correla-

---

[1] *Probably this is an overestimation, based on the assumption that these six behaviors are uncorrelated, which is an assumption hard to maintain.*

tions were negative, and three were positive; even worse news is that only two of the correlations concerned transformations (changes at the word level were negatively related to text quality, while changes at the sentence level were positively related to quality). The other four behaviors were rereading the passage just written (positive correlation), rereading the whole previous text (negative), evaluating a passage (positive) and evaluating formal characteristics (negative) (Van den Bergh et al., 1994). So when we extend our concept of revision from making transformations to the whole set of activities involved in revision, we study something that is strongly connected to the quality of the text. This allows us to study something from which valid inferences can be made concerning the relation between revision activities and text quality. In sum, this relationship has often been neglected in previous research, but is an important area for future work.

Another important issue for revision studies is taking into account the quality of revision skill. The sheer number of instances of rereading, evaluating and transforming already-written text during writing is of less interest than the quality of the execution of these cognitive activities. Carrying our a few appropriate evaluations of an already-written passage is a better indication of a good writing than simply the number of evaluations. A study by Van der Hoeven (1997) may elucidate this remark. In her study, she tried to relate linguistic, planning and revision skills on the one hand, writing processes and written text quality on the other hand. Thirty-one students (sixth grade, half from special education, half from regular classes) wrote four texts (two descriptive and two narrative), two of them under think-aloud conditions. To measure planning skills, participants had to choose, evaluate and elaborate on five out of ten ideas presented by the researcher. To measure revision skills, participants were provided with a virtual student's text, and were invited to evaluate and change the text under conditions of procedural facilitation, similar to those in Scardamalia and Bereiter (1983). Several scores were obtained from the planning and revision protocols. Linguistic skills were measured with a standardized test, indicating lexical and grammar skills. Revision skill was found to be positively related to most of the cognitive activities appearing in the writing-aloud protocols: structuring, writing (production of written text), rereading, evaluating and transforming already-written text. The higher the student's competence in evaluating already-written text, the more instances of rereading, evaluating and transforming were observed, and the better the resulting text. Interestingly, the competence of evaluating already-written text was negatively related with the quality of text. Only by exploiting writing process activities of revision was this negative relation changed into a positive relation. This implies that the skill itself is not sufficient; writers have to apply the skill when they write.

Another important conclusion was that revision skill was not only related to the number of cognitive activities, but also to the temporal distribution of the whole writing process. Participants with low revision skills generated fewer ideas in the beginning of the writing process than participants with relatively high revision skills scores. While the number of ideas gradually decreased in the high revision skills group, this number increased in the low revision skills group. Students with high revision skills scores reread, evaluated and revised relatively little in the beginning and more towards the end of the writing process (Van der Hoeven, 1997). These findings suggest that the quality of revision – revision skill – is related to the way the writer organizes the writing process, and thus affects the quality of the resulting text.

4.   EXCURSION 3: REVISION IN EDUCATION

From a scientific point of view, studying revision may be an aim in itself. However, from an educational standpoint, we want to use research to determine how to teach students of various ages and expertise levels to write more effectively and efficiently, and how revision activities can help them to do so. Knowledge from descriptive and explanatory research on revision may facilitate the design of learning environments that support students learning to write. Moreover, we need creative teachers and researchers who experiment with teaching strategies and instructional arrangements. Good teaching is creative and in some ways experimental teaching. Examples can be found in classrooms where teachers design, try out and evaluate – if possible in co-operation with students – different learning activities, and decide what worked well, and for whom (Rijlaarsdam, Braaksma, & Couzijn, 2002). A classroom is a communicative learning environment where learning takes place as a joint responsibility and a joint interest of both teachers and students. For teaching language (and writing), setting up communicative learning situations fulfils a double goal: learning to communicate while communicating. Designing a learning environment or teaching sequences is a goal-directed activity, based on some strong theoretical assumptions. In this section, we will present some of the assumptions we discuss with teachers during initial and in-service training.

4.1 Thinking about Writing

Many researchers have reported that young writers carry out relatively few higher-order revision activities. MacArthur, Graham, and Harris (this volume) show that clear tasks (such as inducing a task representation: What should be done with this text?) can stimulate children to evaluate their texts at higher levels. Wallace et al. (1996) showed something similar in university students. But the pressing question is why children do not develop such task representations themselves (some stronger writers do, the weaker writers do not appear to do so). But, in fact, why should they? What is the motive to develop such task schemas? It is important for teachers to understand how the concept of writing develops and how education contributes, mostly implicitly, to the construction of that concept.

Young writers, in preschool and the early primary grades, are glad when they succeed in producing something on paper or on a screen. Their first and foremost concern is to produce a text, to make up a story, and they are usually proud if they succeed. They feel like they are real writers! Such as the authors they know from their storybooks. "Mama, I can write!" It is the same with drawing: children have pleasure in making drawings, irrespective of whether they meet adult standards or not. Writing starts as a form of play. The concept of writing in younger children is the concept of the creator, the narrator or the storyteller. Little revision takes place because young writers are easily pleased with any kind of story they produce. In the content-generation phase, some thoughts may get revised or elaborated upon, but after a sentence has been written down, it rarely changes. And when young children "read" their story, they sometimes read the intended and not the written story.

At a certain moment in the educational process, text quality is introduced as a concept: children learn that a text must "look good." Writing becomes part of the language curriculum, and the function of writing texts becomes ambiguous: writing is fun and writing is part of communication. For children, this can be a confusing phase, because fun in writing is mixed with feelings of uncertainty. Writing texts is now also understood as an exercise in which newly learned things must be implemented, that is, neat handwriting, correct spelling, and correct grammar. Correctness becomes the norm for good writing; in the best cases, this norm is combined with sharing texts with other class members (reading aloud in the classroom, exhibits of texts). Now the teacher not only reacts to the fact that the pupil succeeded in writing a text ("Fine! Well done!"), but also becomes the gatekeeper of correct language. Here children start to revise what writing researchers call "lower-order" aspects of their texts, but these aspects are absolutely not "lower order" things in children's minds. Many children fail to correct all mistakes, it seems that they simply cannot see them all, although they steadily do improve in the correct application of all kinds of linguistic rules (see Largy, Chanquoy, & Dedeyan, this volume).

During primary education, some kind of instruction on the textual or stylistic level, or with respect to genre, is introduced: how to start a story, how to describe characters, how to use adjectives in descriptions, etc. Another concept about writing tasks emerges: writing texts demands the competency to include newly learned textual features. Writing becomes more and more loaded down with requirements. As the complexity of the task increases, teachers make stronger attempts at embedding these activities in an inspiring motivational context. Otherwise writing becomes something that "has to be done for school", like mathematics, writing is "doing writing exercises". At the same time, writing is increasingly used in other disciplines: writing projects are carried out, individually as well as cooperatively, about all kinds of topics in geography, history, etc. Here pupils have to cope with the acquisition of relatively complex content and the delivery in written format, with or without restrictions set by the teacher. At this stage, revision takes place on the content level as well as the word and sentence level. Thus writers must learn to juggle with various levels of text quality, with obligatory, rule-based elements (spelling), and more diffuse qualities (genre knowledge, rhetorical quality), that cannot all be taken care of simultaneously.

At the end of primary education, functional writing becomes part of the curriculum: writing texts with a communicative intent or writing transactional texts as they can occur in real life. At this stage, it becomes possible to put (part of) the evaluation of text quality in the hands of readers: Will they accept the text and will they respond as the writer intended?

Within a very limited number of years of schooling, pupils are confronted with different concepts of written texts. They have to cope with an increasing number of requirements, while still developing vocabulary and linguistic forms and structures (i.e., syntax, spelling, grammar). In these early years, attitudes towards writing and feelings about authorship also develop: representations of what writing is, how it can be done, what kind of fun it may offer. In our view, the way in which writing is taught greatly influences all aspects of children's thinking about writing.

4.2 *Thinking about Learning to Write*

A writing task is an educational means for learning. When writing a project for history, children learn two different things: something about history, and as a side-effect, something about writing. When the writing task is used as a means for learning to write, children learn something about an educational subject, which is writing ("how to make a text understandable") and about the learning activity, which is also writing. These two learning outcomes are different for teachers and for children. A good learning-to-write task yields improvement of the student's writing skills, and, as a side-effect, it usually also yields a good text. From an educational point of view, the latter (the text) is of secondary importance, but it is usually the only way to arrive at the former (improved writing skill).

So a writing student has to do two things at the same time: learning and writing. Yet how difficult it is for children to learn while they write. Writing is in itself such a mentally demanding task, that learning while writing is extremely demanding. For this phenomenon, we use the metaphor of the "dual agenda" (Rijlaarsdam & Couzijn, 2000a, 2000b; Braaksma, Van den Bergh, Rijlaarsdam, & Couzijn, 2001). The most dominant of the two goals is writing: to create a product that meets the requirements of the writing task. It is difficult for a child to know beforehand whether the text she is writing will meet these requirements: writing is often just an attempt to see if and how one can meet the requirements or not. When the text is finished, the task may be accomplished. But that does not necessarily mean that the parallel learning task has also been brought to a good end, that is, that knowledge, attitude, and skills have been improved. Writing is not only a productive skill (making something) but also a reflective skill (monitoring one's own knowledge and performance). Therefore, it is an important teacher activity to provide opportunities to reflect before, during, and after writing. If there are no such opportunities, only the better and more autonomous students will purposely develop writing skill, on their own.

Learning to write is building theories about text and communication. Theories are arrived at by setting goals, for instance in the form of producing and checking hypotheses, such as (1) if I have to write a text with a beginning that attracts readers' attention, I could start with an actual fact, or (2) if my writing should be more interesting for readers, I could include more concrete examples.

We recognize three problems that hinder learning in writing:

1) The fact that most students are not competent, routine writers, and therefore have to pay considerable attention to the text production process itself (the "writing" part of the double agenda).

2) The fact that many hypotheses about communication and writing, if present, are en-passant, implicit, tacit, or unconscious. They may play a certain role in learning, but the testing of these hypotheses is rarely conscious or overt. For in-

stance, a writer may start an essay about "the meaning of homework" with a concrete example because she thinks her classmates will recognize and accept it. Or she does not feel like inserting counter-arguments in her essay because she fears it will weaken her defense of her own viewpoint. Such ideas are intuitions rather than explicit hypotheses, and their effects may be never checked during or after the drafting process. They merely guide the writer's activities for a moment and may actually have a strong impact on the text quality, but the writer is not capable of externalizing and purposely checking these hypotheses.

3) Even when some of these hypotheses are consciously evoked, it is often beyond the capability of the writer to check whether the text meets the requirements or not, or whether the hypothesis can be confirmed or rejected. One reason is that the learner is constrained by her own perspective on her self-produced text. If she has included a certain news fact in her text and has to decide whether the intended passage is really recognizable as a news fact or not, the answer will be positive, because she knows she intended this as a news fact. When she asks herself whether this news fact is really interesting for readers or not, she will again answer "yes", because she intended to write something interestingly and has chosen this news fact for this purpose. It needs to be realized, however, that the answer to such questions is not in fact a simple "yes" or "no." Text quality is a relative and continuous property, not an absolute one. Whether a particular sentence or passage adds to overall text quality is difficult to determine: A text may not be badly written, yet it could still be improved. This implies that learners will hardly ever reach the "best possible text": they make one attempt, drawing from a small repertoire of knowledge and experiences, and produce one imperfect solution, not aware of the multiple solutions that would be possible.

A writing task that is not accompanied by support for learning cannot be very effective. Writing tasks are a necessary but insufficient condition for learning. Here the contributions of the creative teacher come in with attempts to use revision as a tool for supporting learning. In the next section, we will explain how this may happen.

4.3 *Thinking about Teaching-to-Write: Revision as a Learning Tool that includes Feedback*

Once they have completed a version of their text, most writers feel relieved: "Ah, finally done." They need some kind of stimulus to reconsider or rewrite their draft. For most writers, this stimulus comes from outside[2]. They need readers – colleagues,

---

[2] *Even expert writers call for external feedback when writing is difficult or important. When they write a strategic document, or a letter which is intended to have important implications, they ask colleagues to read the piece to check to what extent the text could raise unintended resistance with its audience. Writing difficult texts requires extra "hands-on" advice: even in the SIG Writing group of EARLI, composed of experts on writing, very few members have experienced an occasion where a submitted article was accepted without requests for revisions.*

peers – to estimate effects on readers, to detect flaws or omissions in the line of thinking, to detect redundancy (relics of the thinking process during writing), etc. By invoking the help of readers, writers create an opportunity to learn from their writing: They know that their text is not perfect and that it can be improved, and they look for ways in which to do that.

In writing instruction, systematic attention paid to revision activities may serve as a powerful learning tool. Revision, including feedback, guides the student's attention specifically to potential improvements of written texts and text plans. It reflects what adult/expert writers do (improving first drafts) and it involves real audience (teacher and/or peer readers). It disconnects the burden of writing (producing text) from the burden of learning (evaluating and improving text), thus making way for the "double agenda."

Implementing revision as a learning tool requires at least two components: (1) incentives for evaluation of the written text (e.g., readers' feedback) and (2) opportunities to apply the results from component (1) while writing.

Hillocks (1986) characterized both of these learning activities as "post-writing instruction." His meta-analysis of intervention studies on writing showed that the largest effect sizes were observed in studies that implemented specific feedback criteria, and included comments from both peers and the teacher. Non-specific feedback from peers and teachers was less effective, but still more effective than non-specific feedback from teachers only. Unfortunately, Hillocks could not find enough studies that met his methodological criteria to identify the effects of specific feedback from peers only. But from our own analysis of studies in which peer response was confronted with teacher feedback, we know that peer feedback results in at least the same quality of texts as that resulting from teacher feedback, and that in eight out of twenty studies, peer feedback outperformed teacher feedback (Rijlaarsdam, 1987).

So two important features of the feedback component have been identified: (1) involving peers, and (2) working with specific comments or feedback criteria. Specific feedback sheets are important, because they help students to focus their evaluation and connect evaluation to the learning goal (Why should I evaluate my peers' texts on criterion X? Because I had to write a text meeting criterion X and now I can learn by evaluating my peers' texts how to improve my own text on criterion X). When instruction is provided on writing an introduction that attracts readers' attention, then "attracting readers interest" is one of the response categories to use in evaluation/revision of texts. When writing a text of instructions is the learning goal, then a reader's success in carrying out the instructions could constitute the ultimate concrete feedback (see, for such experiments, Couzijn & Rijlaarsdam, 1996; Holliway & McCutchen, this volume).

The way in which peers are involved as feedback providers may vary (Elbow, 1981). First, they can be the intended readers of the text: for example, in the case

---

That is not to say that such writers do not have some ideas about text quality: in most instances, the readers' feedback supports evaluations already made by the author. Nevertheless, writers need multiple readers to inform them about effects of the text.

that a text of instructions was aimed at this audience, or when a persuasive text about the organization of a school outing was meant to convince them to go to a certain place. Readers react subjectively, which is a valid and normal behavior that may result in multiple and varied responses. That is an important thing to learn for any writer: responses to one's text will probably vary. After all, the concept of "the" reader is a mere abstraction. Variation in readers' responses is valid, although difficult for the author to process when a text has to be revised on the base of multiple and varied responses. There is no one-to-one relationship between text and reader.

Second, peers can act as commentators. Commenting includes reading, but requires a more objective stance with respect to the text. It means that peers not only respond to the rhetorical quality of the introduction, but can also provide some analyses about why a particular passage fails to attract readers' attention, and they may even add suggestions to improve the introduction (see Hayes et al.'s (1987) distinctions between detection, diagnosis, and remedy). "Commentators" often provide more assistance with diagnosis and remedy than mere "readers" do. They may identify more strongly with the writer and her task than with the task of reading.[3]

Getting multiple feedback stimulates the writing student to reconsider her text. This is even more the case when she can compare her writing with that of peers and become aware of other solutions to the same task. She thus extends her repertoire and knowledge about texts beyond her own production. She may be more receptive of the feedback she gets and develop more ability to choose from the feedback, because of her better understanding of the relative quality of her own text.

To sum up, to make revision useful as a learning tool, three instructional decisions play a role: (1) to involve peers as feedback providers (readers, users of texts; or commentators), (2) to provide peers with specific feedback tasks related to the learning aims of the particular writing lesson, (3) to provide multiple texts to read for each reader, and multiple readers to comment on each writer's text. This assures multiple feedback per text, as well as multiple opportunities to discover various texts in the reader role.

Two further decisions about how to create an optimal revision phase have to be made, concerning the content and the form of feedback. Regarding the *content* of peer feedback, we consider comments from peers in their role of co-readers as the most valid peer evaluations, particularly on aspects of communicative effectiveness, content and organization of the text, audience-orientation, etc. Evaluation can also be related to rhetorical aspects of the texts: does the text do what it should do, and is there something to delete, change, and/or add to improve the communicative effect? Peers in their role of co-readers are real language users. They are interested in the topic and in what the writer has to say about it. Their opinions about what works, whether something is missing in the text, or something is unclear, redundant or not

---

[3] *The distinction between the role of "reader" and the role of "commentator" corresponds in reality to a continuum. The underlying theoretical dimension is conceived as follows a reader responds in a natural way, being the intended reader, undergoing the communicative impact of the piece of writing, while a commentator estimates the communicative effect, and estimates whether the piece of writing includes elements that contributes to that effect. The reader is a participant in the communication; the commentator fulfils also another role.*

related to the communicative aim, are valid – even though they are not expert writers themselves. These *opinions* are more valid than their marking of spelling errors and linguistic problems. Their role is that of an assistant, a helper; they are not expected to stand in the shoes of the red pencil-marking teacher.

The *form* of feedback is usually written. This has some advantages over oral feedback. In a study on the effects of feedback, Couzijn (1995; Couzijn & Rijlaarsdam, 1996; Couzijn & Rijlaarsdam, 2002) found that written comments had additional effects on learning results for both the feedback giver as the feedback receiver. Also, reading texts aloud, while inserting online reader feedback, which is audio-taped and played back to the learner, can have strong effects (see Berner, Boswell & Kahan, 1996; see also Lumbelli, Paoletti, Camagni & Frausin, 1996; Boscolo & Asorti, this volume). Another possibility is to show real readers on videotape, who "use" or respond to the text. This is particularly the case when the text has an observable communicative effect, as in texts of instructions. For instance, seeing a video that shows a peer who reads your instructions, and tries to follow them, proved to result in a strong learning gain. Moreover, a videotape showing a reader's usage of a text written by someone else than the writing student resulted in learning gains for this student (Couzijn & Rijlaarsdam, 1996).

After having received feedback, and having acquired more knowledge about texts and a better understanding of what a good text in this situation entails, the learner should have the opportunity to use this new knowledge in a subsequent revision task. The most obvious task is to return to the starting task (to revise the text, to rewrite the text) or to undertake a transfer task (a different but similar writing assignment). In both conditions, it is useful to implement a planning task consisting of processing the feedback into a plan for rewriting or revising. Not all feedback needs to be included into the revision, so some thoughtful selection needs to be made. The reflection on the quality of one's own written text could be enhanced if the learner processes the feedback she got: making categories of the feedback, relating remarks to particular texts passages, evaluating the remarks, and accounting for what feedback she accepts (i.e., sees as valid comments). From this insight, the learner can plan a revision or rewriting phase: What should be improved and how should the improvement be realized? Because the content generation and organization is done beforehand, the learner can then concentrate on the learning agenda, leaving the writing agenda aside. From a learning psychology perspective, one might say that when writing a first version, the writing student shows her ability or *present developmental stage* as a writer, and when revising her text, she now purposefully moves forward in her *zone of proximal development*.

5.   TWO PROSPECTIVE RESEARCH AGENDAS

5.1 *Revision as a Writing Process: A Prospective Research Agenda*

Research into writing processes, or more specifically into the revision process, should at least try to relate process variables with text quality and cognitive skills, as described above. As we have advocated, an exclusive focus on process variables may well yield hard to interpret and even misleading conclusions. Thus, a general framework and a multi-method approach could make a difference in research progress.

Our minimal and therefore favorite description of a model of writing processes is "a certain configuration of certain cognitive activities" (Rijlaarsdam & Van den Bergh, 1996). The minimal assumption in this model is that all writing processes rely on the same set of cognitive activities. In principle, all activities can occur in all combinations at any time during the writing process. In different combinations, at different moments in the writing process, a cognitive activity can function differently: for example, reading already-written text can be the input for a generating activity but also for a text-evaluation activity. The actual function of these activities depends to some extent on their environment. Although all possible configurations can exist, some will be more effective under some circumstances than others. It seems reasonable to assume that not all activities contribute to the quality of the resulting texts: At certain moments during writing, writers will suffer from lack of concentration and will cognitively doodle and dazzle. Some differences in processes within and between writers can be called "free variation," while other differences are "effective variation." What writing process research aims at is to describe which configurations of cognitive activities are better predictors of text quality. We can use this definition of writing processes in trying to set an agenda for the study of revision.

5.1.1 Definitions and Main Research Questions

We have already discussed the definition of revision. In our proposal for the research agenda, we focus on revision as reflecting/reconsidering already-written text. We take (nearly) automatic processes of editing into account, however, in order to distinguish them from more deliberate (non-automatic) processes of revision. Too often, little effort is made to distinguish these processes. When transformations are the focus of study, distinctions need to be made between obligatory-optional (see Allal, this volume) and target-not targeted transformations (Piolat et al., this volume).

The main descriptive research questions concerning revision in our opinion are:

1) How can we conceptually define and how can we operationally measure, the distinction between automatic correction of text and the goal directed non-automatic reflection on already-written text?

2) When does non-automatic reflection on already-written text occur during the writing process?

3) How is this activity related to other cognitive activities, and do these relations changes during the writing process? Do some activities trigger non-automatic reflection on already-written text, and under what circumstances?

4) What is the relation of this activity with the text quality? Does that relation change during the course of the writing process?

These rather simple questions will give insight when we take other variables into account while searching for generalization and explanation.

5.1.2   Generalization

One problem in writing process research is the generalization of findings across tasks, task conditions, and writers' characteristics. No such thing as "the" writing process exists, since processes in reality show large variances across tasks, situations, and writers. On second thought then, the issue of generalization is not so much a problem as a set of research perspectives and a way to stipulate areas of study for a research agenda. In the following paragraphs we will describe a number of distinctions that deserve systematic study.

Across Writing Tasks. In one of our studies (Van den Bergh et al., 1994), all participants wrote two argumentative essays on similar topics; topics were counterbalanced across sessions. Writing processes were recorded by means of thinking-aloud protocol analysis. For thirteen out of eighteen processes, the within-writer-variance proved to be task-dependent. Sub-processes of all the three main processes (rereading, evaluating, and changing) obviously were task dependent. This implies that it is not possible to generalize findings across writing tasks, although in many studies on writing processes, participants wrote just one essay and researchers suggested that the findings were not task-dependent. In our view, writing process research that involves writing-aloud protocols, observation, key-logging, or dual task loadings (Piolat et al., this volume) should implement multiple tasks per participant. As a result, the task-dependency of the findings can be controlled.

Across Task Conditions. Are the answers on the main questions different for different task contexts? Writers may differ in the degree and the way they adapt their default skills and strategies to task conditions: the writing goal or purpose, the intended audience, the writing medium, acquaintance with the text type, etc. Van Waes (1991), for instance, found that if we compare pen-and-paper with computer writing conditions, some writers do not show varying writing profiles, while other writers clearly do. Writers apparently differ in the extent to which they recognize assignment features, resulting in different task representations. If task representation governs the writing process, task conditions may trigger revision differently.

Across Writers' Profiles. Are the answers to the main questions different for different writers, who have different writing profiles, monitor configurations (Hayes & Flower, 1980) or default task schemata (Hayes, 1996) or revision task schemes (Hayes, this volume)? Writers may differ with regard to the "default" of the parameter setting that corresponds to the way they accomplish writing tasks. Some writers are accustomed to carrying out planning activities in the first part of the process, then moving on to formulating in the second episode of writing, and then to reviewing, revising and editing. Other writers first attempt to "say as much as they can" on the topic, trying to find a particular focus. They write in order to find meaning and are prepared to completely redraft the paper in a later stage. These two types of writers can be identified by their default settings of the probabilities of occurrence of particular writing activities. For instance, the first type will show a high probability of generating and structuring activities in the beginning of the process, while the second type will show a high probability of generating in the beginning and a low probability of structuring (see Galbraith & Torrance, this volume). When we study revision, we should be aware that our "general findings" include a number of different writers' profiles for which revision may have a different function in their writing strategy.

Across Writers' Cognitive Functioning. Are the answers to the main question different for different levels of cognitive functioning? A good divergent thinker will generate text with a different quality than a writer with a lower level of divergent thinking. And this difference will influence the configuration of cognitive writing activities. For instance, while writers at the beginning of the writing process may perform the activity "reading the writing assignment" to an certain extent, differences between writers may show up later in the process as a result of their ability to read the writing task *well*. Good readers will return less often to this activity than less-able readers, who may process the task demands one-by-one.

Two studies illustrate the importance of including cognitive functioning in writing research. Piolat et al. (this volume) observed that undergraduate writers with a high working memory were better when revising text than writers with a relatively low working span. Van den Bergh showed that cognitive skill, measured as Structure of intellectual abilities (Guilford, 1971), accounted for 52% of the variance in text quality (Van den Bergh, 1988). In this study, however, it appeared that especially the interactions between such cognitive skills are relevant for writing. That is, students with high working memory scores, and good evaluation skills, or good working memory skills and good formulation skills proved to be better writers: students who did not do well at one of these tasks clearly did not write as well.

Across Writers' Writing Expertise. Are the answers to the main question different for different levels of writing competence, for instance for "good" and "weak" novices (Elshout, 1994; Rijlaarsdam, 1993; Torrance, 1996)? How do good novices adapt their processes under new and maybe therefore difficult circumstances, and how do they learn from such events? How do different levels of competence contribute to different representations of the assignment? How do writers compensate for weaknesses in their default configuration and/or cognitive functioning? The fact that one writer more often reads the assignment during the writing process, as a consequence of a low reading ability, may have a *compensatory* function, as compared to the more able reader who analyzes and synthesizes the gist of the task almost immediately. If the writer compensates sufficiently, then the difference in process frequency will not be related to text quality. Hence, writing is to be considered an interactive and compensatory process.

5.2 *Revision as a Learning Tool: A Prospective Research Agenda*

In section 4.3, we laid out a meta-script, including several options for the use of revision as a learning tool in writing education. We see four main questions for educational research in this domain:

1) Is there a separate effect of the feedback component and the revision component on declarative knowledge (awareness of readers, genre, repertoire of rhetorical strategies, insight about coherence, etc.), on writing process and skill, and on transfer (e.g., to reading skill)?

2) Is it necessary to receive feedback on one's own text or is it possible to reach the same learning effects when one evaluates and revises texts written by others? In other words, is the writing and revision of one's own original text a necessary condition to learn from revision activities? (Cf. Hillocks's (1986) description of working with essay scales).

3) If the answer to question 2 is yes, is it then necessary to implement the meta-script in a "post-writing" instructional format or can we recreate it in the form of pre-writing instruction with the same or even more effect? In our meta-script, the learning phase is the reconsideration phase, or revision phase, applied on the text the learner wrote as a response to a writing prompt, aimed at the acquisition of a new learning content ("how to attract readers' attention in the beginning", "writing instructions for a physics experiment"). But more or less the same activities could be organized before writing the beginning or instructional text. In that case, learners work on a set of given texts, evaluate them, share comments, build knowledge about rhetoric and instructional texts, and then write texts themselves.

4) In the meta-script in section 4, the text used as input for the revision phase was a first version, meant to be read by others. Depending on the writer's profile, such a version could result from multiple drafts. From Galbraith's studies (Galbraith, 1996, 1999; Galbraith & Torrance, this volume), it becomes clear that different writers make different use of the revision phase. Writers who use the first draft to find out what they have to say about the topic must analyze this draft very thoroughly and must learn to use this text only as a springboard for thinking, but not for writing. How can these writers be effectively trained to do so?

6.   CONCLUSION

In this chapter, we discussed three issues in writing process and writing education research. We considered the definition of revision, and questioned the attention which writing researchers give to revision. Thirdly, we analyzed the role of revision in writing education, pointing at the necessity of an incentive to revise texts, and the role of readers' and/or peer feedback. We concluded this chapter with two research agendas, one for writing research on revision, and one for educational research on the conditions for revision as an instructional device in language education.

To conclude this chapter, we would like to raise awareness about some methodological issues in writing research and educational research on writing.

Instrumentation: Measuring Text Quality. More than half of the studies reported in this volume discussed the effects of revision activities on text quality. We agree that quality of the resulting text is what we strive for in education, not for a higher number of revisions *per se*. However, in the reported studies, text quality is hardly defined, operationalized, or validated. It would help enormously if researchers could agree upon a well-defined set of writing prompts, rating procedures, and essay scales.

Unit of Analysis. In our opinion, much of present-day writing research uses a too small unit of analysis, irrespective of the research methodology applied (process studies, think-aloud studies, dual task methodology, key-logging, etc.). Revision seems to be regarded as the number of times that a writer makes a transformation. However, the longer we studied writing-aloud protocols, the more we become aware that the meaningful unit is not the mere occurrence of revision. Just as a sentence is built on constituents larger than a word, writing processes are strings of cognitive activities. These strings form certain patterns. Writers differ in the type and length of these constituents and patterns. In other words, we have to take into account the context of each act of revision in order to find the rhythm in the process, that is, the recurring patterns.

Writers and not revisions should be the unit of analysis. In writing research, we try to generalize over writers, not over revisions. Revisions are nested within persons: the meaning of a certain revisions is different for different writers. We should not equate the correction of a spelling error by a young writer with the same correction by an expert writer.

Educational studies: Measurements. Measures of knowledge about texts, writing skill and transfer should be included where possible. The same holds for measures on writing processes, even if – for reasons of efficiency and costs – only a small sample of the students included in effect studies can be measured (see, for an example, Braaksma et al., in press). Measures of implementation should be included to explain differences in the way students allocated time and effort to different subtasks. Relating these differences to learning gains will help us understand the contribution of the various components to the learning gains (see Braaksma et al., 2001). This type of *post hoc* analysis may contribute to theoretical insights about the elements of the molar instructional arrangement which are effective.

Educational Studies: Different Writers, Different Interventions. Variations of the treatment for different writers should be included in research (see Galbraith & Torrance, this volume). It is quite remarkable that, in many studies, differences in writers' profiles are neglected, although we are aware that different writers have different needs to exploit their strengths and to improve their weaknesses.

ACKNOWLEDGEMENTS

We would like to thank our colleague Martine Braaksma for her thoughtful comments. Linda Allal and Lucile Chanquoy, volume editors, skillfully helped us with their critical review through the first versions of this chapter.

REFERENCES

Alamargot, D., & Chanquoy, L. (2001). *Studies in writing: Vol. 9. Through the models of writing.* Dordrecht: Kluwer Academic Publishers.

Alamargot, D., Favart, M., & Galbraith, D. (2000, September). *Evolution of ideas in argumentative writing: Writing as a knowledge-constituting process.* Paper presented at 7th EARLI SIG Writing conference, Verona, Italy.

Alexander, P. A., Schallert, D. L., & Hare, V. C. (1991). Coming to terms: How researchers in learning and literacy talk about knowledge. *Review of Educational Research, 61*, 315-343.

Allal, L. (1988). Vers un élargissement de la pédagogie de maîtrise: Processus de régulation interactive, rétroactive et proactive. In M. Huberman (Ed.), *Assurer la réussite des apprentissages scolaires* (pp. 86-126). Neuchâtel: Delachaux & Niestlé.

Allal, L. (2000). Metacognitive regulation of writing in the classroom. In A. Camps & M. Milian (Eds.), *Studies in writing: Vol. 6. Metalinguistic activity in learning to write* (pp. 145-166). Amsterdam: Amsterdam University Press.

Allal, L. (2001). Situated cognition and learning: From conceptual frameworks to classroom investigations. *Revue Ssuisse des Sciences de l' Education, 23*, 407-422.

Allal, L., Bétrix Köhler, D., L. Rieben, L., Rouiller Barbey, Y., Saada-Robert, M., & Wegmuller, E. (2001). *Apprendre l' orthographe en produisant des textes.* Fribourg: Editions Universitaires.

Allal, L., & Saada-Robert, M. (1992). La métacognition: Cadre conceptuel pour l'étude des régulations en situation scolaire. *Archives de Psychologie, 60*, 265-296.

Allal, L., Rouiller, Y., & Saada-Robert, M. (1995). Autorégulation en production textuelle: Observation de quatre élèves de 12 ans. *Cahier d' Acquisition et de Pathologie du Langage, 13*, 17-35.

Anderson, J. R. (1983). *The architecture of cognition.* Cambridge, MA: Harvard University Press.

Anderson, J. R. (1993). *Rules of the mind.* Hillsdale, N.J.: Laurence Erlbaum.

Anderson, J. R. (1995). *Learning and memory: An integrated approach.* New York: John Wiley.

Anderson, J. R., & Fincham, J. M. (1994). Acquisition of procedural skills from examples. *Journal of Experimental Psychology: Learning, Memory, and Cognition, 20*(6), 1322-1340.

Baddeley, A. D. (1986). *Working Memory.* Oxford: Oxford University Press.

Baddeley, A. D. (1990). *Human memory: Theory and practice.* Boston: Allyn & Bacon.

Baddeley, A. D. (1996). Exploring the central executive. *Quarterly Journal of Experimental Psychology, 49A*, 5-28.

Baddeley, A. D. (2000). The episodic buffer: A new component of working memory? *Trends in Cognitive Sciences, 4*(11), 417-423.

Bangert-Drowns, R. L. (1993). The word processor as an instructional tool: A meta-analysis of word processing in writing instruction. *Review of Educational Research, 63*, 69-93.

Bartlett, E. J. (1982). Learning to revise: Some component processes. In M. Nystrand (Ed.), *What writers know: The language, process, and the structure of written discourse* (pp. 345-363). New York: Academic Press.

Beal, C. R. (1990). The development of text evaluation and revising skills. *Child Development, 61*, 247-258.

Beal, C. R. (1996). The role of comprehension monitoring in children's revision. *Educational Psychology Review, 8*, 219-238.

Beal, C. & Flavell, J. (1984). Development of the ability to distinguish communicative intention and literal message. *Child Development, 55*, 920-928.

Benson, N. L. (1979). *The effect of peer feedback during the writing process on writing performance, revision behavior, and attitude toward writing.* Unpublished doctoral dissertation, University of Colorado at Boulder.

Bereiter, C., & Scardamalia, M. (1987). *The psychology of written composition.* Hillsdale, NJ: Lawrence Erlbaum.

210

Berkenkotter, C. (1981). Understanding a writer's awareness of audience. *College Composition and Communication, 32,* 388-399.

Berner, A., Boswell, W., & Kahan, N. (1996). Using the tape recorder to respond to student writers. In G. Rijlaarsdam, H. Van den Bergh, & M. Couzijn (Eds.). *Studies in writing: Vol. 2. Effective teaching and learning of writing. Current trends in research* (pp 339-357). Amsterdam: Amsterdam University Press.

Berninger, V. W., Abbott, R. D., Whitaker, D., Sylvester, L., & Nolen, S. B. (1995). Integrating low- and high-level skills in instructional protocols for writing disabilities. *Learning Disability Quarterly, 18,* 293-309.

Berninger, V. W., & Swanson, H. L. (1994). Modification of the Hayes and Flower model to explain beginning and developing writing. In E. Butterfield (Ed.), *Advances in cognition and educational practice, Vol. 2: Children's writing: Toward a process theory of development of skilled writing* (pp. 57-82). Greenwich, CT: JAI Press.

Berninger, V. W., Whitaker, D., Feng, Y., Swanson, H. L., & Abbott, R. D. (1996). Assessment of planning, translating and revising in junior high writers. *Journal of School Psychology, 34*(1), 23-52.

Bétrix Köhler, D. (1995). *Orthographe en questions.* Lausanne: Centre Vaudois de Recherches Pédagogiques.

Bialystok, E. (1991). *Language processing in bilingual children.* Cambridge, UK: Cambridge University Press.

Bisaillon, J. (1992). La révision de textes: Un processus à enseigner pour l'amélioration des productions écrites. *The Canadian Modern Language Review, 48*(2), 276-291.

Bock, J. K. (1995). Producing agreements. *Current Directions in Psychological Science, 4,* 56-61.

Bock, J. K., & Cutting, J. C. (1992). Regulating mental energy: Performance units in language production. *Journal of Memory and Language, 31,* 99-127.

Bock, J. K., & Eberhard, K. M. (1993). Meaning, sound and syntax in English number agreement. *Language and Cognitive Processes, 8,* 57-99.

Bock, J. K., & Miller, C. A. (1991). Broken agreement. *Cognitive Psychology, 23,* 45-93.

Bonitatibus, G. J. & Flavell, J. (1985). Effect of presenting a message in written form on young children's ability to evaluate its communicative adequacy. *Developmental Psychology, 21*(3), 455-461.

Bonk, C. (1990). A synthesis of social cognition and writing research. *Written Communication, 7,* 136-163.

Boscolo, P. (1995). The cognitive approach to writing and writing instruction: A contribution to a critical appraisal. *Current Psychology of Cognition, 14*(4), 343-366.

Boscolo, P., & Cisotto, L. (1999). On narrative reading-writing relationships: How young writers construe the reader's need for inferences. In S. R. Goldman, A. C. Graesser, & P. Van den Broek (Eds.), *Narrative comprehension, causality, and coherence: Essays in honor of Tom Trabasso* (pp. 161-178). Mahwah, NJ: Lawrence Erlbaum.

Bourdin, B., & Fayol, M. (1994). Is written language production more difficult than oral language production? A working memory approach. *International Journal of Psychology, 29,* 591-620.

Bourdin, B., & Fayol, M. (1996). Mode effects in a sentence production span task. *Current Psychology of Cognition, 15*(3), 245-264.

Braaksma, M. A. H., Rijlaarsdam, G., Van den Bergh, H., & Van Hout-Wolters, B. (in press). Observational learning and effects on orchestration of writing processes. *Cognition and Instruction, 22*(1).

Braaksma, M. A. H., Van den Bergh, H., Rijlaarsdam, G., & Couzijn, M. (2001). Effective learning activities in observation tasks when learning to write and read argumentative texts. *European Journal of Psychology of Education, 1,* 33-48.

Bracewell, R., Scardamalia, M., & Bereiter, C. (1978). The development of audience awareness in writing. *ERIC Document, ED* 154 433.

Breetvelt, I., Van den Bergh, H., & Rijlaarsdam, G. (1994). Relations between writing processes and text quality: When and how? *Cognition and Instruction, 12*(2), 103-123.

Breetvelt, I., Van den Bergh, H., & Rijlaarsdam, G. (1996). Rereading and generating and their relation to text quality: An application of multilevel analysis on writing process data. In G. Rijlaarsdam, H. Van den Bergh, & M. Couzijn (Eds.), *Studies in writing: Vol. 1. Theories, models and methodology in writing research* (pp. 10-21). Amsterdam: Amsterdam University Press.

Bridwell, L. S. (1980). Revising strategies in twelfth grade students' transactional writing. *Research in the Teaching of English, 14,* 197-222.

Britton, J., Burgess, T., Martin, N., McLeod, A., & Rosen, H. (1975). *The development of writing abilities*. London: MacMillan Education.

Brown, A. L., & Palinscar, M. S. (1982). Inducing strategic learning from texts by means of informed, self-control training. *Topics in Learning & Learning Disabilities, 2*, 1-17.

Brown, J. S., Collins, A., & Duguid, P. (1989). Situated cognition and the culture of learning. *Educational Researcher, 18*(1), 32-42.

Bruner, J. S. (1960). *The process of education*. New York: Vintage

Bruner, J. (1996). *The culture of education*. Cambridge, MA: Harvard University Press.

Butterfield, E. C., Hacker, D. J., & Albertson, L. R. (1996). Environmental, cognitive, and metacognitive influences on text revision: Assessing the evidence. *Educational Psychology Review, 8*(3), 239-260.

Butterfield, E. C., Hacker, D. J., & Plumb, C. (1994). Topic knowledge, linguistic knowledge, and revision processes as determinants of text revision. In J. S. Carlson, & E. C. Butterfield (Eds.), *Advances in cognition and educational practice: Vol. 2: Children's writing: Toward a process theory of the development of skilled writing* (pp. 83-143). Greenwich, CT: JAI Press.

Calkins, L. M. (1986). *The art of teaching writing*. Portsmouth, NH: Heinemann.

Cameron, C. A., Edmunds, G., Wigmore, B., Hunt, A. K., & Linton, M. J. (1997). Children's revision of textual flaws. *International Journal of Behavioral Development, 20*(4), 667-680.

Cameron, C. A., Hunt, A. K., & Linton, M. J. (1996). Written expression as recontextualization: Children write in social time. *Educational Psychology Review, 8*, 125-150.

Canale, M., & Swain, M. (1980). Theoretical bases of communicative approaches to second language teaching and testing. *Applied Linguistics, 1*, 1-47.

Chafe, W. L. (1986). Writing in the perspective of speaking. In C. R. C. S. Greenbaum (Ed.), *Studying writing: Linguistic approaches*. Beverly Hills, CA: Sage.

Chandler, D. (1992). The phenomenology of writing by hand. *Intelligent Tutoring Media, 3*, 65-74.

Chandler, M. (1977). Social cognition: A select review in current research. In W. Overton & J. McCarthy Gallagher (Eds.), *Knowledge and development* (pp. 93 -148). New York: Plenum Press.

Chanquoy, L. (1997). Thinking skills and composing: Examples of text revision. In J. H. M. Hamers, & M. Overtoom (Eds.), *Inventory of European Programmes for teaching thinking* (pp. 179-185). Utrecht: Sardes.

Chanquoy, L. (2001). How to make it easier for children to revise their writing: A study of text revision from 3rd to 5th grades. *British Journal of Educational Psychology, 71*, 15-41.

Chanquoy, L., & Negro, I. (1996). Subject-verb agreement errors in written productions. Study in French children and adults. *Journal of Psycholinguistic Research, 25*(5), 553-570.

Chanquoy, L., Piolat, A., & Roussey, J. Y. (1996, September). Effects of self questionning on text revising: A study with children of 7, 9, and 13 years of age. Paper presented at the International Congress "The Growing Mind", Geneva, Switzerland.

Chenoweth, N. A., & Hayes, J. R. (2001). Fluency in writing: Generating text in L1 and L2. *Written Communication, 18*, 80-98.

Chenoweth, N. A., & Hayes, J. R. (2003). The inner voice in writing. *Written Communication, 20*, 99-118.

Clifford, J. (1981). Composing in stages: The effects of a collaborative pedagogy. *Research in the Teaching of English, 15*(1), 37-58.

COROME (Commission romande des moyens d'enseignement). (1997). *Français – Expression. Conception d'ensemble*.

Couzijn, M. J. (1995). *Observation of writing and reading activities. Effects on learning and transfer*. Unpublished dissertation, University of Amsterdam.

Couzijn, M., & Rijlaarsdam, G. (1996). Learning to write by reader observation and written feedback. In G. Rijlaarsdam, H. Van den Bergh, & M. Couzijn (Eds.), *Studies in writing: Vol. 2. Effective teaching and learning of writing: Current trends in research* (pp 224-253). Amsterdam: Amsterdam University Press.

Couzijn, M., & Rijlaarsdam, G. (2002, September). *Learning about physics by explaining to peer students*. Paper presented at the conference on Foundations for language and science literacy research: philosophical, psychological, linguistic and cultural. Conference Victoria University, Victoria: Canada.

Crook, C. (1994). *Computers and the collaborative experience of learning*. London: Routledge.

Crowhurst, M., & Piché, G. L. (1979). Audience and mode of discourse effects on syntactic complexity in writing at two grade levels. *Research in the Teaching of English, 13*, 101-109.

Daiute, C. (1986). Do 1 and 1 make 2? Patterns of influence by collaborative authors. *Written Communication, 3,* 382-408.

Daiute, C. (1989). Play as thought: Thinking strategies of young writers. *Harvard Educational Review, 59*(1), 1-23.

Daiute, C. (1990). The role of play in writing development. *Research in the Teaching of English, 24,* 4-47.

Daiute, C., & Dalton, B. (1988). "Let's brighten it up a bit": Collaboration and cognition in writing. In B. A. Rafoth, & D. L. Rubin (Eds.), *The social construction of written communication* (pp. 249-269). Norwood, NJ: Ablex.

Daiute, C., & Dalton, B. (1993). Collaboration between children learning to write: Can novices be masters? *Cognition and Instruction, 10,* 281-333.

Dale, H. (1994). Collaborative writing interactions in one ninth-grade classroom. *Journal of Educational Research, 87,* 334-344.

Daneman, M., & Carpenter, P. A. (1980). Individual differences in comprehending and producing words in context. *Journal of Memory and Language, 25,* 1-18.

Daneman, M. & Stainton, M. (1993). The generation effect in reading and proofreading: Is it easier or harder to detect errors in one's own writing? *Reading & Writing, 5,* 297-313.

Daniles, H. (1990). Young writers and readers read out: Developing a sense of audience. In T. Shanahan (Ed.), *Reading and writing together: New perspectives for the classroom* (pp. 100 – 126). Norwood, MA: Christopher-Gordon Publishers.

Davies, A., Clarke, M. A., & Rhodes, L. K. (1994). Extended text and the writing proficiency of students in urban elementary schools. *Journal of Educational Psychology, 86,* 556-566.

De Keyser, R. (1995). Learning second language grammar rules: An experiment with a miniature linguistic system. *Studies in Second Language Acquisition, 17,* 379-410.

De La Paz, S., Swanson, P., & Graham, S. (1998). The contribution of executive control to the revising of students with writing and learning difficulties. *Journal of Educational Psychology. 90,* 448-460.

Demorest, A., Silberstein, L., Gardner, H., & Winner, E. (1983). Telling it as it isn't: Children's understanding of figurative language. *British Journal of Developmental Psychology, 1,* 121-134.

Deshler, D. D., & Schumaker, J. B. (1986). Learning strategies: An instructional alternative for low-achieving adolescents. *Exceptional Children, 52,* 583-590.

Desmette, D., Hupet, M., Schelstraete, M. A., & Van der Linden, M. (1995). Adaptation en langue française du 'Reading Span Test' de Danaman et Carpenter (1980). *L'Année Psychologique, 95,* 459-482.

DiPardo, A., & Freedman, S. W. (1988). Peer response groups in the writing classroom: Theoretic foundations and new directions. *Review of Educational Research, 58,* 119-149.

Dolz, J., & Schneuwly, B. (1998). A la recherche du coupable: Métalangage des élèves dans la rédaction d'un récit d'énigme, *Recherches, 27,* 40-61.

Doughty, C., & Williams, J. (1998). *Focus on form in classroom second language acquisition.* Cambridge, UK: Cambridge University Press.

Dubois, J. (1965). *Grammaire structurale du Français: Nom et pronom.* Paris: Larousse.

Duffy, G. G., Roehler, L. R., & Rackliffe, G. (1986). How teachers' instructional talk influences students' understanding of lesson content. *The Elementary School Journal, 87,* 357-366.

Dunn, D. S. (1996). Collaborative writing in a statistics and research methods course. *Teaching of Psychology, 23,* 38-40.

Dyson, A. & Freedman, S. (1991). Writing. In J. Flood, J. M. Jensen, D. Lapp, and J. R. Squire, (Eds.), *Handbook on teaching the English language arts* (pp. 754 -774). New York: Macmillan.

Eberhard, K. M. (1999). The accessibility of conceptual number to the processes of subject-verb agreement in English. *Journal of Memory and Language, 41,* 560-578.

Ede, L. (1984). Audience: An introduction to research. *College Composition and Communication, 35*(2), 140-154.

Ehri, L. C. (1986). Sources of difficulty in learning to spell and read. *Advances in Developmental and Behavioural Paediatricks, 7,* 121-195.

Elbow, P. (1981). *Writing with power: Techniques for mastering the writing process.* New York: Oxford University Press.

Elbow, P. (1987). Closing my eyes as I speak: An argument for ignoring audience. *College English, 49* (1), 51-69.

Elbow, P. (1998). *Writing without teachers* (second edition). Oxford: Oxford University Press.

Ellis, N. C. (1994). *Implicit and explicit learning of language.* London: Academic Press.

Ellis, N. C. (1996). Sequencing in SLA: Phonological memory, chunking and points of order. *Studies in Second Language Acquisition, 18*, 91-126.

Elshout, J. J. (1984). Experts en beginners. [Experts and novices]. In G. A. M. Kempen, & C. Sprengers (Eds.), *Kennis, mensen en computers* [Knowledge, people, and computers] (pp. 25-30). Lisse: Swets & Zeitlinger.

Englert, C. S. (1992). Writing instruction from a sociocultural perspective: The holistic, dialogic, and social enterprise of writing. *Journal of Learning Disabilities, 25*, 153-172.

Englert, C.. S., Berry, R., & Dunsmore, K. (2001). A case study of the apprenticeship processes: Another perspective on the apprentice and the scaffolding metaphor. *Journal of Learning Disabilities, 34*, 152-171.

Englert, C. S., Garmon, A., Mariage, T., Rezendale, M., Tarrant, K., & Urba, J. (1995). The early literacy project: Connecting across the literacy curriculum. *Learning Disability Quarterly, 18*, 253-275.

Englert, C. S., Raphael, T. E., Anderson, L. M., Anthony, H. M., & Stevens, D. D. (1991). Making writing strategies and self-talk visible: Cognitive strategy instruction in writing in regular and special education classrooms. *American Educational Research Journal, 28*, 337-372.

Englert, C. S., Raphael, T. E., Anderson, L. M., Gregg, S. L., & Anthony, H. M. (1989). Exposition: Reading, writing, and the metacognitive knowledge of learning disabled students. *Learning Disabilities Research, 5*, 5-24.

Faigley, L., & Witte, S. (1981). Analysing revision. *College Composition and Communication, 32*, 400-414.

Faigley, L., & Witte, S. P. (1984). Measuring the effects of revisions on text structure. In R. Beach, & L. S. Bridwell (Eds.), *New directions in composing research* (pp. 95-108). New York: Guilford Press.

Farrell, K. J. (1977). *A comparison of three instructional approaches for teaching written composition to high school juniors: Teacher lecture, peer evaluation, and group tutoring.* Unpublished doctoral dissertation, Boston University School of Education.

Fayol, M. (1997). *Des idées au texte: Psychologie cognitive de la production verbale, orale et écrite.* Paris: PUF.

Fayol, M., Gombert, J. E., & Baur, V. (1987). *La révision de textes écrits dans l'activité rédactionnelle précoce.* Communication au Congrès Annuel de la Société Française de Psychologie, Nanterre (France).

Fayol, M., & Got, C. (1991). Automatisme et contrôle dans la production écrite. *L'Année Psychologique, 91*, 187-205.

Fayol, M., Hupet, M., & Largy, P. (1999). The acquisition of subject-verb agreement in written French: From novices to experts'errors. *Reading and Writing: An Interdisciplinary Journal, 11*, 153-174..

Fayol, M., & Largy, P. (1992). Une approche cognitive fonctionnelle de l'orthographe grammaticale. *Langue Française, 95*, 80-98.

Fayol, M., Largy, P., & Ganier, F. (1997). Le traitement de l'accord sujet-verbe en français écrit: Le cas des configurations Pronom1 Pronom2 Verbe. *Verbum, 1-2*, 103-120.

Fayol, M., Largy, P., & Lemaire, P. (1994). When cognitive overload enhances subject-verb agreement errors. A study in French written language. *The Quarterly Journal of Experimental Psychology, 47*, 437-464.

Fitzgerald, J. (1987). Research on revision in writing. *Review of Educational Research, 57*, 481-506.

Fitzgerald, J. (1992). Variant views about good thinking during composing: Focus on revision. In, M. Pressley, K. Harris, and J. Guthrie (Eds.). *Promoting academic competence and literacy in school* (pp. 337-360). San Diego, CA: Academic Press.

Fitzgerald, J., & Markham. L. R. (1987). Teaching children about revision in writing. *Cognition and Instruction, 4*(1), 3-24.

Flavell, J. H. (1976). Metacognitive aspects of problem solving. In L. B. Resnick (Ed.), *The nature of intelligence* (pp. 231-235). Hillsdale, NJ: Lawrence Erlbaum.

Flavell, J. (1992). Perspectives on perspective taking. In H. Belin & P. B. Pufall (Eds.), *Piaget's theory: Prospects and possibilities* (pp. 107-139). Hillsdale, NJ: Lawrence Erlbaum.

Flower, L. (1994). *The construction of negotiated meaning: A social cognitive theory of writing.* Detroit: Wayne State University Press.

Flower, L. S., & Hayes, J. R. (1980). The dynamics of composing: Making plans and juggling constraints. In L. W. Gregg, & E. R. Steinberg (Eds.), *Cognitive processes in writing* (pp. 31-50). Hillsdale, NJ: Lawrence Erlbaum.

214

Flower, L., & Hayes, J. R. (1981). A cognitive process theory of writing. *College Composition and Communication, 32,* 365-387.

Flower, L. S., Hayes, J. R., Carey, L., Schriver, K., & Stratman, J. (1986). Detection, diagnosis and the strategies of revision. *College Composition and Communication, 37*(1), 16-55.

Flower, L. S., Wallace, D. S., Norris, L., & Burnett, R. E. (Eds.). (1994). *Making thinking visible: Writing, collaborative planning, and classroom inquiry.* Urbana, IL: National Council of Teachers of English.

Francis, W. N. (1986). Proximity concord in English. *Journal of English Linguistics, 19,* 309-318.

Frank, L. (1992). Writing to be read: Young writers' ability to demonstrate audience awareness when evaluated by their readers. *Research in the Teaching of English, 26,* 277-298.

Gafi (1998). *Méthode d'apprentissage de la lecture, C.P. livrets 1 et 2.* Paris: Nathan.

Galambos, S. J., & Goldin-Meadow, S. (1990). The effects of learning two languages on levels of metalinguistic awareness. *Cognition, 34,* 1-56.

Galbraith, D. (1992). Conditions for discovery through writing. *Instructional Science, 21,* 45-72.

Galbraith, D. (1996). Self-monitoring, discovery through writing and individual differences in drafting strategy. In G. Rijlaarsdam, H. Van den Bergh, & M. Couzijn. (Eds.), *Studies in writing: Vol. 1. Theories, models and methodology in writing research* (pp. 121-144). Amsterdam: Amsterdam University Press.

Galbraith, D. (1999). Writing as a knowledge-constituting process. In M. Torrance, & D. Galbraith (Eds.), *Studies in writing: Vol. 4. Knowing what to write: Conceptual processes in text production* (pp. 139-160). Amsterdam: Amsterdam University Press.

Garcia-Debanc, C. (1990). *L'élève et la production d'écrits.* Metz: Centre d'analyse syntaxique de l'université de Metz.

Garner, R. (1990). When children and adults do not use learning strategies: Toward a theory of settings. *Review of Educational Research, 60,* 517-529.

Gathercole, S. E., & Baddeley, A. D. (1993). *Working memory and language.* Hillsdale, NJ: Lawrence Erlbaum.

Gehrke, N. J., Knapp, M. S., & Sirotnik, K. A. (1992). In search of the school curriculum. *Review of Educational Research, 18,* 51-110.

Gentry, J. R. (1982). Analysis of developmental spelling in GNYS AT WORK. *The Reading Teacher, 36,* 192-200.

Glucksberg, S. & Krauss, R. (1967). What do people say after they have learned how to talk? Studies of the development of referential communication. *Merill-Palmer Quarterly, 13,* 309-316.

Glynn, S. M., Britton, B., Muth, D., & Dogan, N. (1982). Writing and revising persuasive documents: Cognitive demands. *Journal of Educational Psychology, 74,* 557-567.

Goldberg, G. L., Roswell, B. S., & Michaels, H. (1996). Empirical investigations: Can assessment mirror instruction? A look at peer response and revision in a large-scale writing test. *Educational Assessment, 3* (4), 287-314.

Grabe, W. (2001). Notes towards a theory of second language writing. In T. Silva, & P. K. Matsuda (Eds.), *On second language writing* (pp. 39-57). Mahwah, NJ: Laurence Erlbaum.

Graham, S. (1990). The role of production factors in learning disabled students' compositions. *Journal of Educational Psychology, 80,* 781-791.

Graham, S. (1997). Executive control in the revising of students with learning and writing difficulties. *Journal of Educational Psychology, 89,* 223-234.

Graham, S., Berninger, V. W., Abbott, R. D., Abbott, S. P., & Whitaker, D. (1997). The role of mechanics in composing of elementary school students: A new methodological approach. *Journal of Educational Psychology, 89,* 170-182.

Graham, S., & Harris, K. R. (1997). Whole language and process writing: Does one approach fit all? In I. W. Lloyd, E. J. Kameenui, & D. Chard (Eds.), *Issues in education students with disabilities* (pp. 239-258). Mahwah, NJ: Lawrence Erlbaum.

Graham, S., Harris, K., MacArthur, C. A., & Schwartz, S. S. (1991). Writing and writing instruction with students with learning disabilities: A review of a program of research. *Learning Disability Quarterly, 14,* 89-114.

Graham, S., & MacArthur, C. (1988). Improving learning disabled students' skills at revising essays produced on a word processor: Self-instructional strategy training. *Journal of Special Education, 22,* 133-152.

Graham, S., MacArthur, C. A., & Schwartz, S. S. (1995). The effects of goal setting and procedural facilitation on the revising behavior and writing performance of students with writing and learning problems. *Journal of Educational Psychology, 87,* 230-240.

Graham, S., Schwartz, S., & MacArthur, C. (1993). Learning disabled and normally achieving students' knowledge of the writing and composing process, attitude toward writing, and self-efficacy. *Journal of Learning Disabilities, 26,* 237-249.

Graves, D. H. (1983). *Writing: Teachers and children at work.* Portsmouth, NH: Heinemann.

Graves, D. H. (1994). *A fresh look at writing.* Portsmouth, NH.: Heinemann.

Guerrero, M. C., & Villamil, O. S. (1994). Social-cognitive dimensions of interaction in L2 peer revision. *The Modern Language Journal, 78,* 484-496.

Guilford, J. P. (1971). *The nature of human intelligence.* London: McGraw-Hill.

Hacker, D. J. (1994). Comprehension monitoring as a writing process. In E. C. Butterfield, & J. S. Carlson (Eds.), *Advances in cognition and educational practice: Vol. 2. Children's writing: Toward a process theory of the development of skilled writing* (pp. 143-172). Greenwich, CT: JAI Press.

Hacker, D. J., Plumb, C., Butterfield, E. C., Quathamer, D., & Heineken, E. (1994). Text revision: Detection and correction of errors. *Journal of Educational Psychology, 86*(1), 65-78.

Halford, G. S., Wilson, W. H., & Philipps, S. (1998). Processing capacities defined by relational complexity: implications for comparative, developmental and cognitive psychology. *Behavioral and Brain Sciences, 21*(6), 803-831.

Harper, L. (1997). The writer's toolbox: Five tools for active revision instruction. *Language Arts, 74,* 193-200.

Harris, K. R., & Graham, S. (1992). Self-regulated strategy development: A part of the writing process. In M. Pressley, K. R. Harris, & J. T. Gutherie (Eds.), *Promoting academic literacy in schools* (pp. 277-309). San Diego: Academic Press.

Harris, K. R., & Graham, S. (1995). *Making the writing process work: Strategies for composition and self-regulation.* Cambridge, MA: Brookline Press.

Harris, K. R., Schmidt, T., & Graham, S. (1998). Every child can write: Strategies for composition and self-regulation in the writing process. In K. R. Harris, S. Graham, & D. Deshler (Eds.), *Teaching every child every day: Learning in diverse schools and classrooms* (pp. 131-167). Cambridge, MA: Brookline.

Hayes, J. R. (1996). A new framework for understanding cognition and affect in writing. In C. M. Levy, & S. Ransdell (Eds.), *The science of writing: Theories, methods, individual differences and applications* (pp. 1- 27). Mahwah, NJ: Lawrence Erbaum Associates.

Hayes, J. R., & Flower, L. (1980). Identifying the organization of writing processes. In L. W. Gregg, & E. R. Steinberg (Eds.), *Cognitive processes in writing: An interdisciplinary approach* (pp. 3–30). Hillsdale, NJ: Lawrence Erlbaum.

Hayes, J. R., Flower, L. S., Schriver, K. A., Stratman, J., & Carey, L. (1987). Cognitive processes in revision. In S. Rosenberg (Ed.), *Advances in psycholinguistics: Vol. 2. Reading, writing, and language processing* (pp. 176-240). Cambridge: Cambridge University Press.

Heap, J. L. (1989a), Sociality and cognition in collaborative computer writing. In D. Bloome (Ed.), *Classrooms and literacy* (pp. 135-157). Norwood, NJ: Ablex.

Heap, J. L. (1989b). Collaborative practices during word processing in a first grade classroom. In C. Emihovich (Ed.), *Locating learning: Ethnographic perspectives on classroom research* (pp. 263-288). Norwood, NJ: Ablex.

Higgins, L., Flower, L., & Petraglia, J. (1992). Planning text together: The role of critical reflection in student collaboration. *Written Communication, 9,* 48-84.

Hillocks, G. (1984). What works in teaching composition: A meta-analysis of experimental treatment studies. *American Journal of Education, 93,* 133-170.

Hillocks, G. (1986). *Research in written composition: New directions for teaching.* Urbana, IL: ERIC Clearinghouse on Reading and Communication Skills and National Conference on Research in English.

Holliway, D. & McCutchen, D. (2000, September). Reading as the reader: The role of audience perspective in children's composing and revising. Paper presented at the Writing Conference 2000, Verona, Italy.

Howden, J., & Kopiec, M. (2000). *Ajouter aux compétences: Enseigner, coopérer et apprendre au postsecondaire.* Montréal: La Chenelière.

216

Hulstijn, J. H. (1997). Second-language acquisition research in the laboratory: Possibilities and limitations. *Studies in Second Language Acquisition, 19*(2), 131-143.

Hunt, K. W. (1983). Sentence combining and the teaching of writing. In M. Martlew (Ed.), *The psychology of written language* (pp. 99-125). Chichester: Wiley.

Jaffré, J.-P. (1986). Construire des savoirs sur la langue: Le cas de l'orthographe. *Communiquer, ça s'apprend* (Rencontres pédagogiques, no. 11). Paris: Institut National de Recherche Pédagogique.

James, W. (1890). *The principles of psychology.* New York: Holt.

Jarema, G., & Kehayia, E. (1992). Impairment of inflectional morphology and lexical storage. *Brain and Language, 43,* 541-564.

Johnson, D. W., & Johnson, R. T. (1990). Cooperative learning and achievement. In S. Sharan (Ed.), *Cooperative learning: Theory and research* (pp. 23-38). New-York: Praeger.

Johnson, D. W., Johnson, R. T., & Holubec, E. J. (1994). *Cooperative learning in the classroom.* Alexandria, VA: Association for Supervision and Curriculum Development.

Just, M. A., & Carpenter, P. A. (1992). A capacity theory of comprehension: Individual differences in working memory. *Psychological Review, 99,* 122-149.

Kahneman, D. (1973). *Attention and Effort.* Englewood Cliffs, NJ: Prentice-Hall.

Karegianes, M. L., Pascarella, E. T., & Pflaum, S. W. (1980). The effects of peer editing on the writing proficiency of low-achieving tenth grade students. *Journal of Educational Research, 73,* 203-207.

Kastra, J., Tollefson, N., & Gilbert, E. (1987). The effects of peer evaluation on attitude toward writing and writing fluency of ninth grade students. *Journal of Educational Research, 80* (3), 168-172.

Kaufer, D. S., Hayes, J. R., & Flower, L. (1986). Composing written sentences. *Research in the Teaching of English, 20*(2), 121–140.

Kellogg, R. T. (1987). Effects of topic knowledge on the allocation of processing time and cognitive effort to writing processes. *Memory and Cognition, 15*(3), 256-266.

Kellogg, R. T. (1988). Attentional overload and writing performance: Effects on rough draft and outline strategies. *Journal of Experimental Psychology: Learning, Memory and Cognition, 14*(2), 355-365.

Kellogg, R. T. (1990). Effectiveness of prewriting strategies as a function of task demands. *American Journal of Psychology, 103,* 327-342.

Kellogg, R. T. (1994). *The psychology of writing.* New York: Oxford University Press.

Kellogg, R. T. (1996). A model of working memory in writing. In C. M. Levy & S. Ransdell (Eds.), *The science of writing: Theories, methods, individual differences and applications* (pp. 57-71). Mahwah, NJ: Lawrence Erbaum.

Kemp, J. H. (1979). *A comparison of two procedures for improving the writing of developmental writers.* Unpublished doctoral dissertation, University of Georgia.

Keys, C. W. (1994). The development of scientific reasoning skills in conjunction with collaborative writing assignments: An interpretative study of six ninth-grade students. *Journal of Research in Science Teaching, 31,* 1003-1022.

Keys, C. W. (1995). An interpretative study of students' use of scientific reasoning during a collaborative report writing intervention in ninth grade general science. *Science Education, 79,* 415-435.

Krashen, S. D. (1981). *Second language acquisition and second language learning.* Oxford: Pergamon.

Krashen, S. (1982). *Principles and practice in second language learning.* New York: Pergamon.

Kroll, B. (1978). Cognitive egocentrism and the problem of audience awareness in written discourse. *Research in the Teaching of English, 12* (3), 269-281.

Kroll, B. (1984). Writing for readers: Three perspectives on audience. *College Composition and Communication, 35* (2), 172-185.

Kroll, B. M. (1985). Rewriting a complex story for a young reader: The development of audience-adapted writing skills. *Research in the Teaching of English, 19,* 120-139.

Kroll, B. M. (1986). Explaining how to play a game: The development of informative writing skills. *Written Communication, 3,* 195-218.

Kumpulainen, K. (1996). The nature of peer interaction in the social context created by the use of word processors. *Learning and Instruction, 6,* 243-261.

Langer, J. A. (1984). Literacy instruction in American schools: Problems and perspectives. *American Journal of Education, 93,* 107-132.

Langer, J. A., & Flihan, S. (2000). Writing and reading relationships: Constructive tasks. In R. Indrisano & J. R. Squire (Eds.), *Perspectives on writing* (pp. 112-139). Newark, DE: International Reading Association.

Largy, P. (1995). *Production et gestion des erreurs en production écrite: Le cas de l'accord sujet-verbe.* Unpublished doctoral dissertation, Université de Bourgogne, Dijon (France).

Largy, P. (2001). La révision des accords nominal et verbal chez l'enfant. *L'Année Psychologique, 101,* 221-245.

Largy, P., Chanquoy, L., & Fayol, M. (1994). Automatic and controlled writing: Subject-verb agreement errors in French native speakers. In G. Eigler & T. Jechle (Eds.), *Writing: Current Trends in European Research* (pp. 109-119). Freiburg: Hochschule Verlag.

Largy, P., & Fayol, M. (2001). Oral cues improve subject-verb agreement. A study in French language. *International Journal of Psychology, 36*(2), 121-132.

Largy, P., Fayol, M., & Lemaire, P. (1996). The homophone effect in written French: The case of verb-noun inflection errors. *Language and Cognitive Processes, 11*(3), 217-255.

Levelt, W. J. M. (1989). *Speaking: From intention to articulation.* Cambridge, MA: MIT Press.

Levy, C. M, & Ransdell, S. (1995). Is writing as difficult as it seems? *Memory and Cognition, 23,* 767-779.

Levy, C. M., & Ransdell, S. (1996). Writing signatures. In C. M. Levy & S. Ransdell (Eds.), *The science of writing: Theories, methods, individual differences and applications* (pp. 149-162). Mahwah, N.J.: Lawrence Erlbaum.

Littleton, E. B. (1998). Emerging cognitive skills for writing: Sensitivity to audience perspective in five-through nine-year-olds' speech. *Cognition and Instruction, 16,* 399-430.

Logan, G. D. (1988a). Toward an instance theory of automatization, *Psychological Rewiew, 95,* 492-527.

Logan, G. D. (1988b). Automaticity, resources, and memory: Theoretical controversies and practical implications. *Human Factors, 30,* 583-598.

Logan, G. D. (1992). Automaticity and memory. In W. E. Hockley & S. Lewandowsky (Eds.), *Relating theory and data: Essays in Honor of Bennett Murdock* (pp. 234-248). Hillsdale, N.J.: Lawrence Erlbaum.

Long, M. H. (1991). Focus on form: A design feature in language teaching methodology. In K. d. Bot & R. Ginsberg, & C. Kramsch (Eds.), *Foreign language research in cross-cultural perspective* (pp. 39-52). Amsterdam: John Benjamins.

Lumbelli, L., Paoletti G., & Frausin, T. (1999). Improving the ability to detect comprehension problems: From revising to writing. *Learning and Instruction, 9,* 143-166.

Lumbelli, L., Paoletti, G., Camagni, C., & Frausin, T. (1996). Can the ability to monitor local coherence in text comprehension be transferred to writing? In G. Rijlaarsdam, H. Van den Bergh, & M. Couzijn (Eds.), *Studies in writing: Vol. 2. Effective teaching and learning of writing. Current trends in research.* (pp 207-223). Amsterdam: Amsterdam University Press.

MacArthur, C., & Graham, S. (1987). Learning disabled students' composing under three methods of text production: Handwriting, word processing, and dictation. *Journal of Special Education, 21,* 22-42.

MacArthur, C. A., Graham, S., & Schwartz, S. (1991). Knowledge of revision and revising behavior among learning disabled students. *Learning Disability Quarterly, 14,* 61-73.

MacArthur, C. A., Graham, S., Schwartz, S. S., & Schafer, W. (1995). Evaluation of a writing instruction model that integrated a process approach, strategy instruction, and word processing. *Learning Disabilities Quarterly, 18,* 278-291.

MacArthur, C. A., Schwartz, S. S., & Graham, S. (1991). Effects of a reciprocal peer revision strategy in special education classrooms. *Learning Disabilities Research and Practice, 6,* 201-210.

McCarthey, S. J., & McMahon, S. (1992). From convention to invention: Three approaches to peer interactions during writing. In R. Hertz-Lazarowitz & N. Miller (Eds.), *Interaction in cooperative groups: The theoretical anatomy of group learning* (pp. 17-35). Cambridge: Cambridge University Press.

McCutchen, D. (1984). Writing as a linguistic problem. *Educational Psychologist, 19,* 226-238.

McCutchen, D. (1988). "Functional automaticity" in children's writing: A problem of metacognitive control. *Written Communication, 5,* 306-324.

McCutchen, D. (1995). Cognitive processes in children's writing: Developmental and individual differences. *Issues in Education: Contributions from Educational Psychology, 1,* 123-160.

McCutchen, D. (1996). A capacity theory of writing: Working memory in composition. *Educational Psychology Review, 8*(3), 299-325.

McCutchen, D., Covill, A., Hoyne, S. H., & Mildes, K. (1994). Individual differences in writing: Implications of translating fluency. *Journal of Educational Psychology, 86,* 256-266.

McCutchen, D., Francis, M., & Kerr, S. (1997). Revising for meaning: Effects of knowledge and strategy. *Journal of Educational Psychology, 89,* 667-676.

218

McCutchen, D., Kerr, S., & Francis, M. (1994). *Editing and revising: Effects of knowledge of topic and error location.* Paper Presented at the Annual Meeting of the American Educational Research Association, New Orleans, LA.

McCutchen, D., & Perfetti, C. A. (1982). Coherence and connectedness in the development of discourse production. *Text, 2,* 113-139.

McLane, J. B. (1990). Writing as a social process. In L. C. Moll (Ed.), *Vygotsky and education* (pp. 304-318). Cambridge: Cambridge University Press.

Miller, P., Kessel, F., & Flavell, J. (1970). Thinking about people thinking about people thinking about. . . : A study of socio-cognitive development. *Child Development, 41,* 613-623.

Morani, R., & Pontecorvo, C. (1995). Invenzione e scrittura di storie in coppie di bambini. *Età Evolutiva, 51,* 81-92.

Morocco, C., Dalton, B., & Tivnan, T. (1990, April). *The impact of computer-supported writing instruction on the writing quality of 4th grade students with learning disabilities.* Paper presented at the annual meeting of the American Educational Research Association, Boston.

Morris, D. (1983). Concept of word and phoneme awareness in the beginning reader. *Research in the Teaching of English, 17,* 359-373.

Murray, D. M. (1978). Internal revision: A process of discovery. In C. R. Cooper & L. Odell (Eds.), *Research on composing: Points of departure* (pp. 85-103). Urbana, IL: National Council of Teachers of English.

NAEP (National Assessment of Educational Progress). (1977). *Write/rewrite: An assessment of revision skills. Selected results from the second national assessment of writing.* Washington, DC.: Government Printing Office.

National Joint Commission on Learning Disabilities. (1998). Position papers by the National Joint Committee on Learning Disabilities. *Learning Disability Quarterly, 21,* 182-193.

Negro, I., & Chanquoy, L. (1999). Subject-verb agreement errors: Phonological and semantic control in adults. In G. C. Jeffery & M. Torrance (Eds.), *Studies in writing: Vol. 3. The cognitive demands of writing. Processing capacity and working memory effects in text production* (pp. 83-98).. Amsterdam: Amsterdam University Press.

Negro, I., & Chanquoy, L. (2000a). Subject-verb agreement with present and imperfect tenses: A developmental study from second to seventh grade. *European Journal of Psychology of Education, 15*(2), 113-133.

Negro, I., & Chanquoy, L. (2000b). Etude des erreurs d'accord sujet-verbe au présent et à l'imparfait. Analyse comparative entre des collégiens et des adultes. *L'Année Psychologique, 100,* 209-240.

Nelson, N., & Calfee, R. C. (Eds.) (1998). *The reading-writing connection. The Ninety-seventh Yearbook of the National Society for the Study of Education. Part 2.* Chicago: National Society for the Study of Education.

Newell, A., & Simon, H. A. (1972). *Human problem solving.* Englewood Cliffs, NJ: Prentice-Hall.

Newkirk, T. (1982). Young writers as critical readers. *Language Arts, 59,* 451-457.

Newman, D., Griffin, P., & Cole, M. (1984). Social constraints in laboratory and classroom. In B. Rogoff & J. Lave (Eds.), *Everyday cognition: Its development in social context* (pp. 172-193). Cambridge, MA: Harvard University Press.

Nold, E. W. (1981). Revising. In C. H. Frederiksen & J. F. Dominic (Eds.), *Writing: The nature, development and teaching of written communication* (Vol. 2). Hillsdale, NJ.: Lawrence Erlbaum.

Norris, J. M., & Ortega, L. (2000). Effectiveness of L2 instruction: A research synthesis and quantitative meta-analysis. *Language Learning, 50,* 417-528.

Nunn, G. (1982). *Peer interaction during collaborative writing at the 4th/5th grade level.* ERIC document No. ED 257074.

Nystrand, M. (1986a). Learning to write by talking about writing: A summary of research on intensive peer review. In M. Nystrand (Ed.), *The structure of written communication: Studies in reciprocity between writers and readers* (pp. 179-211). Orlando: Academic Press.

Nystrand, M. (1986b). *The structure of written communication: Studies in reciprocity between writers and readers.* New York: Academic Press.

O'Donnell, A. M. (1999). Structuring dyadic interaction through scripted cooperation. In A. M. O'Donnell & A. King (Eds.), *Cognitive perspectives on peer learning* (pp. 179-196). Mahwah, NJ: Lawrence Erlbaum.

Olive, T. (1999). *Economie de la production de textes. Gestion des ressources attentionnelles et mode d'activation des processus rédactionnels.* Unpublished doctoral dissertation of the University de Provence, France.

Olive, T., & Kellogg, R. T. (2002). Concurrent activation of high- and low-level production processes in written composition. *Memory and Cognition, 30*(4), 594-600.

Olive, T., & Levy, C. M. (Eds.) (2001). *Studies in writing: Vol. 10. Contemporary tools and techniques for studying writing.* Dordrecht: Kluwer Academic Publishers.

Olive, T., Kellogg, R. T., & Piolat, A. (2001). The triple task technique for studying the processs of writing. In T. Olive & C. M. Levy (Eds.), *Studies in writing: Vol. 10. Contemporary tools and techniques for studying writing* (pp. 31-59). Dordrecht: Kluwer Academic Publishers.

Olive, T., Piolat, A., & Roussey J. Y. (1997). Effort cognitif et mobilisation des processus: Effet de l'habileté rédactionnelle et du niveau de connaissances. In D. Mellier & A. Vom Hofe (Eds.), *Attention et contrôle cognitif: Mécanismes, développement des habiletés, pathologies* (pp. 71-85). Rouen: P.U.R.

Oliver, E. (1995). The writing quality of seventh, ninth, and eleventh graders, and college freshman: Does rhetorical specification in writing prompts make a difference? *Research in the Teaching of English, 29*(4), 422-450.

Olson, D. (1994). *The world on paper.* Cambridge, MA: Cambridge University Press.

Oostdam, R. J., & Rijlaarsdam, G. C. W. (1995). *Towards strategic language learning.* Amsterdam: Amsterdam University Press.

Pacton, S., Fayol, M., & Perruchet, P. (2002). The acquisition of untaught orthographic regularities in French. In L. Verhoeven, C. Erlbro, & P. Reitsma (Eds.), *Precursors of functional literacy* (pp. 121-137). Dordrecht: Kluwer Academic Publishers.

Pacton, S., Perruchet, P., Fayol, M., & Cleeremans, A. (2001). Implicit learning out of the lab: The case of orthographic regularities. *Journal of Experimental Psychology: General, 130*, 401-426.

Palincsar, A. S., & Brown, D. A. (1984). Reciprocal teaching of comprehension-fostering and comprehension-monitoring activities. *Cognition and Instruction, 1*, 117-175.

Palincscar, A., & Klenk, L. (1992). Fostering literacy learning in supportive contexts. *Journal of Learning Disabilities, 25*, 211-225.

Park, D. (1982). The meanings of "audience." *College English, 44*(3), 247-257.

Perkins, D. N. (1993). Person-plus: A distributed view of thinking and learning. In G. Salomon (Ed.), *Distributed cognitions: Psychological and educational considerations* (pp. 88-110). Cambridge, UK: Cambridge University Press.

Perl, S. (1979). The composing process of unskilled college writers. *Research in the Teaching of English, 13*, 317-336.

Perruchet, P. (1998). L'apprentissage implicite: un débat théorique. *Psychologie Française, 43-1*, 13-25.

Piolat, A. (1998). Writers' assessment and evaluation of their texts In C. Clapham (Ed.), *The encyclopedia of language and education: Vol. 7. Language testing and assessment.* Dordrecht: Kluwer Academic Publishers.

Piolat, A., Kellogg, R. T., & Farioli, F. (2001). The triple task technique for studying writing processes: On which task is attention focused? *Current Psychology Letters: Brain, Behavior and Cognition, 4*, 67-83.

Piolat, A., & Olive, T. (2000). Comment étudier le coût et le déroulement de la rédaction de textes? La méthode de la triple tâche: Un bilan méthodologique. *L'Année Psychologique, 100*, 465-502.

Piolat, A., Olive, T., Roussey, J. Y., Thunin, O., & Ziegler, J. C. (1999). SCRIPTKELL: a tool for measuring cognitive effort and time processing in writing and other complex cognitive activities. *Behavior Research Methods, Instruments, & Computers, 31/1*, 113-121.

Piolat, A., & Roussey, J. Y. (1991-1992). A propos de l'expression « stratégie de révision » de texte en psychologie cognitive. *Texte en Main: "Lis tes raptures", 10/11*, 51-64.

Piolat, A., Roussey, J. Y., Olive, T., & Farioli, F. (1996). Charge mentale et mobilisation des processus rédactionnels: Examen de la procédure de Kellogg. *Psychologie Francaise, 41*, 339-354.

Plumb, C., Butterfield, E.C., Hacker, D. J., & Dunlosky, J. (1994). Error correction in text: Testing the processing-deficit and knowledge-deficit hypotheses. *Reading and Writing: An Interdisciplinary Journal, 6*, 347-360.

Pontecorvo, C., & Paoletti, G. (1991). Planning story completion in a collaborative computer task. *European Journal of Psychology of Education, 6*, 199-212.

Pressley, M., & Wharton-McDonald, R. (1997). Skilled comprehension and its development through instruction. *School Psychology Review, 26,* 448-466.

Pressley, M., El-Dinary, P. B., Gaskins, I., Schuder, T., Bergman, J. L., Almasi, J., Brown, R. (1992). Beyond direct explanation: Transactional instruction of reading comprehension strategies. *Elementary School Journal, 92,* 513-555.

Rafoth, B. (1989). Audience and information. *Research in the Teaching of English, 23*(3), 273-290.

Rafoth, B. & Rubin, D. (Eds.). (1988). *The social construction of written communication.* Norwood, NJ: Ablex Publishing Corporation.

Reber, A. S. (1967). Implicit learning of artificial grammars. *Journal of Verbal Learning and Verbal Behavior, 77,* 317-327.

Reber, A. S. (1989). Implicit learning and tacit knowledge. *Journal of Experimental Psychology, 118,* 219-235.

Resnick, L. B. (1990). Literacy in school and out. *Daedalus, 119,* 169-185.

Rieben, L., Fayol, M., & Perfetti, C. A. (Eds.). (1997). *Des orthographes et leur acquisition.* Neuchâtel: Delachaux & Niestlé.

Rijlaarsdam, G. (1987, March). *Effects of peer evaluation on writing performance, writing processes, and psychological variables.* Paper presented at the 38th Annual Meeting of the Conference on College Composition and Communication, Atlanta, USA. ED 284 288.

Rijlaarsdam, G. (1993). Research in L1-Education: A Review and preview of applied linguistics research for the benefit of mother tongue education. *Toegepaste taalkunde in artikelen* [Papers in applied linguistics], *46/4,* 238 -254.

Rijlaarsdam, G., Braaksma, M., & Couzijn, M. (2002, July). *What makes teaching writing effective in secondary education?* Paper presented at the 8th International Conference of the Special Interest Group of Writing of EARLI, Stafford, UK.

Rijlaarsdam, G., & Couzijn, M. (2000a). What do writers learn from peer comments on argumentative texts? In A. Camps, & M. Milian (Eds.), *Studies in writing: Vol. 6. Metalinguistic activity in learning to write* (pp. 167-202). Amsterdam: Amsterdam University Press.

Rijlaarsdam, G., & Couzijn, M. (2000b). Writing and learning-to-write: A double challenge. In R. Simons, J. Van der Linden, & T. Duffy (Eds.), *New learning* (pp. 157-190). Dordrecht: Kluwer Academic Publishers.

Rijlaarsdam, G., & Van den Bergh, H. (1996). An agenda for research into an interactive compensatory model of writing: Many questions, some answers. In C. M. Levy & S. Ransdell (Eds.), *The science of writing* (pp. 107-126). Mahwah, NJ: Lawrence Erlbaum.

Robinson, P. (1996). Learning simple and complex second language rules under implicit, incidental, rule-search and instructed conditions. *Studies in Second Language Acquisition, 18,* 27-67.

Robinson, P. (1997). Individual differences and the fundamental similarity of implicit and explicit adult second language learning. *Language Learning, 47*(1), 45-99.

Roen, D. H., & Willey, R. J. (1988). The effects of audience awareness on drafting and revising. *Research in the Teaching of English, 22,* 75-88.

Rosen, M. (1973). *A structured classroom writing method: An experiment in teaching rhetoric to remedial college English students.* Unpublished doctoral dissertation, New York University.

Rosow, E. G. (1996). *The effects of analytic assessment strategies on second graders' ability to identify revision needs in their writing.* Unpublished doctoral dissertation, University of Connecticut.

Rouiller, Y. (1996). Metacognitive regulations, peer interactions and revisions of narratives by sixth graders. In G. Rijlaarsdam, H. Van den Bergh, & M. Couzijn (Eds.), *Studies in writing: Vol. 2. Effective teaching and learning of writing: Current trends in research* (pp. 274-286). Amsterdam: Amsterdam University Press.

Rouiller, Y. (1998). *Approche contextualisée de la révision textuelle: Effets d'une situation de coproduction dyadique.* Unpublished doctoral dissertation, University of Geneva.

Roussey, J. Y. (1991) Text schemas in a modeling paradigm: Improvement of a narrative and a description by ten-year-olds. *European Journal of Psychology of Education, 5,* 233-242.

Roussey, J. Y. (1999). *Le contrôle de la rédaction de textes. Perspective cognitive.* Synthèse d'Habilitation à Diriger des Recherche, Université de Provence, Aix-en-Provence.

Rubin, D. (1984). Social cognition and written communication. *Written Communication, 1,* 211-245.

Rubin, D. L., & Piché, G. L. (1979). Development in syntactic and strategic aspects of audience adaptation skills in written persuasive communication. *Research in the Teaching of English, 13,* 293-316.

Rumelhart, D. E., Smolensky, P., McClelland, J. L., & Hinton, G. E. (1986). Schemata and sequential thought processes in PDP models. In D. Rumelhart, J. McClelland, & the PDP research group (Eds.), *Parallel distributed processing: Vol. 2. Psychological and biological models* (pp. 7-57). Cambridge, MA: MIT press.

Russell, M. (1999). Testing Writing on Computers: A Follow-up Study Comparing Performance on Computer and on Paper. *Educational Policy Analysis Archives, 7*(20). http://epaa.asu.edu/epaa/v7n20

Sager, C. (1973). *Improving the quality of written composition through pupil use of rating scale.* Unpublished doctoral dissertation, Boston University School of Education.

Saunders, W. M. (1989). Collaborative writing tasks and peer interaction. *International Journal of Educational Research, 13*, 101-112.

Scardamalia, M. (1981). How children cope with the cognitive demands of writing. In C. H. Frederiksen & J. F. Dominic (Eds.), *Writing: The nature, development and teaching of written communication* (Vol. 2). Hillsdale, NJ.: Lawrence Erlbaum.

Scardamalia, M., & Bereiter, C. (1983). The development of evaluative, diagnostic, and remedial capabilities in children's composing. In M. Martlew (Ed.), *The psychology of written language: Development of educational perspectives* (pp. 67-95). London: Wiley.

Scardamalia, M., & Bereiter, C. (1986). Research on written composition. In M. C. Wittrock (Ed.), *Handbook of research on teaching* (pp. 778-803). New York: Collier-Macmillan.

Scardamalia, M., & Bereiter, C. (1991). Literate expertise. In K. A. Ericsson & J. Smith (Eds.), *Toward a general theory of expertise* (pp. 172-194). Cambridge, MA: Cambridge University Press.

Schmidt, R. (1992). Psychological mechanisms underlying second language fluency. *Studies in Second Language Acquisition, 14*, 357-385.

Schmidt, R. (1993). Awareness and second language acquisition. *Annual Review of Applied Linguistics, 13*, 206-226.

Schneuwly, B., & Dolz, J. (1997). Les genres scolaires: Des pratiques scolaires aux objets d'enseignement. *Repères, 15*, 27-40.

Schober, M. F. (1993). Spatial perspective-taking in conversation. *Cognition, 47*, 1-23.

Schriver, K. A. (1992). Teaching writers to anticipate readers' needs: A classroom-evaluated pedagogy. *Written Communication, 9*, 179–208.

Schunk, D. H. (1989). Social cognitive theory and self-regulated learning. In B. J. Zimmerman & D. H. Schunk (Eds.), *Self-regulated learning and academic achievement: Theory, research, and practice* (pp. 83-109). New York: Springer-Verlag.

Segalowitz, N., Poulsen, C., & Komoda, M. (1991). Lower level components of reading skill in higher level bilinguals: Implications for reading instruction. *Aila Review, 8*, 15-30.

Sijtstra, J. (1991). *Doel en inhoud van taalonderwijs; de ontwikkeling van een model voor domeinbeschrijvingen van taalonderwijs* [Objective and content of language instruction: Ihe development of a model for domain descriptions of language instruction]. Arnhem: CITO.

Slavin, R. E. (1983). Non-cognitive outcomes of cooperative learning. In L. J. M. Levin & M. C. Wang (Eds.), *Teacher and students perceptions: Implications for learning* (pp. 341-366). Hillsdale, NJ: Laurence Erlbaum.

Snellings, P., Van Gelderen, A., & De Glopper, K. (2002). Lexical retrieval: An aspect of fluent second language production that can be enhanced. *Language Learning, 54*(4), 723-754.

Snyder, M. (1986). *Public appearances, private realities: The psychology of self-monitoring.* New York: W. H. Freeman and Company.

Sommers, N. (1980). Revision strategies of student writers and experienced writers. *College Composition and Communication, 31*, 378-387.

Sontag, S. (2000, December 18). Writers on writing; Directions: Read, write, rewrite. Repeat steps 2 and 3 as needed. *The New York Times.*

Spivey, N. N. (1997). *The constructivist metaphor: Reading, writing, and the making of meaning.* San Diego, CA: Academic Press.

Squire, L. (1992). Declarative and non declarative memory: Multiple brain systems supporting learning and memory. *Journal of Cognitive Neuroscience, 4*, 232-243.

Stoddard, B., & MacArthur, C. A. (1993). A peer editor strategy: Guiding learning disabled students in response and revision. *Research in the Teaching of English, 27*, 76-103.

Sweller, J., & Chandler. P. (1994). Why some material is difficult to learn. *Cognition and Instruction, 12*, 185-233.

Taylor H. A., & Tversky, B. (1996). Perspective in spatial descriptions. *The Journal of Memory and Language, 35,* 371-391.

Thibadeau, R., Just, M., & Carpenter, P. (1982). A model of the time course and content of reading. *Cognitive Science, 6,* 157-203.

Tierney, R. J., Carter, M. A., & Desai, L. E. (1991). *Portfolio assessment in the reading-writing classroom.* Norwood, MA: Christopher-Gordon.

Tierney, R. J., Leys, M., & Rogers, T. (1984). *Comprehension, composition, and collaboration: Analysis of communicative influences in two classrooms.* Paper presented at the Conference on Contexts of Literacy, Snowbird, UT.

Tierney, R. J., & Shanahan, T. (1991). Research on the reading-writing relationship: Interactions, transactions, and outcomes. In R. Barr, M. L. Kamil, P. B. Mosenthal, & P. D. Pearson (Eds.), *Handbook of reading research* (Vol. 2, pp. 246-280). New York, London: Longman.

Torrance, M. (1996). Is writing expertise like other kinds of expertise?. In G. Rijlaarsdam, H. Van den Bergh, & M. Couzijn (Eds.), *Studies in writing: Vol. 1. Theories, Models and Methodology in Writing Research,* (pp. 3-9). Amsterdam: Amsterdam University Press.

Torrance, M., & Jeffery, G. (Eds.). (1999). *Studies in writing: Vol. 3. The cognitive demands of writing: Processing capacity and working memory effects in text production.* Amsterdam: Amsterdam University Press.

Torrance, M., Thomas, G. V., & Robinson, E. J. (1994). The writing strategies of graduate research students in the social-sciences. *Higher Education, 27*(3), 379-392.

Torrance, M., Thomas, G. V., & Robinson, E. J. (1999). Individual differences in the writing behaviour of undergraduate students. *British Journal of Educational Psychology, 69,* 189-199.

Torrance, M., Thomas, G. V., & Robinson, E. J. (2000). Individual differences in undergraduate essay-writing strategies: A longitudinal study. *Higher Education, 39*(2), 181-200.

Totereau, C., Barrouillet, P., & Fayol, M. (1998). Overgeneralizations of number inflections in the learning of written French: The case of noun and verb. *The British Psychological Society, 16,* 447-464.

Totereau, C., Thevenin, M. G., & Fayol, M. (1997). The development of the understanding of number morphology in French. In C. Perfetti, M. Fayol, & L. Rieben (Eds.), *Learning to spell* (pp. 97-114). Hillsdale, NJ: Lawrence Earlbaum.

Traxler, M. & Gernsbacher, M. (1992). Improving written communication through minimal feedback. *Language and cognitive process, 7,* 1-22.

Traxler, M. & Gernsbacher, M. (1993). Improving written communication through perspective-taking. *Language and cognitive process, 8*(3), 311-334.

Tynjälä, P. (2001). Writing, learning, and the development of expertise in higher education. In P. Tynjälä, L. Mason, & K. Lonka (Eds.), *Studies in writing: Vol. 7. Writing as a learning tool* (pp. 37-56). Dordrecht: Kluwer Academic Publishers.

Tynjälä, P., Mason, L., & Lonka, K. (Eds.) (2001). *Studies in writing: Vol. 7. Writing as a learning tool.* Dordrecht: Kluwer Academic Publishers.

Vacc, N. N. (1987). Word processor versus handwriting: A comparative study of writing samples produced by mildly mentally handicapped students. *Exceptional Children, 54,* 156-165.

Van den Bergh, H. (1988). *Examens geëxamineerd.* [Exams examined]. 's-Gravenhage: Institute of Educational Research.

Van den Bergh, H., & Rijlaarsdam, G. (1999). The dynamics of idea generation during writing: An online study. In M. Torrance, & D. Galbraith (Eds.), *Studies in writing: Vol. 4. Knowing what to write: Cognitive perspectives on conceptual processes in text production* (pp. 99-120). Amsterdam: Amsterdam University Press.

Van den Bergh, H. & Rijlaarsdam, G. (2001, July). *What revisions can tell about writing processes.* Paper presented at the Third International IAIMTE Conference on the Learning and Teaching of Language & Literature, Amsterdam, The Netherlands.

Van den Bergh, H., Rijlaarsdam, G., & Breetvelt, I. (1994). Revision process and text quality: An empirical study. In G. Eigler & T. Jechle (Eds.), *Writing: Current trends in European research.* (pp. 133-148). Freiburg: Hochschul Verlag.

Van der Hoeven, J. (1997). *Children's composing: A study into the relationships between writing processes, text quality, and cognitive and linguistic skills.* Utrecht Studies in Language and Communication, vol. 12. Amsterdam: Rodopi.

Van Gelderen, A. (1994). Prediction of global ratings of fluency and delivery in narrative discourse by linguistic and phonetic measures; oral performances of students aged 11-12 years. *Language Testing, 11*(3), 291-319.

Van Gelderen, A. (1997). Elementary students' skills in revising: Integrating quantitative and qualitative analysis. *Written Communication, 14*, 360-397.

Van Gelderen, A., Couzijn, M., & Hendrix, T. (2000). Language awareness in the Dutch mother-tongue curriculum. In L. J. White, B. Maylath, & A. Adams & M. Couzijn (Eds.), *Language awareness: A history and implementations* (pp. 57-88). Amsterdam: Amsterdam University Press.

Van Waes, L. (1991). *De computer en het schrijfproces. De invloed Van de tekstverwerker op het pauzeen revisiegedrag Van schrijvers.* [The computer and the writing process. The influence of the text processor on the pausing and revision behavior of writers]. Enschede: WMW Publikaties.

Wallace, D. L., & Hayes, J. R. (1991). Redefining revision for freshmen. *Research in the Teaching of English, 25*(1), 54-66.

Wallace, D. L., Hayes, J. R., Hatch, J. A., Miller, W., Moser, G., & Silk, C. M. (1996) Better revision in eight minutes? Prompting first-year college writers to revise globally. *Journal of Educational Psychology, 88*(4), 682-688.

Willingham, D. B., Nissen, M. J., & Bullemer, P. (1989). On the development of procedural knowledge. *Journal of Experimental Psychology: Learning, Memory and Cognition, 15*, 1047-1060.

Witte, S. P. (1985). Revising, composing theory, and research design. In S. W. Freedman (Ed), *The acquisition of written language: Response and revision* (pp. 250-284). Norwood, NJ: Ablex.

Witte, S. (1992). Context, text, intertext: Toward a constructionist semiotic of writing. *Written Communication, 9*, 237-308.

Wollman-Bonilla, J. E. (2001). Can first-grade writers demonstrate audience awareness? *Reading Research Quarterly, 36*, 184-201.

Wong, B. Y. L., Butler, D. L., Ficzere, S. A., Kuperis, S., Corden, M., & Zelmer, J. (1994). Teaching problem learners revision skills and sensitivity to audience through two instructional modes: Student-teacher versus student-student interactive dialogues. *Learning Disabilities Research and Practice, 9* 78-90.

Wong, B. Y. L., Wong, R., & Blenkinsop, J. (1989). Cognitive and metacognitive aspects of learning disabled adolescents' composing problems. *Learning Disability Quarterly, 12*, 300-322.

Wright, N. J. (1975). *The effect of role playing on the improvement of freshman composition.* Unpublished doctoral dissertation, Texas A & M University.

Writer's Digest, May, 2001.

Yagelski, R. P. (1995). The role of classroom context in the revision strategies of student writers. *Research in the Teaching of English, 29*(2), 216-238.

Zammuner, V. L. (1995). Individual and cooperative computer-writing and revising: Who gets the best results? *Learning and Instruction, 5,* 101-124.

AUTHOR INDEX

SUBJECT INDEX

LIST OF CONTRIBUTORS

Linda Allal, Professor of Education, Faculty of Psychology and Sciences of Education, University of Geneva, Switzerland. Linda.Allal@pse.unige.ch

Muriele Amada, doctoral student, Center for Research in Psychology of Cognition, Language and Emotion, University de Provence, France.

Katia Ascorti, Educational psychologist, Department of Developmental and Socialization Psychology, University of Padova, Italy. katia.ascorti@libero.it

Pietro Boscolo, Professor of Educational Psychology, Department of Developmental and Socialization Psychology, University of Padova, Italy. pietro.boscolo@unipd.it

Lucile Chanquoy, Professor of cognitive and developmental psychology, Faculty of Psychology, University of Nantes, France. lucile.chanquoy@humana.univ-nantes.fr

Michel Couzijn, Senior lecturer in Language Education, Graduate School of Teaching and Learning, University of Amsterdam, The Netherlands. couzijn@ilo.uva.nl

Alexandra Dédéyan, PhD candidate, Department of Psychology, University of Rouen, France

David Galbraith, Senior Lecturer in Psychology, Department of Psychology, Staffordshire University, U.K. d.galbraith@staffs.ac.uk

Steve Graham, Professor of Special Education, Department of Special Education, University of Maryland, U.S.A. Sg@umail.umd.edu

Karen R. Harris, Professor of Special Education, Department of Special Education, University of Maryland, U.S.A. kh9@umail.umd.edu

John R. Hayes, Professor of Psychology, Department of Psychology, Carnegie Mellon University, Pittsburgh, U.S.A. Jh50@andrew.cmu.edu

David R. Holliway, Assistant Professor, Human Development and Cognition, Educational Foundations and Technology, Marshall University, Huntington, U.S.A. holliway@marshall.edu

Pierre Largy, Professor of cognitive and developmental psychology, Department of Psychology, University of Toulouse Le Mirail, France. e-mail: largy@univ-tlse2.fr

Charles A. MacArthur, Professor of Special Education, School of Education, University of Delaware, U.S.A. macarthu@udel.edu

Deborah McCutchen, Professor, Educational Psychology and Cognitive Studies in Education, College of Education, University of Washington, Seattle, U.S.A. maccutch@u.washinton.edu

Thierry Olive, Research Scientist, Laboratory of Language and Cognition, University of Poitiers, France. thierry.olive@univ-poitiers.fr

Ron Oostdam, Senior researcher, SCO-Kohnstamm Institute, Centre for the Study of Language Learning, University of Amsterdam, The Netherlands. ron@educ.uva.nl.

Annie Piolat, Professor of Psychology, Center for Research in Psychology of Cognition, Language and Emotion, University de Provence, France. annie.piolat@up.univ-mrs.fr

Gert Rijlaarsdam, Professor of Language Education, Graduate School of Teaching and Learning, University of Amsterdam, The Netherlands. rijlaars@ilo.uva.nl

Yviane Rouiller, Professor, School for Teacher Education, Lausanne, Switzerland. yviane.rouiller@edu-vd.ch.

Jean-Yves Roussey, Professor of Education,, Center for Research in Psychology of Cognition, Language and Emotion, University of Provence, France. jy.roussey@aix-mrs.iufm.fr

Mark Torrance, Senior Lecturer in Psychology, Department of Psychology, Staffordshire University, U.K. m.torrance@staffs.ac.uk

Amos Van Gelderen, Senior researcher, SCO-Kohnstamm Institute, Centre for the Study of Language Learning, University of Amsterdam, The Netherlands. amos@educ.uva.nl

Huub Van den Bergh, Associate Professor in Language Behavior, University of Utrecht, The Netherlands. Huub H.vandenbergh@let.uu.nl.

Studies in Writing

For Volumes 1-6 please contact Amsterdam University Press, at www.aup.nl

KLUWER ACADEMIC PUBLISHERS – DORDRECHT/BOSTON/NEW YORK/LONDON